Cooking Vegetables the Italian Way

~ ~ ~

Cooking Vegetables the Italian Way

~ ~ ~

Judith Barrett

Illustrations by
Claudia Karabaic Sargent

Collier Books
Macmillan Publishing Company
New York

Maxwell Macmillan Canada
Toronto

Maxwell Macmillan International
New York   Oxford   Singapore   Sydney

Collier Books   Maxwell Macmillan Canada, Inc.
Macmillan Publishing Company   1200 Eglinton Avenue East
866 Third Avenue   Suite 200
New York, NY 10022   Don Mills, Ontario M3C 3N1

Macmillan Publishing Company is part of the Maxwell Communication Group of Companies.

Library of Congress Cataloging-in-Publication Data
Barrett, Judith, 1948–
    Cooking vegetables the Italian way / Judith Barrett ; illustrations
by Claudia Karabaic Sargent. — 1st Collier Books ed.
        p.   cm.
    Includes index.
    ISBN 0-02-009078-1
    1. Cookery (Vegetables)   2. Cookery, Italian.   I. Title.
TX801.B296   1994   93-32920   CIP
641.6′5—dc20

Macmillan books are available at special discounts for bulk purchases for sales promotions, pre-
miums, fund-raising, or educational use. For details, contact:

Special Sales Director
Macmillan Publishing Company
866 Third Avenue
New York, NY 10022

First Collier Books Edition 1994

10   9   8   7   6   5   4   3   2   1

Printed in the United States of America

Design by Laura Hough

For Annie and Rachel

~ ~ ~

Contents

~ ~ ~

Acknowledgments

~ ~ ~

MANY PEOPLE gave me wonderful support and help for this project.

In Italy, I was given great assistance by Faith Willinger, and also owe many thanks to Annie Brodie, Dania Lucherini and Ceasare Casella, Marquese Sersale, Lorenza de' Medici, and Roberto Stucchi. And in Boston, I am grateful to my colleagues Michela Larsen, Jane Lavine, Ann Robert, Nina Simonds, and Barbara Haber, who gave me advice and counsel.

I am greatly indebted to Susan Mason for her cheerfulness and invaluable help in testing recipes, to Barbara Lloyd and Anne Glickman for their thoughtful comments on the manuscript, and to my agent, Robert Cornfield, and my editor, Pam Hoenig, for their work in seeing this project through.

And I am especially grateful to my family: to my parents for sharing their passion for Italian food and culture with me at home and in Italy; to my brother, Jimmy, and sister-in-law, Susan, and their family for first giving me an appreciation of a healthful approach to eating centered on vegetables; to my sister, Jane, and Rob Robinson for their enthusiasm in this project; to my children, Annie and Rachel, who cheerfully tasted almost everything I prepared, tactfully gave me their honest evaluations, put up with my absences when I traveled, and made the most out of months of irregular meals; and to my husband, David—my co-eater and traveling companion, advisor and confidant, my greatest supporter and biggest fan—who really made it possible for me to write this book.

Preface

~ ~ ~

ITALIAN COOKING, it has been said, begins in the garden. Italy is a traditionally agricultural and poor country where preparing whole meals from the fields has been necessary and customary. When meat is scarce, produce becomes the backbone, heart, and soul of the cuisine. While in many cuisines vegetables seem to be afterthoughts, when Italian cooks take to sautéing or roasting their vegetables, the results are full of imagination and flavor: baby eggplants are baked with sun-dried tomatoes until they are infused with flavor; sautéed red and yellow peppers are bathed in balsamic vinegar and paired with pasta; fennel and broccoli are steeped in a rich broth to make an intensely flavorful soup.

I became intrigued by the role of vegetables in Italian cuisine when I was writing a cookbook on the northern Italian rice dish, risotto. The list of vegetable risotto recipes was the longest and most varied, and included some of the tastiest and most inventive versions. That, combined with a longstanding interest in eating lighter, leaner, and more healthfully, led me to look beyond risotto to the other Italian dishes that are prepared with vegetables and fruit. And I found plenty.

For recipes, ideas, and inspiration I traveled throughout Italy to explore and experience the foods of the different regions. I delved into the culinary collection at the Schlesinger Library at Radcliffe College in Cambridge, Massachusetts. I gained a wealth of information and got background and inspiration from the classic books by some of the great Italian food writers such as Pellegrino Artusi and Ada Boni, from the 1899 book *Leaves From Our Tuscan Kitchen*, and from writers Elizabeth David and Waverley Root, and many contemporary writers as well, including Marcella Hazan and Giuliano Bugialli. I scoured markets at home and abroad to compare produce and ingredients, and sought out Italian cooks and restaurant owners.

I talked with Italians everywhere I could and found a regional pride in produce that may explain why this part of their cuisine offers so many delicious possibilities. During a visit to Venice in the summer of 1988, I mentioned to Arrigo Cipriani, the owner of Harry's Bar, that I was writing a cookbook about Italian vegetables and fruit. His eyes lit up and he said to me, "You must come back to Venice in May. We have the best vegetables in the Veneto and then they are at their peak." Months later, in Positano on the Amalfi coast south of Naples, I talked with the Marquese Sersale, the proprietor of the Hotel Sirenuse there, about the progress on my cookbook. He looked at me and said, "So it is a good thing you have come to Positano since our vegetables are the best in all of Italy." Faith Willinger, the author of the guidebook *Eating in Italy* and a Florentine for the last twenty years, directed me to Tuscany for firsthand information about how Italian cooks prepare vegetables. And at home, Magda Brosio, a native of Turin but a Bostonian for many years, said with great assurance, "In Piedmont, the vegetables are the best in Italy."

I set out to discover what Italian cooks do to prepare vegetable and fruit dishes in Italy that taste so good, and then to find ways to cook them at home in my American kitchen, using local produce, to make them as authentic as possible and as delicious as they are in Italy. In addition, I have created recipes that reflect my own interpretation of Italian cuisine. Ultimately, I have tried to make the Italian way with vegetable dishes accessible to American cooks, their families and friends.

Introduction

~ ~ ~

THERE ARE THOUSANDS of different vegetable and fruit dishes prepared in Italy. Every region has its specialties and every city or town its characteristic versions. In *From an Italian Garden*, I have tried to bring you a broad—traditional and unconventional—selection from this vast variety. I aimed to be as inclusive as possible, but ultimately this is a personal selection of my favorite recipes.

I have organized this book in a way that I hope makes the information accessible and easy to use.

The first three chapters give the background and introductory information you will need to prepare the recipes in this book. Included here are descriptions and recommendations for the essential nonvegetable ingredients (olive oil, cheeses, etc.) called for in the recipes, descriptions of the basic equipment you will need, and the cooking techniques that are used in the recipes.

Chapter Four, The Vegetables of Italy, provides a brief history of vegetables in Italian cuisine, and a complete guide on how to select and prepare for cooking each of the vegetables called for in the recipes in this book.

In the remaining chapters you will find over two hundred recipes for antipasti, soups, crostini, bruschetta, pizza, pasta, risotto, polenta, gnocchi, beans, *torte*, *frittate*, salads, and fruit desserts. The majority of the recipes are concise and easy to prepare. Many of the recipes have been adapted from my research. Others are personal interpretations of Italian cuisine.

Although the place in a traditional Italian meal for many of the vegetable dishes in this book is at the beginning as antipasti and *primi piatti*, many are hearty and substantial preparations that you should feel free to serve as either a first or main course. One of the wonderful aspects of Italian vegetable dishes is that they are so versatile.

The recipes do not call for meat, fish, or poultry, though those who follow a vegetarian diet should note that when broth is called for, as in the soup and risotto recipes, the traditional Italian version is a meat-based broth. However, in the introductory part of the book I have given recipes for meat-based as well as vegetable broths, which will also produce excellent results.

At a time when so many of us are looking for meat alternatives, for healthier foods, and for diets lower in fat, the Italian way with vegetables and fruit offers unlimited possibilities. I hope this book will help you take advantage of the delights they have to offer.

Chapter One

~ ~ ~

Essential Ingredients of Italian Cooking

THE SIMPLICITY OF Italian cooking is evident in the pantry. A well-stocked Italian kitchen requires only a few basic ingredients. When combined with the fresh produce and foods from the market, they give the distinctive Italian character and flavor of the dishes in which they are used. For example, Italian food is inseparable from the olive oil that serves as the cooking medium for so many recipes. Any oil won't provide the particular taste to the dish. Similarly, authentic Reggiano Parmesan cheese—not just any cheese—lends its characteristic tangy, nutty flavor to soups, pasta, risotto, and many other dishes. Following is a guide to the essential ingredients that are called for in the recipes in this book. I hope that it will help you when you are shopping for ingredients as well as when you are in your kitchen preparing recipes.

Olive Oil

~ ~ ~

OLIO D'OLIVA

Perhaps the most important ingredient in Italian cooking, olive oil is used in the preparation of most of the recipes in this book.

Throughout the centuries olive oil has maintained a prominent place in Italian culture as well as its cuisine. We know that the Romans used olive oil for many things, including fuel for their lamps, cosmetics, and as a body treatment for athletes. To the Romans, olive oil was also the *olio santo*, or sacred oil, and it was considered a healing balm for illnesses and as a restorer of youth to the aged.

But in Italian cooking olive oil has achieved and maintained, over thousands of years, its most important status. Although there are strong regional differences in Italian foods, olive oil has remained the single common ingredient and the unifying factor in the cuisine of Italy. Olive oil, it is fair to say, is at the very heart of Italian cuisine.

When it comes to choosing olive oil, there is really only one consideration and that is taste. But, interestingly enough, that will probably lead you to use at least two different olive oils—one for cooking and one for dressing salad, various soups, pastas, and antipasti before serving. The oil you use for cooking should not have a particularly strong or distinctive flavor. As one respected chef in Italy told me, "Food that is cooked in oil should taste like the food, not the oil." On the other hand, the oil that you add to salads and other dishes can—and should—have a particular and characteristically fruity olive taste that adds to and complements the dish.

Like wine, olive oil and its production are regulated and controlled, and the different oils are classified. The type of olives used (green, ripe, or overripe) and how they are processed to extract the oil (stone-pressed, mechanically pressed, and/or chemically treated) will determine the flavor, color, classification, and ultimately price of the oil.

The best olive oil has a low level of acidity, less than one percent, is made with green, unripe olives, and is classified as "extra virgin." But there is still variation within the group of oils that fall into the "extra virgin" category, and as a cook you shouldn't just assume that all extra virgin oils will be the same. Lesser-quality oils are made from a mixture of green and ripe olives, are usually mechanically pressed, and have higher levels of acidity. Some have a heavy, fruitier flavor, while others are lighter tasting.

My own approach is to use a relatively light pure olive oil for cooking, and fruitier (and more expensive) extra virgin oil for salads and other dishes. I recommend that you do the same. One of the easily affordable minor luxuries is to buy one or two small bottles of fine extra virgin olive oil such as the Badia a Coltibuono, explore the differences in flavor they offer, and then pick your own favorites.

Vegetable Oil

~ ~ ~

OLIO DI VERDURE

Olive oil is unquestionably the primary oil used in Italian cooking, but other vegetable oils are also used. Safflower oil is very popular in Italy, evidenced by the vast fields of sunflowers growing all around the Italian countryside. Other oils used to a lesser degree by Italian cooks include corn and peanut oils. These vegetable oils are used specifically for deep-frying vegetables and other foods, but can also be substituted for olive oil as the cooking medium. However, when olive oil is called for as a dressing, do not substitute any other oil.

Bread

~ ~ ~

PANE

"Senza il pane tutto diventa orfano" is an Italian saying that probably best describes the importance of bread in Italian life. It means, "Without bread, one is deprived of everything."

So important is bread in Italy that in many places loaves are incised with the symbol of the cross before they are put into the oven to bake. No meal is ever served without bread. And no crust or crumb is ever allowed to go to waste. And in Tuscany, bread, not pasta or rice, is the principal starch of the cuisine.

Bread is also the basis for some of Italy's best-known and most-loved dishes, notably pizza, and the foundation for such specialties as bruschetta, crostini, and the numerous Tuscan bread soups and salads. Bread that is no longer fresh finds its way into stuffings, toppings, or coatings for vegetable dishes from all over Italy.

Although the term "Italian bread" is often used in much the same manner as "French bread" to mean crusty white loaves, there is actually an enormous variety of breads in Italy—some estimates are as high as a thousand different types of bread that can be found from the northern to the southern regions of Italy.

Most daily bread is baked with only flour, water, and yeast. Variations come from the type of flour (wheat, rye, etc.) used, the coarseness or refinement of the flour (which produces a range in textures and the whiteness or darkness of the bread), and the addition of or lack of salt. In Tuscany, bread is surprisingly tasteless, but that's because little or no salt is added to it.

There are also special breads for occasions and holidays which may be made with shortening, milk, sugar, nuts, and fruits. And there are the hearth breads, which the Italians call *focaccia*—rustic flat breads that are baked with wonderful seasonings.

When bread is called for in a recipe, you should always try to use a firm-textured bread with a good crust. In other words, avoid soft sandwich loaves. When bread crumbs are called for, the best are the fresh ones you make yourself. If you use packaged bread crumbs, avoid the ones that are flavored or seasoned, since they can spoil the flavor of the dish you are preparing.

Home-Style Bread
~ ~ ~
PANE CASERECCIO

This recipe produces two impressive round, crusty loaves. You can prepare the dough and do all the kneading in an electric mixer that's fitted with a dough hook, or by hand. This recipe was given to me by my neighbor Barbara Lloyd, a professor of Italian at Boston University and a splendid cook.

1 envelope active dry yeast
2½ cups warm water (about 90°F)
2 teaspoons salt
7 to 8 cups unbleached white flour, plus extra for kneading
Coarse semolina flour or cornmeal for dusting

1. In the large work bowl of your electric mixer, combine the yeast with the water and allow it to stand for about 15 minutes. (If the mixture doesn't froth up, the yeast is dead and must be discarded.) Add the salt and turn on the machine to kneading speed (check the manufacturer's directions for kneading bread dough). Add the flour ½ cup at a time until

the dough forms a ball on the hook. Knead for 25 to 30 minutes. The dough will be slightly sticky and soft. (To knead by hand, you will add about 1 cup additional flour to the dough, which will be less sticky when fully kneaded.)

2. Remove the work bowl from the mixer, cover with plastic wrap and a dish towel, and place it in a warm, draft-free place to rise until the dough is tripled in bulk, about 3½ hours.

3. Without punching the dough down, turn it out onto a floured work surface. Pull the dough apart (do not cut it) into two equal pieces. Using your hands, and working around each piece, turn the edges of the dough under to form two round shapes. Place the two round forms on a baking sheet or pizza stone dusted with semolina or cornmeal. Cover with a well-floured dish towel and allow to rise until doubled in bulk, about 1 hour.

4. Brush the loaves with water and bake in a preheated 400°F oven for 1 hour, until the loaves are well browned and hollow sounding when tapped on top. Bake for an additional 5 to 10 minutes for a harder, browner crust.

MAKES TWO 1-POUND LOAVES

Cheese

~ ~ ~

FORMAGGIO

Cheese is widely used in the preparation of Italian vegetable dishes. It is also eaten with fruit, as a dessert.

Over the centuries numerous cheeses have been developed throughout Italy—both soft, fresh varieties without rinds as well as aged, hard-rind cheeses. It was the ancient Greeks who first brought cheese to the Italian peninsula and taught the Etruscans how to take the curds from sour milk and form them into cheeses. The Etruscans took the process a step further and developed hard-rind cheese, specifically what is now known as Parmesan cheese, which was aged and could last much longer than soft, fresh cheeses. The Romans were the first to use animal rennet (the lining from a milk-fed calf's stomach) to induce the curdling process of the milk—before then milk was left to sour naturally. In his book *Rei rusticae* ("On Rustic Matters," A.D. 65), Columella recorded the cheese-making process of his day, which does not differ much from the process today.

It is always a good idea to allow cheeses to come to room temperature before you serve or cook them.

PARMESAN/*PARMIGIANO-REGGIANO* AND *GRANA*. The most important Italian cheese—the one that is most used in cooking—is Parmesan. There are two basic types of Parmesan—Parmigiano-Reggiano and Grana. The best is the Parmigiano-Reggiano, which is made in a narrowly defined area around Parma, Reggio-Emilia, Modena, Bologna, and Mantova.

Unlike so many other cheeses in Italy that have succumbed to modern industrial techniques, Parmigiano-Reggiano is produced today the same way it has been produced for centuries: The milk comes from local cows that feed only on fresh grass. The milk, gathered from two milkings a day, is partially skimmed and is augmented with whey from the previous day's milkings to encourage fermentation. The cheese is curdled with rennet, shaped, and salted. The end products are 60- to 70-pound wheels of cheese that are aged for at least a year and as much as seven years. According to some sources, no other cheese in the world is aged as long or formed into such large wheels. You can always tell real Reggiano Parmesan by the distinctive "Reggiano" imprint stamped on the yellow rind. Reggiano has a nutty, mild flavor and is only slightly salty.

Grana is made under less stringent guidelines than Reggiano and is, therefore, generally less expensive. Its flavor, while still relatively mild and nutty-tasting, is sharper than that of Reggiano and also slightly saltier. However, it is comparable to Reggiano in that it has a hard, crumbling texture that makes it good for grating. There are three types of Grana: Grana Padano from Piedmont, Lombardy, the Veneto, and Reggio-Emilia; Grana Lodigiano from the town of Lodi in southern Lombardy; and Grana Piacentino from the town of Piacenza. Grana can always be used in any recipe calling for Parmesan cheese.

(*Note*: There are Parmesan-type cheeses from other countries including Argentina and the United States. I would recommend these only if no Italian varieties are available.)

Whether you buy Reggiano or Grana, you should always buy it by the piece and grate it just before you are ready to use it for the best flavor. Grated Parmesan will take on a sour flavor—even in the refrigerator—after several days. A chunk of Parmesan, on the other hand, will keep in the refrigerator for at least a month if wrapped well and kept airtight.

You can easily grate Parmesan in a food processor; although I don't particularly like the powdery texture this method produces, it is fast and efficient, especially if you are using the cheese to cook with, rather than to serve at the table. In restaurants in Italy, Parmesan is rarely served already grated in a dish. Instead, it is usually grated at the table with a fine-toothed hand-grater directly onto each serving. (See page 23 for information on cheese-grating equipment.)

PECORINO. Pecorino is the generic name for Italian cheeses made with ewe's (sheep's) milk and the rennet from the stomach of the milk-fed lamb, or *abbacchio*, which is a Roman delicacy. Pecorino cheeses are made throughout the central and southern regions of Italy, although the best-known pecorino cheeses are the sardo from Sardinia and romano from Rome. Pecorino Toscano, although not well known or available in the United States, is an essential ingredient in Tuscan cuisine. It is a very strong-flavored and odoriferous cheese. In general, the *pecorini* are aged two weeks (for the sardo) to eight months (for the romano). They are all typically very salty and sharp-tasting. The longer these cheeses are aged, the better they become for grating. That is why the romano cheese is usually grated and often used as a substitute for Parmesan cheese.

GORGONZOLA. Named for the town where it was first produced, strong-scented, flavorful Gorgonzola cheese is made from cow's milk in the area north of Milan. It is one of the most formidable of Italian cheeses. Originally the moldy blue streaks in the cheese developed when fresh milk was added to old. Today, while Gorgonzola is still aged in caves in the alpine towns of Valsassina and Val Brembana, long copper pins are inserted into the cheeses to allow air in and the mold to form.

There are two types of Gorgonzola: *naturale*, which is the more pungent and strongly flavored; and the *dolcelatte*, which is not aged as long and is therefore milder and creamier. Most stores that carry Gorgonzola usually have the *dolcelatte* because it appeals to a wider clientele. Gorgonzola is wonderful eaten with some crusty bread or with pears for dessert. It can also be cooked with risotto, polenta, and pasta, as well as with certain vegetables.

MOZZARELLA. Naples and the region around it are known for mozzarella cheese. Although it is widely made from cow's milk, the best (and consequently the most expensive) mozzarella, the *fior di latte* (flower of the milk) as it is called, is made from the milk of the water buffalo that were introduced to southern Italy in the sixteenth century. Unlike the flavorless, rubbery mozzarella cheese that you can buy almost anywhere, *mozzarella di bufala*, which is available in specialty shops, has a soft, uncommonly creamy texture and an almost sweet aroma. When you cut into it, it should drip with its own buttermilk. Buffalo milk mozzarella imported from Venezuela is now becoming available and is often comparable in quality to the Italian variety. Another good choice is locally made fresh mozzarella if you can find it in shops in your area or by mail order (see pages 295–96 for sources).

You can use almost any mozzarella cheese for cooking. However, when it is called for in salads, try to use the buffalo milk mozzarella or fresh mozzarella. It's worth it.

FONTINA. Fontina comes from Italy's smallest region, the Valle d'Aosta, which shares its borders with France and Switzerland. It is a semisoft cheese made from unpasteurized cow's milk with 45 percent butterfat. It has a mild and slightly nutty flavor, and is an excellent creamy cheese, perfect for melting. Fontina has a soft, reddish brown rind that can be cut away easily. A comparable cheese is Taleggio.

BEL PAESE. "Beautiful country" is the name of this mild, good melting cheese. I like to use it in place of mozzarella in many recipes because it has more flavor and doesn't become as stringy when cooked. Another comparable cheese is Asiago fresco.

GOAT CHEESE. *Caprino* is the general name used for goat cheese, of which many different versions are produced throughout Italy. In general, goat cheese has a crumbly, soft texture and a pungent, piercing flavor and salty taste. It does not melt particularly well because it is low in butterfat, but it is just as delicious hot and cooked as it is cold. Goat cheese is not widely used in traditional Italian cooking, but it has recently become popular with younger, more adventurous chefs in restaurants. I like to add it as a topping to pizza and crostini and to some pasta dishes, as well as risotto, because its sharp flavor adds a nice contrast to these rich and creamy dishes. If you can't find Italian goat cheese, you can use one of the many American-made or French goat cheeses available.

Butter

~ ~ ~

BURRO

Butter is one of the staples of northern Italian cooking where the pasta sauces, the risotti, and even the desserts are made with butter. Historians have credited the French with introducing butter to Italy, and certainly Catherine de' Medici's affection for French cooking was influential in spreading the use of butter. However, butter is a natural product of the Italian alpine valleys and the cattle that graze there. So it is not surprising for it to be a common ingredient in the cooking from that region.

Some recipes call for melted butter. To melt butter without browning or burning it, either put it in a small pot over boiling water or use a microwave; to do so, remove the wrapping on the butter, place it in a microwave-safe container, cover loosely with waxed paper or a paper towel, and cook on high power for about 1 minute (depending on how much butter, and how cold it is).

While butter is used for cooking in Italy, it is rarely served at the table with bread except in some hotel restaurants catering to travelers from other countries, and even then only occasionally. This is because bread is considered to be an accessory to the food—not a dish in itself—to retrieve every last drop of sauce, to *fare una scarpetta*, make a little shoe with their piece of bread for scooping up sauce.

When butter is called for in these recipes, you should always use unsalted butter.

Broth

~ ~ ~

BRODO

Broth is the base for soups, risotto, and other dishes. Since it will be an important flavor in the dish you are preparing, you should always use a flavorful broth—one you enjoy the taste of—whether it is the kind you prepare yourself from raw ingredients or a ready-made, instant variety.

"Broth" is technically the term for the cooking liquid that results from the preparation of another dish (for example, a French *pot-au-feu* or an Italian *bollito misto*). However, *brodo* can describe any flavorful liquid that's been made by cooking water with the meat or bones from beef, chicken, or fish, or with vegetables. Traditionally, broth was prepared in earthenware pots and simmered, never boiled, for hours.

Meat Broth

~ ~ ~

The most common type of broth used in Italian kitchens is a meat broth made from a combination of meat (veal or beef) and chicken. Unlike French stock, which is prepared with well-browned bones and is cooked down to almost its essence, Italian broth is made with meat and bones and is altogether lighter. Even so, this type of broth is time-consuming to prepare. If you want the added quality that homemade broth can provide, I recommend preparing a large quantity and freezing it in small-size containers to have on hand when you need it. You should use inexpensive cuts of meat, such as veal or beef ribs and shank and chicken backs and necks. Cold water and a few aromatic ingredients make this a most flavorful broth.

2 pounds veal bones
2 pounds chicken backs and necks
1 large onion, peeled
4 ribs celery
2 medium-size carrots, scraped

1 small bunch fresh parsley, rinsed in cold water

1 tablespoon salt

5½ quarts cold water

1. Place all the ingredients in an 8- or 10-quart stockpot and bring to a boil over high heat. Skim the foam from the top of the broth.

2. Reduce the heat to low and simmer, partially covered, for 2 to 3 hours, occasionally skimming the foam from the top.

3. Strain the broth through a wire-mesh sieve into a large container or bowl. Let cool slightly and allow to stand in the refrigerator until cold and the fat has settled on top. Remove the fat with a spoon. The broth can be used immediately, covered tightly and stored in the refrigerator for up to 5 days, or frozen for 2 to 3 months.

MAKES ABOUT 4 QUARTS

Chicken Broth

~ ~ ~

A flavorful chicken broth can be used in any recipe that calls for broth.

3 pounds chicken, whole or parts

2 medium-size carrots, scraped

4 ribs celery

1 medium-size onion, peeled

1 small bunch fresh parsley, rinsed in cold water

1 tablespoon salt

3½ quarts cold water

1. Place all the ingredients in an 8- or 10-quart stockpot and bring to a boil over high heat. Skim the foam from the top of the broth.

2. Reduce the heat to low and simmer, partially covered, for 2 hours, occasionally skimming the foam from the top.

3. Strain the broth through a wire-mesh sieve into a large container or bowl. Let cool slightly. Place in the refrigerator until cold and the fat

has settled on top. Remove the fat with a spoon. The broth can be used immediately, covered tightly and stored for up to 4 days in the refrigerator, or frozen for 2 to 3 months.

MAKES ABOUT 3 QUARTS

Vegetable Broth

~ ~ ~

For vegetarians, or anyone whose diet does not permit a broth made with meat, vegetable broth can be used in any of the recipes in this book that call for broth. As with the meat or chicken broth, you can make your own or use one of the all-vegetable instant bouillons available.

¼ *cup olive oil or other vegetable oil (corn, safflower, but not peanut)*
1 *large onion, coarsely chopped*
1 *large leek, thoroughly cleaned and coarsely chopped (see page 47)*
2 *medium-size carrots, scraped and coarsely chopped*
2 *ribs celery, coarsely chopped*
2 *medium-size turnips, peeled and sliced*
3 *small plum tomatoes, seeded and coarsely chopped*
1 *small bunch fresh parsley, rinsed in cold water*
1 *tablespoon salt*
1 *teaspoon whole black peppercorns*
8 *to 10 cups cold water*

1. Place the oil in a large stockpot over medium-high heat. When the oil is hot add the onion and sauté until it begins to soften, about 2 minutes. Add the leek, carrots, and celery and continue to cook while stirring. Add the turnips, tomatoes, parsley, salt, and peppercorns and pour in the water.

2. Turn the heat to high and bring to a boil. Reduce the heat to medium-low, cover the stockpot, and simmer for 1½ hours.

3. Strain the liquid through a wire-mesh sieve. Use immediately, or cover tightly and refrigerate for up to 5 days or freeze for 2 to 3 months.

MAKES 2 QUARTS

HOW TO MAKE BROTH IN A PRESSURE COOKER: You can use a pressure cooker to prepare meat, chicken, or vegetable broth. Place all the ingredients, except the water, in a 6- or 8-quart pressure cooker. (If you have a 4-quart pressure cooker, use half the recipes.) Add only enough water to fill the cooker two-thirds. Put the top on the cooker and follow the manufacturer's instructions for using the pressure cooker. Bring the pressure up and allow the broth to cook for 45 minutes for meat, 30 minutes for chicken, and 15 minutes for vegetable broth. Turn off the heat and let the pressure drop gradually. Strain as instructed in each of the recipes.

INSTANT BROTH. It is common for Italian cooks at home to use bouillon cubes, called *dadi* (which literally means "dice"), just the way American cooks do. If you want to use instant bouillon, be sure to select the brand you use carefully. Many are salty and flavored with seasonings that give a distinctly artificial taste. Almost all have some preservatives in them. My own preference is for the flavor of the Knorr bouillon cubes. I always overdilute the cubes with 50 percent more water than is called for on the package: 1 bouillon cube and 3 cups of water instead of the 2 cups directed on the package.

All brands of instant broth are usually quite salty. Therefore, when you use it in a recipe, always taste before adding any salt. It is generally not required.

Canned broth, also quite salty, can be used with the recipes in this book. You can improve the flavor of canned broth if you simmer it for 30 minutes with some aromatic flavorings, such as onion, carrots, celery, and parsley, before using it.

Flour

~ ~ ~

FARINA

Flour is an essential ingredient in pasta, bread, pizza, cakes, cookies, and other recipes. Unbleached all-purpose flour can be used in most recipes. For pizza dough I recommend using durum flour, which is made from hard durum wheat and gives the pizza crust more flavor and an authentic pizza crust texture.

Salt and Pepper

~ ~ ~

SALE E PEPE

Two different types of salt are called for in the recipes. Ordinary, fine granular salt is used to season and flavor most recipes. You'll be wise to stick with one brand, because different brands of salt have more or less saltiness in their taste. Quantities for salt listed in the recipes in this book are approximate and given as "salt to taste." And I mean just that: you should always taste before salting and add only as much as you find necessary. Kosher salt, with its large, coarse crystals, is used for roasting vegetables. Most directions call for "lightly sprinkling" with kosher salt. This is because it is easier to get a light coating of kosher salt than of ordinary salt, which, if used too heavily, can form a crust on the vegetables.

Whenever pepper is called for, unless otherwise specified, freshly ground black pepper should be used.

Vinegar

~ ~ ~

ACETO

WINE VINEGAR/*ACETO DI VINO*. A byproduct of the great Italian wine-making industry, wine vinegar is made everywhere wine is in Italy, and usually from good red and white wines. It is principally used in salad dressing in relatively small quantities—approximately 1 part vinegar to 4 parts olive oil. It is also used in the preparation of sweet and sour sauces (*agrodolce*), in pickling brines for vegetables, and in marinades. The best wine vinegars are made in wooden barrels. Good white wine vinegar should have a pale pinkish color, and good red wine vinegar can range in color from pink to deep, dark red. Good wine vinegars are always transparent.

BALSAMIC VINEGAR/*ACETO BALSAMICO*. With its sweet and sour flavor, thick, syrupy texture, and rich, dark brown color, balsamic vinegar is in a league by itself. Since the Middle Ages it has been made in the area around Modena, north of Florence, from the cooked and concentrated juice of white trebbiano grapes that is aged in progressively smaller wooden barrels. Like extra virgin olive oil and Reggiano Parmesan cheese, balsamic vinegar is controlled by law. The only real product is the *aceto balsamico tradizionale*. In order to be labeled that way, it must have been aged at least ten years and sometimes as long as fifty years or more. Other products that are sold as balsamic vinegar, but don't have the official label, have either not been aged as long or are only red wine vinegar that has been flavored with caramel. The difference between the two is in the flavor and the price. The *tradizionale* can cost as much as $40 for a 100-gram bottle.

Balsamic vinegar is used in special dishes—with strawberries, in some soups and marinades, and, of course, in salad dressings. Even though the flavor of balsamic vinegar is not as sharp as regular wine vinegar, you should still use only a small quantity in salad dressings.

Wine

~ ~ ~

VINO

The wines of Italy are varied and diverse, with almost every region producing local varieties. Italy produces more than a fifth of the world's wine, and it has been estimated that over four million acres of Italian countryside are devoted to growing wine grapes. In general, wine used in cooking will be white wine, unless otherwise specified, and should be dry, light, and crisp rather than fruity. Wine used in cooking should also be drinkable. If you don't enjoy the taste of the wine, you won't enjoy the flavor it gives to the food you're preparing. Some good white wines to use when cooking include Pinot Grigio, Soave, Chardonnay, white Corvo, Verdicchio, and Orvieto. I recommend using less expensive bottles of these wines. You can also substitute dry white vermouth in place of the wine. If wine is called for in a recipe, and you want to omit it, simply replace the wine with an equivalent amount of water or broth, depending on the recipe, or omit it altogether.

Chapter Two

~ ~ ~

Basic Techniques for Cooking Vegetables

ITALIAN COOKS are renowned for cooking simply, with the emphasis not on how much but how little can be done so that the minimum amount of natural flavor is lost. The basic cooking techniques used for vegetables in Italian cooking are described here; some will be quite familiar to most cooks, while others—such as roasting vegetables—are less common.

Steaming

~ ~ ~

A VAPORE

Steaming cooks food indirectly by the heated vaporization of boiling water or other liquid, with the benefit that the steamed food retains most of its nutrients and flavor. In the steaming process, a small amount of liquid (usually water, about 1 cup) is heated to a boil in a large saucepan or steamer-pot. The vegetables are placed in a basket or perforated tray and placed above, not in, the water. The pot is covered, and as the steam circulates throughout the pot, it gently cooks the food. Steamed vegetables should be briefly rinsed, or refreshed, under cold running water as soon as they reach the desired level of doneness, in order to stop the cooking process and (in the case of green vegetables) preserve the bright green color.

Steamed vegetables can be lightly coated with olive oil or other dressing and served as is, or cooked further.

Boiling

~ ~ ~

BOLLIRE

Boiling cooks vegetables (or other foods) in liquid, usually water, at 212°F and brings the entire surface of the food into contact with the cooking liquid so that it cooks evenly. Boiling is the best method for preparing broths and soups.

Blanching and Parboiling

~ ~ ~

SCOTTARE

Blanching a vegetable means to submerge it briefly—1 to 2 minutes—in a pot of briskly boiling water and then to remove it immediately.

Parboiling refers to the process of covering the food with cold water, bringing it just to a boil, and then immediately draining it.

These two methods for partially cooking vegetables as a preliminary step rather than as a final preparation can be used interchangeably. My own preference is for blanching since you have more control over the process and can achieve more consistent results. With parboiling, there are more variables: the quantity of vegetables and water when you start, and how fast or slow your stove works, which means a greater risk of accidentally overcooking the vegetables.

Microwave-Steaming

~ ~ ~

MICROONDE

Although it is not widely used in kitchens in Italy yet, the microwave oven has become a common kitchen appliance in the United States and is an excellent way to quickly steam-cook most vegetables. The results you get with a microwave oven match those from a steamy pot on top of the stove, and sometimes the cooking times are faster. You also gain a measure of convenience with the microwave because you eliminate a pot to wash when you're finished. In addition, there are other uses for the microwave oven in the preparation of Italian vegetable dishes. Wherever I have found that using the microwave oven does apply, directions for using it are included in the recipe.

The microwave oven works as follows: the microwaves enter the oven cabinet and transfer energy to the water, fat, and sugar molecules in the food, accelerating their movements, which results in friction and therefore heat, causing the food to cook.

The less food you put into the microwave, the higher the ratio of microwaves to food, so the food cooks faster. The more food you put into your oven, the slower it will cook. Also, the bigger (more wattage) and more powerful your microwave oven, the faster it will work.

Here are some tips to follow that will help ensure even, fast results when microwaving vegetables.

- Vegetables to be cooked in the microwave should be cut into approximately equal-size small pieces.
- The pieces should be arranged or distributed evenly, preferably in a single layer, on a microwave-safe plate or in a cooking container.
- ALWAYS cover the cooking container securely, either with a tight-fitting cover or with microwave-safe plastic wrap.
- Vegetables to be steam-cooked in the microwave should be rinsed but not dried.
- You NEVER need to add water to vegetables that are being steam-cooked in the microwave; the water left on them from rinsing will be enough.
- NEVER salt vegetables before cooking them in the microwave. Microwaves are affected by salt (as well as fats and sugar), so food tends to overcook in those places where there are concentrations of salt.
- Always cook vegetables on the "high" setting.
- Cooking times vary for each vegetable. (For specific cooking times, see the section on vegetables.)
- After microwave steam-cooking, vegetables should stand while still covered for approximately 5 minutes. This finishes the cooking process.
- You don't have to rinse microwave-cooked vegetables in cold water to stop the cooking process or preserve color.

Aside from preparing foods, the microwave does a wonderful job in heating ingredients—for example, if you need to heat milk to prepare a *balsamella* (bechamel) sauce, or heat stock before adding it to a dish.

Pressure Cooking

~ ~ ~

PENTOLA A PRESSIONE

Pressure cookers are widely used in Italian kitchens. You can cook vegetables, beans, sauces, and even risotto in the pressure cooker, and in a significantly shorter time than you can in a pot on top of the stove. Pressure cooking cooks food faster because the water used in cooking can be heated to a higher temperature under pressure than it can in an ordinary pot.

Using a pressure cooker is similar to using an ordinary pot on top of the stove except that the top of a pressure cooker seals and locks closed. Before using any pressure cooker, you should carefully read and follow the manufacturer's instructions that come with the pot.

Pressure cookers are now safer than ever before. If you are still using your old one, you might consider looking into one of the newer models. Made of heavy stainless steel with practically foolproof and fail-safe safety mechanisms, the new pressure cookers are pleasurable and efficient to use.

Roasting

~ ~ ~

ARROSTIRE

To roast means to cook food in an uncovered pan in an oven using indirect, very high, dry heat. Although this cooking method is more typically applied to meats, roasted vegetables are a wonderful treat. When vegetables are lightly coated with olive oil, flavored with a dusting of salt, and cooked in a very hot oven, the water in the vegetables quickly cooks away and the natural sugars in the vegetables caramelize. The result is vegetables with an intense and delicious flavor.

You can roast almost any vegetable—particularly good are asparagus, onions (red and white), fennel, leeks, and eggplant. Roasted vegetables are an essential component of almost every antipasti table in Italy. They make a wonderful first course or can be served as an accompaniment to a main course.

Until as recently as the 1940s, ovens were not commonly found in Italian home kitchens. A baked dish, such as lasagna, would be taken to the local baker. Meat and vegetables, therefore, were "roasted" in a pan on top of the stove—seared in a preheated very hot pan and cooked slowly until tender. There are still many dishes in the repertoire of Italian cooking that are pan-roasted.

Baking

~ ~ ~

CUOCERE AL FORNO

Baking, like roasting, requires an oven, indirect dry heat, and an uncovered pan. However, baking is probably the older term. It is also the more general term and refers to oven-cooking almost anything from bread to casseroles at a range of heat from very low, 225°F, to very high, 500°F.

There are many baked vegetable dishes in the Italian cuisines. Aside from breads and sweets, there are the savory baked vegetable dishes such as pasta, polenta, and pizza.

Grilling

~ ~ ~

ALLA GRIGLIA

Grilling means placing food over an open flame on a rack. It is one of the great pleasures of summertime, when so many of us take our cooking out of doors.

For most of the year, however, when cooking must be done indoors, the oven broiler can be a fully satisfactory substitute for the grill; it produces excellent results, though without the burned-wood flavoring.

Sautéing or Pan Frying

~ ~ ~

ROSOLARE

To sauté means to quickly fry food in a small amount of fat. In Italian cooking, the fat is usually olive oil, vegetable oil, or a mixture of butter and olive oil. I recommend using a mild-flavored oil such as pure olive oil (rather than extra virgin), or corn or safflower oil.

Deep Frying

~ ~ ~

FRIGGERE

Deep frying, the process of cooking food while it is completely submersed in hot oil (or other fat), is widely used in Italian cooking. Deep-fried vegetables are a traditional antipasto in Rome. Vegetables that are fried are coated first either with seasoned flour, bread-crumbs that adhere to the surface of the food with the help of a beaten whole egg or egg white, or with a light batter of flour and egg. A mixture of different deep-fried vegetables, or *fritto misto* (see page 95), is a classic antipasti dish, as is fried zucchini. Eggplant, coated with bread crumbs and deep-fried, is also a traditional component of the Italian antipasti table.

Chapter Three

~ ~ ~

Basic Equipment

WITH FEW EXCEPTIONS, you will not need specialized kitchen equipment for preparing the recipes in this book. The following is an alphabetical listing of the equipment that will come in handy, most of which you probably already have on hand.

BAKING EQUIPMENT. Baking dishes are used for preparing a variety of recipes, from vegetable antipasti to baked pasta, polenta, and desserts. I like to use heatproof glass baking dishes because you can see what's going on inside, but you can also use lighter-weight (compared to roasting pans) metal pans, porcelain, enameled cast iron, or steel pans. Baking pans are usually square or rectangular in shape. You can also use oval pans that make a nice serving dish. A useful selection would include:

- 1 square baking dish, 10 × 10 inches
- 1 rectangular baking dish, 10 × 14 inches
- 2 oval baking dishes, 14 inches long

In addition:

- 1 plastic pastry scraper—a stiff plastic tool that resembles a spatula without a handle. It is essential when preparing doughs by hand— and handy for cleaning up your work surface after preparing dough.
- 1 rolling pin—a French-style tapered wooden rolling pin is ideal. You can also use an American ball-bearing rolling pin.
- 1 pie crimper—a rotating wheel with a curvy edge on a handle. A pie crimper allows you to cut pastry without tearing it.
- 1 springform pan—a pan with removable sides. The springform pan

is essential for preparing Italian *torte* (sweet and savory), which are meant to be freestanding.

- 2 cookie sheets

CASSEROLE. A heavy 6-quart casserole will be useful and versatile for preparing soups, beans, and risotto, as well as some of the desserts. I like to use enameled cast iron casseroles because they hold the heat extremely well and are also easy to clean.

CHEESE GRATER. It's always best to buy your Parmesan cheese in a piece and grate it just before you want to use it, whether for cooking or at the table. Hand-grating at the table adds to the pleasure of the meal. You can grate Parmesan in a food processor, but I prefer to use a hand-grater because the processor actually chops rather than grates the cheese and heats it in the process. You can also use a traditional three- or four-sided grater, but they are not usually sturdy enough to stand up to the firmness of aged Parmesan. There are a number of Parmesan graters on the market, some of which are battery operated. For grating cheese at the table, I recommend a small, hand-held single-sided grater and pass the cheese, please.

COLANDER. One large wire-mesh colander is essential for draining steamed or boiled vegetables, as well as cooked pasta, beans, and other foods.

FOOD MILL. Long before food processors were invented, cooks used food mills of various shapes and sizes for pureeing vegetables and soups. I have used an American-made food mill, which has served me well, for over twenty-five years. It looks like a strainer with a handle on one side, but it has a central blade that you turn to force the cooked food through the perforated bottom. European food mills are typically cone-shaped and work by forcing the food through with a wooden pestle. Food mills will come in handy when preparing some soups, pureed bean dishes, and gnocchi.

FOOD PROCESSOR. The food processor is traditionally not prescribed in the preparation of Italian cuisine; however, it has become an integral and labor-saving part of the way we cook and has many uses in the preparation of the recipes in this book, particularly for grating large quantities of mozzarella or other soft cheeses for pizzas or lasagna, for slicing pounds of mushrooms, for preparing *sformati*, the savory vegetable custards that are served as antipasti, and for pureeing some vegetables for soup or fruit for *sorbetti* and *granite*. You will also find a processor helpful in the preparation of some of the doughs, but it is hardly essential. In fact, many Italian cooks disdain a processor for the preparation of dough. They find that preparing dough by hand is faster and easier, gives the cook more control over the ingredients, and makes the results tastier. Wherever a food processor can be used, directions are included in the recipe. When a food processor should not be used—such as in the preparation of gnocchi because it makes the potato dough a dense paste—that is also stated.

GRILL. The backyard barbecue is ideal for preparing many of the grilled vegetable dishes described in this book. However, inclement weather often makes outdoor grilling less than pleasurable, and outdoor grilling can also be more work than seems desirable for some dishes, so you should consider alternatives. Stove-top, cast iron grills work very well to give your food a grilled effect but without the wood-burning flavor. An oven-broiler can also give a grilled effect.

KNIVES. A good set of sharp knives makes any kind of food preparation vastly easier, and that applies equally to the recipes in this book. You should have on hand:

- 1 large chef's knife (an 8-inch is an excellent all-purpose size)
- 1 bread knife with a serrated edge
- two 4-inch paring knives
- 1 tomato knife (with a serrated edge)

MICROWAVE OVEN. The microwave oven can be a helpful tool in the kitchen, even though it's an unconventional shortcut as far as traditional Italian cooking goes. However, many Italian vegetable recipes can be prepared either in part or entirely in the microwave and they have been included in this book. (*Note*: See pages 17–18 for more general microwave-cooking information.) Whenever a microwave recipe is given, so is the standard conventional cooking method. All microwave recipes in this book have been tested in a 700-watt oven. If your oven has a lower wattage, you will have to increase the cooking times given. Remember, the more food you have in your microwave, the longer the cooking time will be.

OLIVE/CHERRY PITTER. This is a small, inexpensive, and highly specialized hand tool that is indispensable for removing the pits from olives and cherries. It looks like a modified hole puncher: it has an elongated punch on one side and a little cup with a hole in the bottom on the other side. The olive/cherry is placed in the little cup; when the handle is squeezed the puncher goes right through the olive, forcing the pit through.

PASTA EQUIPMENT. Fresh pasta is ever more widely available in specialty stores and refrigerator cases in supermarkets, and often works superbly, but there are irreplaceable satisfactions in making your own.

Pasta machine. A hand-cranked or electric pasta machine is not essential for rolling out pasta dough—you can use good old elbow grease and a rolling pin—but it makes the job a lot easier. Once you make the dough, the pasta machine kneads and stretches the dough into paper-thin sheets and cuts it into strands. If you want different lengths or widths of pasta—pasta for lasagna, ravioli, or pappardelle—you'll have to cut them by hand.

Pasta pot. Any large 6- to 8-quart pot will be sufficient. There are specialized pasta pots fitted with colander/steamer inserts that can also be used for steaming, boiling, and/or blanching vegetables. These are convenient since you can quickly and efficiently lift the pasta from the water, instead of pouring the boiling water off. Pasta pots are also very helpful if you are cooking gnocchi, which must be cooked in small batches, or two or more different types of pasta since with this type of pot you can strain out the pasta and reuse the water, saving time and energy.

Pasta utensils. There are dozens of specialized pasta tools you can buy, but the only essential utensil I have come to rely on is a pastry crimper, which is indispensable for cutting and sealing ravioli. A wooden pasta "spoon" with perpendicular dowels is also handy for sampling pasta strands to test for doneness.

PRESSURE COOKER. Pressure cookers that are manufactured today are very different from the cookers made in the 1950s and '60s—they are extremely safe. They are often made with several safety features which help ensure that you can't make a mistake and hurt yourself. In addition, the better models today are made of heavy stainless steel, which makes them more durable and better cooking vessels than their predecessors. Pressure cookers are ideal for preparing soups, stocks, and beans.

RISOTTO POT. A 4- or 6-quart heavy-bottom saucepan or casserole is important for making the risotto recipes. I like to use an enameled cast iron casserole such as LeCreuset or Copco because the heavy bottom ensures an even distribution of heat, cooking the risotto evenly, while the enamel surface helps keep the rice from sticking.

ROASTING PANS. Used primarily for roasting vegetable antipasti dishes, roasting pans should be constructed of heavy metal—either stainless steel or coated aluminum—or enamel on cast iron, which makes them able to take excessively high heat. Most vegetables are roasted at the maximum oven heat of 500°F. If the pans are lightweight, you may find that they warp after a few uses. You'll want roasting pans in two sizes, 10 × 14 inches and 14 × 24 inches.

SAUTÉ PANS. Also called fry pans or skillets, these are reserved for stove-top cooking and are used for preparing numerous recipes in this book. A few dishes will require a pan with a nonstick surface. These four pans will cover all your sautéing and frying needs (though you can go for just one 10-inch nonstick model):

- one 8-inch sauté pan
- one 10-inch sauté pan
- one 12-inch sauté pan
- one 10-inch pan with a nonstick surface

SAUCEPANS. You will need saucepans for preparing many of the recipes in this book. I recommend using stainless steel, nonstick-coated, enameled, or anodized aluminum saucepans, which won't react with either acidic or base foods. You'll need:

- one 1½-quart saucepan
- one 2-quart saucepan
- one 4-quart saucepan

STOCKPOT. You will need one very large 8- or 10-quart casserole or stockpot with a lid for cooking soups and beans.

STEAMER. A steamer pot fitted with a steamer basket is most convenient, but you can also use a collapsible steamer tray insert to fit into your large saucepan.

VEGETABLE PEELER. Over the years I have acquired a number of different vegetable peelers in a variety of different shapes and widths. Some were billed as specialty items, such as asparagus peelers, with a price tag to reflect the "specialness." The most reliable peeler, and my favorite for asparagus as well, remains the simplest, or "classic," all-purpose vegetable peeler—a stainless steel peeler with a vertical-swivel two-sided blade that can be found in lots of places, including kitchenware and hardware stores, and some supermarkets.

Chapter Four

~ ~ ~

The Vegetables of Italy

A Brief History
~ ~ ~

ONE OF THE SPECIAL PLEASURES of all things Italian is their connection to the past—the art, the architecture, the music, the landscape, and, of course, the cuisine have old, even ancient sources. Although Italian cooking can be traced back to the ancient Greeks and possibly even earlier, it was the early Romans who established the foundation of Italian cooking today.

It is intriguing to discover how many Romans, known to us as statesmen and authors, left us specific records of their observations and opinions on vegetables and their preparation, giving us insight into the role vegetables played not only in the cuisine but in the culture of Italy as well.

Cato the Elder, the statesman and historian who documented the history of the Roman Empire as well as the agricultural methods of his day during the first half of the second century B.C., wrote in great detail about the cultivation and cooking of asparagus. The first-century epigrammist Martial also left us his opinion on asparagus: Ravenna grew the best asparagus, he wrote, which some Italians maintain is still true today.

The clearest evidence of the interest the Romans had in food preparation is the extensive collection of recipes, in the form of "Ten Books" on dining and cookery, left to us by Apicius, a lover of food and cooking from the first century A.D. Two of Apicius' books are devoted entirely to vegetables and legumes, and many other vegetable recipes are scattered throughout the remaining text.

The Romans didn't care for carrots, but they valued celery as a medicine and food. Apicius provided a number of celery recipes, though you might not want to try them in your own kitchen; a typical one calls for celery cooked in soda water (presumably to keep it green), drained or "squeezed," and finely chopped. The recipe continues, "In the mortar crush pepper, lovage, origany [oregano], onion and mix with wine and stock, adding some oil. Cook this in the boiler and mix the celery with this preparation."

Many vegetables besides celery were consumed in ancient Rome as medications. Cabbage was particularly revered for its healing qualities, but only aristocrats could afford it. Wild fennel was widely eaten for medicinal purposes, according to the writings of Pliny, who attributed twenty-two remedies to fennel. Also used for their healing properties, fresh herbs were cooked with other foods to mask bad tastes as well as to enhance good flavors. The Romans consumed vast quantities of garlic for its health benefits and worshiped it for its mythical effect, especially as an aphrodisiac, on the gods and goddesses of antiquity. Garlic mixed with coriander was considered a love potion. The Romans—who ate garlic for strength before going into battle—are credited with first using garlic in cooking.

Onions and leeks were also popular with the ancient Romans. Nero ate leeks, allegedly because he believed they made his voice clearer, and Horace ate them simply because he liked them with chickpeas and pasta.

Many vegetables have been assimilated into Italian cooking from other cultures. Cucumbers, which have been cultivated in the Mediterranean region for over four thousand years, were brought to Italy by the ancient Greeks, as were peas. The Romans took to cultivating peas on a large scale, but always dried them like other podded legumes, not eating them fresh. The Moslems introduced cauliflower to southern Italy.

The most significant influx of vegetables—many of which have come to be synonymous with Italian cooking—occurred during the sixteenth century. It was only then, with the discovery of the Americas, that Italy gained the tomato, and along with it the potato, pepper, corn, and squash. And about the same time, Catherine de' Medici, the great gastronome from Florence who became queen of France in 1547, introduced French cooking techniques to Italy along with such foods as pastries and creamed soups.

The importance of vegetables in Italian cooking in the late sixteenth and early seventeenth centuries is evident in the book *The Fruit, Herbs and Vegetables of Italy*, written by Giacomo Castelvetro, an Italian living in England at the time. Castelvetro documented the preparation of vegetable dishes by season, many of which are still made today.

Today Italy is part of the global market; kiwi and pineapple are airfreighted to markets in major Italian cities and share shelf space with artichokes and eggplants. But as anyone fortunate enough to have spent time in Italy can attest, the Italians have a way of making whatever they have on hand their own, whether it is a dish as ancient as fennel baked with Parmesan cheese or one as contemporary as *macedonia* of fruit with kiwi. The Italian genius for getting the best out of vegetables continues to teach and delight us.

A Guide to the Vegetables of Italy

~ ~ ~

The preparation of Italian vegetable dishes inevitably begins at the market. Freshness is key—that almost goes without saying. Be guided by what's available, as are Italian cooks, who scan the market for the best produce and then plan their meals around it. If you go looking for artichokes only to find pitiful browned and wilted specimens or none at all, look around—perhaps the broccoli is fresh and green or the asparagus spears are firm and tall. It is so much easier to make fine meals with high-quality ingredients than to turn produce past its prime into a delicious repast for family and friends. In supermarkets as well as specialty greengrocers around the country, chances are better today than ever before that you can find some excellent produce most times of the year. And, of course, in spring and summer you can take advantage of your own or friends' gardens, as well as local farm stands.

The following is a guide to the vegetables essential to Italian cooking. I hope this information will help you when you're shopping for produce.

Also included in this section are the preliminary steps needed to prepare vegetables such as artichoke, asparagus, broccoli, or eggplant for cooking. Recipes in the later chapters will regularly refer back to this section when needed.

Artichokes

~ ~ ~

CARCIOFI

Artichokes, which are eaten both raw and cooked, are grown throughout Italy, though they are most closely associated with Rome and the cooking of the region surrounding Rome, called Lazio. Rome has many restaurants that specialize in artichokes. The restaurants, for example, in the area that has been Rome's Jewish quarter since the first century A.D. and in the 1500s was designated as the Jewish ghetto by Pope Paul IV, are the places to go for *carciofi alla giudia* (artichokes, Jewish style), deep-fried artichokes. But almost every Roman restaurant offers a version of *carciofi alla romana*, which are artichokes that have been seasoned with herbs, garlic, and salt and cooked until they are exceptionally tender in a mixture of oil and water—"*Mezzo mezzo*" (half oil and half water), as the proprietress of one restaurant explained. Artichokes are also eaten in regions beyond Lazio, but not with the variety you'll find in Rome.

In the fall in Rome's beautiful open-air fruit and vegetable market, the Campo dei Fiori, there are numerous stalls with crate upon wooden crate of fresh artichokes. Some of the artichokes are purple, others are yellow. Some are thorny, others are thorn-free. Most of the artichokes are elongated, rather than round like the American variety, with stalks 12 to 18 inches long and big leaves that extend almost the full length of the stalk. The seller trims the artichoke stalks and cuts away the leaves as the buyers—older women all in black as well as elegantly dressed *ragazze* (young women) on bicycles—line up for their purchases.

For most Italian artichoke recipes, American-grown artichokes produce excellent results that approximate the Italian version quite well. The principal difference between the American and Italian artichokes is that Italian varieties are spineless, which means the leaves do not have a tough, woody, inedible structure. If you trim away the tough outer leaves, you're left with the tender leaves that cook and taste like Italian artichokes.

Artichokes in the United States are available throughout most of the year, but are considered in season in the late fall and early spring. American artichokes are grown almost exclusively in Castroville, California. Essentially two varieties are grown there which are available in numerous sizes. For the purpose of simplifying the recipes in this book, artichokes will be categorized according to size: the smallest, *carciofini* as they are called in Italy, are about the size of a jumbo-size egg and are the only artichokes you can eat raw; medium-size artichokes are about 3 to 4 inches tall; large artichokes are 5 to 6 inches tall. Greengrocers in America speak of artichokes as "18 count," "120 count," etc., which refers to the number of artichokes that can fit into one standard packing crate. Artichokes are generally shipped within two to three days of picking. They should be wrapped in plastic and refrigerated until they are cooked; otherwise they dry out and lose their fresh flavor.

The directions that follow for cleaning and preparing artichokes for cooking apply to many of the recipes in this book.

TO PREPARE ARTICHOKES FOR COOKING:

1. Combine the juice from 1 whole lemon with 4 cups of cool water in a nonreactive bowl (stainless steel, glass, ceramic, or plastic) and set aside.

2. Peel away the tough dark green leaves of each artichoke: Starting with the leaves closest to the stem, break off the leaves all around the artichoke until only light yellow leaves are visible. Do not use scissors or a knife for this; the leaves will break naturally at the point where the tough part ends and the tender part begins.

3. Using a knife, cut 1 to 2 inches off the top of the artichoke, peel the stem, and trim around the base to make a neat, even surface.

4. Use a grapefruit spoon or melon baller to scrape the fuzzy choke out of larger artichokes.

5. Place the prepared artichoke in the bowl with the lemon and water mixture, to prevent discoloration, until ready to cook.

Arugula

~ ~ ~

RUCOLA

Arugula, with its sharp, peppery flavor, grows wild in fields through-out the Italian countryside and is also grown commercially. Both can be bought in Italian markets. The wild variety tends to have a slightly more pungent taste.

Arugula, which sometimes goes by the name rocket, has become increasingly popular in the last few years. Many big supermarket chains sell it, as do specialty greengrocers. It is available most of the year, and in the summer you can sometimes find locally grown varieties.

When you buy arugula, it is usually very sandy and requires several thorough rinsings in cold water to come clean. It should be dried carefully (a salad spinner does the job well) because it will spoil quickly if left wet.

When using arugula as a salad green, dress it only just before serving, since it is delicate and tends to become soggy more quickly than lettuce.

Asparagus

~ ~ ~

ASPARAGI

Asparagus is available throughout Italy for much of the year because of the temperate climate there. Only in northern Italy are you likely to find the highly regarded white asparagus, a delicacy because it must be carefully cultivated in the absence of light.

Asparagus in the United States does not differ significantly from Italian-grown varieties. The best-tasting asparagus is almost always locally grown and is available for only a short time. Like so much other produce that is grown in mega-quantities and shipped long distances, much of the asparagus that is available most of the year doesn't have the wonderful fresh, grassy flavor that is best associated with it.

Whenever you buy asparagus, you should look for the freshest spears. You can tell a lot from the tips: the older spears tend to look frayed at the tip rather than firm and tight. Older stalks also have a tendency to become dried and shriveled in spots and turn a spoiled, yellowy green color. Always buy spears of uniform thickness, whether fat or thin, so that they cook evenly and uniformly.

If you are cooking thin (no more than ¼ inch in diameter) asparagus spears, they can be prepared for cooking by simply cutting off 1 or 2 inches from the bottom. Thicker spears should also be peeled with a vegetable peeler, because the outer skin toughens as the spears grow. Scrape the skin from the bottom third of each spear.

Italian recipes generally call for the very thin- to medium-thick-size spears because they have a more delicate flavor. Thin-size spears add up to about 16 to 18 spears per pound.

If you don't intend to cook the asparagus the same day you buy it, you can extend its freshness by simply trimming the ends from the spears, like flowers, and placing them in a container of cold water. If placed in the refrigerator they will keep perfectly for a day or two.

BASIC PREPARATION FOR ASPARAGUS. One of the great challenges of cooking asparagus perfectly is to get the stalks tender but still firm while keeping their bright green color. You can boil or steam the spears. To boil asparagus, place the spears in boiling water and cook uncovered. To steam the spears, place them in a steamer basket or tray over boiling water and cook, covered. Whether steaming or boiling, cook for 5 minutes. Refresh spears under cold running water to stop the cooking.

MICROWAVE/STEAMING. My own preference for cooking asparagus is to use the microwave oven. Asparagus cooked in the microwave requires no added water. Simply trim and discard the bottoms of the spears and peel if the spears are medium to thick. Rinse the spears thoroughly—from tip to base—under cold running water, because asparagus can sometimes be sandy. Place the wet spears, all facing in the same direction, on a microwave-safe dish, preferably one that is rectangular or oval. You can also use a square or round plate as long as all of the asparagus lies flat and fits within the sides of the dish. Cover tightly with microwave-safe plastic wrap and place in the oven.

Cooking times on high power: ½ pound of asparagus, cleaned and rinsed, will take 6 minutes to cook in a small (400- to 500-watt) oven or 4 minutes and 30 seconds in a large (600- to 700-watt) oven. One pound of asparagus, cleaned and rinsed, will take 6 minutes to cook in a large oven and 8 minutes in a smaller oven.

Beans

~ ~ ~

FAGIOLI

Once considered the meat of the poor in Italy, many varieties of beans are now popular throughout the country. Like many other vegetables, however, there are strong regional associations with particular beans. For example, lentils are typically grown in Umbria and are associated with the cooking of that region, and chickpeas are almost exclusively grown in the south and are a staple of southern Italian fare.

The most popular beans in Italy include *borlotti*, which are pale pink with red speckles (similar to our pinto beans); *cannellini*, white kidney beans usually associated with Tuscan cooking; chickpeas, or *ceci*, which were brought to Italy from the Middle East and are eaten with pasta as well as with soups; brown lentils, *lenticche*, grown in Umbria; and finally fava beans, the broad flat beans that, more than any other bean, have long held a special place in Italian culture and cooking. At ancient Roman funerals favas were supposedly presented as an offering to deceased relatives. Favas can be eaten either cooked—fresh or dried—or uncooked, although raw fava beans contain toxins to which some people react and can become ill. Unless favas are very young and small, they should be peeled before eating raw.

Although the varieties of dried beans or legumes that are eaten in Italy vary greatly in shape, size, and color, they all have a similar nutritional composition: 1 cup of dried beans contains approximately 210 calories with 14 grams of protein, 36 grams of carbohydrates, 4.3 milligrams of iron, and 740 milligrams of potassium, with traces of vitamins B_1, B_2, and B_3.

(See section on Beans, pages 215–19, for more information on basic preparations, bean types, and cooking times.)

Beets, Beet Greens, and Swiss Chard

~ ~ ~

BARBABIETOLE E BIETOLE

It was only in the late fifteenth century that the beet root (what we know as the beet) was introduced to Italy from Germany. In Italian markets it is often possible to buy beets already cooked. Raw beets are typically treated to one preparation: they are roasted in the oven, sliced, and dressed with olive oil and vinegar. Italian cooks do not peel or cut beets before cooking. Water penetrating the beet root causes a loss of nutritive value. Beets are high in protein and also contain minerals such as iron and calcium.

Beet greens and Swiss chard (essentially two varieties of the same plant) are sautéed, baked, steamed, and used for stuffings for filled pasta dishes.

Broccoli

~ ~ ~

BROCCOLI or BROCCOLETTI

In Italy, broccoli is grown and eaten mostly in the southern regions of Calabria, Abruzzi, Lazio, and Campania where it goes by different names, including *broccoli*, *broccoletti*, and *cavolfiore*, which is actually a purple cauliflower that turns green when cooked and looks and tastes almost the same as what we know as broccoli. When broccoli is eaten in the north it is usually as a *contorni*, or accompaniment to a meat or fish entree. In the south of Italy, broccoli is served in a variety of ways with pasta, as a salad, or as an antipasto.

Broccoli was brought to the United States by Italian immigrants in the late nineteenth century. It retained its Italian name and is still associated with Italian farmers on the West Coast as well as in the East.

BASIC PREPARATION FOR BROCCOLI. Many broccoli dishes require the broccoli to be precooked. You can precook broccoli in the microwave, in a steamer-pot on top of the stove, or by parboiling (see page 17). For one bunch of fresh broccoli (approximately 1½ pounds), trim away the thick stems (save them for Fennel and Broccoli Soup, see page 101), and cut the remaining broccoli into small florets. Place the cut-up broccoli in a large bowl, cover with cold water, and allow to stand for at least 30 minutes. This soaking process helps remove any dirt or sand from the broccoli; simple rinsing doesn't do the job as well.

Microwave technique: Drain, but do not dry the broccoli and arrange the florets in a single layer on a heatproof microwave-safe platter or dish. Cover with microwave-safe plastic wrap and cook on high power for 5 minutes in a 600- to 700-watt oven. When the broccoli has finished cooking, allow to stand for 3 to 5 minutes, carefully remove the plastic wrap, and season with salt to taste. The broccoli can be served immediately, lightly coated with some fruity olive oil and a sprinkling of salt, or prepared in one of the recipes given later in the book.

Stove-top technique: Bring about 1 cup of water to a boil in a large saucepan, place the florets in a steamer basket over boiling water, cover, and cook for 5 minutes. Transfer the broccoli to a colander and refresh under cold running water to stop the cooking process and retain the bright green color.

Cabbage

~ ~ ~

CAVOLO

Three types of cabbage are grown and used in Italian cooking. *Cavolo cappuccio* is the ordinary green or red cabbage that is most common in Italy and the United States. *Cavolo verza* or *cavolo di Milano* is curly-leaf, what we call savoy cabbage, and is used mostly in traditional Milanese dishes. The third type, *cavolo nero*, or black cabbage, is actually very dark green rather than black and has a bitter flavor compared to the other varieties. *Cavolo nero* is commonly found in Tuscan dishes, typically the vegetable soup *ribollita* (see pages 110–11), a version of minestrone.

Unlike in the United States, where cabbage has never been particularly popular, in Italy cabbage is an essential ingredient in almost every variation of minestrone (vegetable soups) and many other dishes as well.

When buying cabbage, look for firm, heavy heads, preferably with their tough outer leaves attached. This usually means that they are fresh and haven't been sitting around for weeks or months, with the greengrocers trimming these leaves as they wilt.

Cardoons

CARDI

Like the artichoke, the cardoon is a prickly thistle, although, with its long stalks, it more closely resembles celery. It has tough outer stalks that are always discarded. The tender inner stalks are cut, cooked, and eaten.

Although cardoons are not widely eaten in Italy, they are a traditional component of the Piedmontese dish *bagna cauda* (see page 94), the hot garlicky dip that is eaten with an array of raw vegetables, of which the cardoon—only the most tender inner stalks—is always one.

Cardoons are rarely available in the United States, but some specialty greengrocers sell them during the winter months. Cardoons vary in size from 12 to 25 inches long. To prepare cardoons, if you should find them, discard the heavy outer stalks and cut the inner stalks into 2– to 3–inch pieces. As with artichokes, after cutting the cardoons you should place them in acidulated water (a mixture of water and lemon juice, see page 32), to prevent them from turning brown, until you are ready to cook them.

Carrots

CAROTE

Carrots are used mainly as a flavoring in soups, stocks, and the *soffritti*, sautéed minced vegetables, that are the bases of many stews and risotti. Carrots also have a place at the antipasti table. Carrot antipasti can be baked, grilled, or marinated.

Cauliflower

CAVOLFIORE

Cauliflower didn't become popular with Italians until the sixteenth century, when it was enjoyed either cold—boiled and dressed with olive oil, salt, and pepper—or served hot in broth, according to Giacomo Castelvetro's early-seventeenth-century book *The Fruit, Herbs and Vegetables of Italy*.

Cauliflower is a variety of cabbage—"cabbage with a college education," as Mark Twain once said—that produces tight florets rather than leaves. When buying cauliflower, choose heads with firm, not wilted green leaves and pure white florets, and avoid heads with brown spots on them. It is important not to overcook cauliflower, because the flavor can become unpleasantly strong and bitter.

HOW TO PRECOOK CAULIFLOWER. As with so many other vegetables used in Italian cooking, cauliflower requires some precooking preparation. The head should be broken or cut into small florets, rinsed well, and drained. You can steam the florets on top of the stove or in a microwave oven. To precook cauliflower in a stove-top steamer, bring about 1 cup of water to a boil in a large saucepan, place the florets in a steamer basket over the boiling water, cover, and cook for 6 minutes. Drain the cauliflower and rinse it under cold running water to stop the cooking. To precook cauliflower in the microwave oven, place the florets in a single, even layer in a shallow microwave-safe dish. Cover securely with microwave-safe plastic wrap and place the dish in the microwave oven. Cook on high power for 5 minutes. Allow the cauliflower to stand for 5 minutes. Carefully remove the plastic.

Celery

~ ~ ~

SEDANO

Celery is an indispensable flavoring ingredient in numerous Italian recipes. It can also be served on its own, baked, fried, or cooked in soup. Celery soup (see page 100) is a typical Italian home-cooked dish that you won't find in restaurants. Most celery in our marketplace is Pascal celery, with large, lightly colored green stalks, which doesn't differ significantly from Italian celery varieties.

Chicory
~ ~ ~
CICORIA, RADICCHIO

There are numerous varieties of chicory used in Italian cooking. The two most popular types are curly green escarole, *scarola*, and red radicchio, either the round-headed *radicchio di Verona* or the elongated *radicchio di Treviso*. (In Italy, you can also find many other varieties, including Catalogna chicory, which is similar in appearance to dandelion with its long, spiky leaves, and is almost always eaten blanched and seasoned with oil and lemon juice. There is also Grumolo chicory from Lombardy, which has a broad, flat leaf that resembles Boston lettuce; it too is usually cooked.)

The most prized types of chicory are the red, or *rosso*, varieties that are grown almost exclusively in the northern Veneto region near Venice. In contrast to green chicories, which tend toward the more bitter, the reds have only a mildly bitter flavor and at the same time are tender to the bite. Although American farmers grow many varieties of green chicory or escarole, all of the red radicchio found in our markets is shipped to us from Italy, which accounts for its high price. Radicchio is probably most commonly found in salads, but it is also wonderful cooked—grilled, baked, or combined with risotto.

Both the green and red varieties can be eaten raw in salads or cooked in a variety of ways.

Cucumbers
~ ~ ~
CETRIOLI

Today in Italy, you usually find small-size cucumbers—like our Kirby or pickling cucumbers. Peeled and sliced, they are a common ingredient in a mixed green salad. The smallest, *cetriolini*, are often pickled in vinegar, similar to the French *cornichons*.

In our markets pickling cucumbers have become more readily available, although they are not as plentiful as the large waxy-skinned cucumbers that commercial farmers grow because they are less perishable and more durable than the small cucumbers.

Dandelion

~ ~ ~

DENTE DI LEONE

Also called *insalatina di campo* ("salad of the field") because it is a salad green commonly found growing wild in the fields, dandelion must be picked while it is still very small and before it flowers. Since it is one of the bitterest of salad greens, some cooks soak the leaves in salted water to help reduce the bitterness before adding it to a salad. Dandelion is almost always eaten uncooked, dressed with oil and vinegar. While it can be cooked, cooking tends to make the dandelion even more bitter.

Eggplant

~ ~ ~

MELANZANE

Although eggplant is a staple of Italian cooking throughout Italy, for hundreds of years it was grown only in Sicily and southern Italy. That accounts for why so many of the classic Italian eggplant dishes—*caponata* (see page 71), *melanzane alla parmigiana* (see page 70)—are traditional southern Italian fare.

Several varieties of eggplant are grown in Italy: small, round, large, or elongated, they can be almost black, pale purple, or even ivory-colored. Whatever the shape or color, almost all eggplants taste pretty much the same and can be interchanged in most recipes.

Different varieties of eggplant can now sometimes be found in markets in the United States. When buying eggplant you should look for firm and shiny ones.

You don't usually have to peel eggplant before cooking. However, most recipes suggest you salt and drain the eggplant after cutting it. This draws out much of the moisture in the eggplant so that when you cook it, the dish does not end up watery. Salting also draws out any bitterness— although really fresh eggplant is not particularly bitter. After salting, you should allow the eggplant pieces to stand for about 30 minutes in a colander. Pat the eggplant pieces dry with paper towels before cooking.

Eggplant can be grilled, baked, roasted, stuffed, stewed, and sautéed.

Fennel

~ ~ ~

FINOCCHIO

An ancient medicinal remedy, fennel began to be cultivated for its culinary attributes in the sixteenth century and has remained a staple of Italian cooking ever since. With its licorice flavor, bulbous celerylike stalks, and wispy green leaves, it is one of the most distinctive vegetables in Italian cooking. Fennel seeds are used as a flavoring in cooking, and the stalks and bulbs can be eaten either raw or cooked. When cooked, fennel's pronounced licorice flavor becomes more subtle and delicate.

Fennel is plentiful throughout the fall and winter months. In American markets fennel is sometimes called anise because of its flavor, although the two are not related.

To prepare fennel, you usually have to discard the outer stalks and trim away the fernlike leaves before cooking.

Garlic

~ ~ ~

AGLIO

Once a purely medicinal remedy, then an indispensable flavoring for food, garlic remains one of the essential ingredients in Italian cooking.

When you buy them, heads of garlic should be firm to the touch. As they age, the bulbs dry out and the paperlike skin starts to flake away. Always store garlic in a dry, preferably cool place. Freshly picked young heads of garlic tend to be less pungent than older ones that have been stored for several months.

The best way to peel a clove of garlic is to use a sharp paring knife and cut away the root end of the clove. The skin on the clove usually comes away easily after that. If you're in a hurry, place the unpeeled garlic clove between your kitchen counter and the flat side of a large chef's knife. Pound the knife blade bluntly with the side of your fist. The garlic clove should flatten slightly and separate from the skin.

Most of the recipes in this book that use garlic call for it to be "finely minced or pressed," which means you can either chop the garlic, with a knife or in a food processor, or force it through a garlic press. It just depends on whether you want to have pieces of garlic in the dish you are preparing. Some garlic purists will tell you that any way of chopping garlic except with a knife will render the clove bitter. I usually can't taste the difference.

In cooking, never burn or overly brown the garlic because it will give a distinctive, unpleasant bitterness to the food. It is also possible to flavor food with garlic without leaving any garlic clove in the dish. Heat a whole peeled clove of garlic in the oil or oil-and-butter to be used for cooking until the clove turns a golden color. At that point remove the garlic and discard it. You can also use garlic-flavored oil to baste vegetables before roasting or grilling them.

Green Beans

~ ~ ~

FAGIOLINI

Green beans, the young pods that eventually grow to be the inedible sacs for mature beans or legumes, are a product of the New World. Like so many other vegetables that are now an integral part of Italian cuisine, they didn't enter the Italian culinary vocabulary until the seventeenth century.

There are several varieties of the skinny green beans grown in Italy. The *cornetti* are the smallest and skinniest. The Tuscan *fagiolini di Sant'Anna* are probably the longest, sometimes measuring as much as 20 inches.

In Italian cooking, green beans are usually steamed first. The steamed beans can be served at room temperature in salads, pan-roasted, or stewed with tomatoes (see page 89–90). You can use any American-grown green beans in Italian recipes provided they are very fresh—they should snap decisively when you break them.

Herbs

~ ~ ~

ERBE

Italian cooking is inseparable from fresh herbs, so dependent is it upon their aromatic leaves for flavoring: it is impossible to imagine roasts without rosemary, beans without sage, or pesto without basil.

Herbs have played several roles in Italian culture and cooking over the centuries. They have been regarded for their medicinal attributes and coveted for religious reasons. Sometimes they have been called upon to mask the bad taste of rancid meat. But more often they have been employed to enhance and embellish the good tastes.

When it comes to cooking, fresh herbs should be used whenever possible, and with a light hand. The flavor of dried herbs, because it is concentrated, is usually stronger if not altogether different from the fresh variety. To substitute, the general rule is for every tablespoon of fresh herbs use 1 teaspoon dried. If a particular fresh herb is not available, I often substitute fresh parsley since it is generally available year-round everywhere. Although the flavor is not the same, you get a fresh-tasting dish.

Storing fresh herbs will vary, depending on the herb. Most can be kept for several days in the refrigerator.

BASIL/*BASILICO*. More than any other herb, basil is associated with Italian cooking. Not only is it the essential ingredient in many Ligurian dishes, most notably pesto; throughout all of the regions of Italy, basil is a fundamental component of fresh tomato sauces, soups, and salads.

The basil plant is an annual and a member of the mint family, with leaves that can be broad or tiny, green or dark purple. It is available—in less or more abundance—throughout most of the year. Cut basil is perishable and should be purchased the day you intend to use it and thoroughly washed and dried just before cooking. Although basil readily wilts and turns brown in the refrigerator from both the cold and the moisture, you can extend its vitality if you wrap it in paper towels, put it in a plastic bag, and place it in the crisper of your refrigerator. You can freeze or dry fresh basil, but you don't get the same flavor that you get from the fresh.

BAY LEAVES/*LAURO*. In Italian cooking, bay leaves are used as a flavoring for soups, stews, and in brines for pickling. Bay leaves are almost always bought in their dry state.

Always use whole bay leaves—and not a leaf broken up into small pieces—and remove it before serving. An ingested whole or piece of bay leaf can cause serious injury to internal organs.

MARJORAM/*MAGGIORANA*. Very similar to oregano, but sweeter and less pungent, marjoram is typically used in Ligurian cooking, where it is added to numerous dishes, including the stuffings for eggplant and zucchini. There are many varieties of marjoram, all of which produce small white flowers tucked within green leaves along a thin stem. Store fresh marjoram wrapped first in a paper towel and then in a plastic bag in the crisper of your refrigerator. To use marjoram, run your fingers along the stems and pull off the leaves and flowers.

MINT/*MENTA*. Many varieties—both cultivated and wild—of mint grow in Italy and are used in cooking. Wild mint, called *mentuccia*, is also used in Italian cooking. This herb has a smaller leaf and much milder flavor and aroma than the cultivated peppermint we know. Another type of mint, *nepitella*, which tastes like a cross between marjoram and mint, is typically used in the cooking of Tuscany and in Lazio (the region around Rome) where the traditional *carciofi alla romana* (see pages 58–59), as well as other dishes, are prepared with it. Because *nepitella* is not available in American markets and specialty stores, I have substituted marjoram and/or parsley in the recipes that traditionally would be prepared with it. To store fresh mint in the refrigerator, wrap in paper towels and store in plastic bags.

PARSLEY/*PREZZEMOLO*. Though there is little taste difference between the flatleaf and curly parsley, it is the flatleaf, the so-called Italian parsley, that is widely used in the preparation of vegetable dishes throughout Italy. It is almost always cooked, rather than added for decoration. You can use flatleaf or curly parsley in the preparation of the recipes in this book.

Parsley is high in nutrients, particularly vitamins C and A as well as potassium, iron, and calcium. The ancient Romans sometimes wore garlands of parsley around their heads and necks, supposedly to fend off drunkenness.

Parsley can be washed and kept for up to a week in the refrigerator.

Wrap it in damp paper towels or place in a plastic bag. For convenience, you can chop parsley and keep it uncovered in a dish in the refrigerator for a day or two; after that it begins to dry out and lose some of its flavor.

CRUSHED RED PEPPER/*PEPERONCINO*. Dried crushed hot red pepper flakes, the dried seeds from hot red chili peppers, are added to many dishes in the southern regions of Italy. The *arrabbiata* sauce of Abruzzi is typically seasoned with *peperoncino*, as is the classic pasta *aglio e olio*, with garlic and oil. *Peperoncino* is also added to olive oil that is used to dress salads or for cooking, to give it a zippier flavor. Because you tend to use only a pinch of *peperoncino* at a time, one container can last for years. You may find that the flavor wanes over time, the heat of the flakes losing some of their spark. At least once a year you should invest in some new pepper flakes.

OREGANO/*ORIGANO*. The herb most closely associated with the cooking of southern Italy, oregano is widely used in the preparation of pizza, tomato sauces, and numerous vegetable antipasti. Fresh oregano has become relatively available in recent years in Italian markets and from specialty greengrocers. Store it in a plastic bag in the refrigerator to prevent it from drying out. Dried oregano has a more intense flavor than the fresh, but, as with most herbs, over time the flavor of dried oregano will weaken, so it is best to restock your dried oregano annually.

ROSEMARY/*ROSMARINO*. In ancient times there were dozens of medicinal and mythological uses for rosemary. A beautiful bush with leaves that resemble a pine tree, rosemary is typically used in Italian cooking as a flavoring for roasted meat and the roasted potatoes that accompany it. Fresh rosemary has a strong, perfumy aroma, but when cooked the fragrance mellows considerably. Fresh rosemary is durable and will keep for up to a week in a plastic bag in the refrigerator.

SAGE/*SALVIA*. Sage is a typical ingredient in Tuscan and northern Italian dishes, often cooked in combination with butter. In ancient times sage was associated with good health—the Italian word *salvia* comes from the Latin *salvere*, which means "to be of good health." The ancient Romans prepared a sage wine that was ingested as a curative for various ailments. Store fresh sage in a plastic bag in the refrigerator.

THYME/*TIMO*. Also called *pepolino* in Tuscany, the Italians favor the wild thyme collected in the countryside as well as cultivated varieties. Thyme is used in cooking meats and fish. It can be stored in a plastic bag in the refrigerator.

Leeks

~ ~ ~

PORRI

With its mild, oniony flavor (although it is not directly related to the onion), the leek is one of the most prized and popular vegetables of northern Italy. Leeks are typically steamed or braised and lightly dressed with olive oil, or preparred in risotto, soups, and vegetable pasta dishes. Very young leeks can be sliced into paper-thin rounds, dressed with oil and vinegar, and eaten raw.

When buying leeks, smaller ones are preferable because they tend to have a more delicate flavor than larger leeks. In any case, you eat only the white part—the green tops can be cooked as a flavoring for broth, or discarded.

It is most important to clean leeks thoroughly before cooking them since they are almost always gritty with sand throughout all their many layers.

TO CLEAN LEEKS. Cut away all but an inch of the green tops (discard or reserve for another use) and the root end. If you want to leave the leeks whole, make two lengthwise cuts down the middle of the leek (45 degrees apart) from the top to the lower third part of the stalk. Then, holding the stalk under cool running water, rinse each layer of the leek carefully. If you plan to julienne the leeks, cut each stalk in half lengthwise. Rinse thoroughly under cold running water and then cut into strips.

Lettuce

~ ~ ~

LATTUGA

Three varieties of lettuce are most commonly used in Italy: *romana* is what we know as romaine, with its stiff spine and crisp leaves; *cappuccio* is most like our Boston lettuce, with soft, tender leaves; and *ricciolina* is like our scallop-edged salad bowl lettuce, with tender leaves and almost no spine at all.

In Italy, lettuce is used in salads, but it can also be cooked—either braised, stuffed with meat or an egg-and-cheese stuffing, or sautéed with a variety of ingredients.

If you wash and spin dry lettuce, and keep it covered or wrapped, it will stay fresh and crisp for a day or two before it begins to turn brown.

Mushrooms and Truffles

~ ~ ~

FUNGHI E TARTUFI

Mushrooms are fungi (hence, the Italian name *funghi*) that grow in usually damp, earthy locations. When Italians speak of mushrooms they are referring to the wonderfully flavorful wild varieties that abound in markets throughout Italy during the spring and fall when they are in season (white cultivated mushrooms are almost nonexistent in Italy). Mushroom hunting and gathering is a livelihood for some Italians and a passion for many others, although there is a limit now in some areas as to how much you can gather to protect the natural crop from being depleted.

The most popular and abundant mushroom in Italy is the porcini (*Boletus edulis*). Also available are morels (*Morchella esculenta*), oyster mushrooms (*Pleurotus ostreatus*), and chanterelles (*Cantharellus cibarius*), among others. The most prized fungi remain truffles. Black truffles (*Tuber melanosporum*) are found mostly in the region around Norcia on the east coast of Italy. The pungently aromatic white truffle (*Tuber magnatum*) comes from Alba and is so closely associated with the area that it is called *tartufo d'Alba*.

In recent years American markets have begun to sell "wild" varieties of mushrooms, most of which are cultivated on specialized mushroom farms, making them available throughout the year and not just during the damp spring and fall seasons as they are in Italy. The most common varieties in American stores are the wide-capped portobello mushrooms, the small round, brown crimini, and the shiitake. Fancier greengrocers might also sell oyster mushrooms, pleurottes as they are sometimes called, as well as the pricier morels and chanterelles. In American markets it is extremely rare to find fresh porcini, although in the future, with new cultivation techniques being developed, that may change. All these varieties are preferable to the white button cap mushrooms, and any one or a mixture can be used in the recipes in this book.

Dried mushrooms, particularly the dried porcini with their intense flavor, are a common ingredient in Italian recipes. Because dried mushrooms are so strong tasting, a little goes a long way. Less than an ounce will flavor enough risotto for four people. When using dried porcini, always soak them in very hot or boiling water to cover for at least 15 minutes before cooking and drain them well before adding to the recipe. If possible, use the strained soaking liquid in the recipe. (Dried mushrooms often have dirt and grit on them which is deposited in the soaking water, and must be strained out through a fine-wire sieve before the liquid can be used.)

You can add some soaked dried porcini to fresh cultivated mushrooms to give them more flavor.

HOW TO CLEAN MUSHROOMS. Never wash mushrooms under running water. They are highly absorbant and the water will spoil their texture and make them spongy. Use a damp paper towel and wipe the caps to remove any dirt. "Portobello" mushrooms are best when the gills along the underside, which give off a black, inky color, are trimmed away.

Olives
~ ~ ~
OLIVE

Olive trees seem to grow everywhere in Italy. As you drive in the countryside you see entire hills covered with their silvery green leaves. The olive makes its biggest contribution to Italian cooking via olive oil (see pages 1–2). Without it, there wouldn't be Italian cooking as we know—and love—it.

Olives are native to the Mediterranean region, where they have been cultivated since about 3000 B.C. Olives are 18 percent oil by weight, and it has been estimated that 90 percent of all olives grown are used to make oil. If you've ever sampled an olive straight from the tree, you know that olives are inedible before they are treated to a curing process. To cure olives, they are packed in salt or soaked in brine or oil. In the different regions of Italy, spices, locally characteristic herbs, and other flavorings—

orange rind, garlic, and bay leaves are traditional in Umbria, for example—are added to flavor the pickling brine.

Cured olives of all types are enjoyed on their own, as an accompaniment to an *antipasto misto* (mixed antipasto plate), and as an ingredient in many Italian recipes, particularly those from Sicily—*caponata* being one of the best known.

The olive crop begins to develop in the early spring, and by fall, usually late November, the first of the olives are ready to be harvested. Green olives, which are also called Sicilian or Spanish olives in the United States, are unripe and in general have a sharper flavor and crunchier texture than black olives, which are picked when ripe and usually have a subtler flavor and softer texture. To my taste the best Italian olives for eating are the small black Gaeta olives that come from Liguria. They are not widely available, but they can usually be found in Italian specialty stores or you can order them from Dean and DeLuca (see the sources section, page 295–96). Greek Calamata, black oil-cured olives, and the tiny French Niçoise olives can also be used in the recipes that call for olives in this book.

Onions

~ ~ ~

CIPOLLE

Many varieties of onions are used in Italian cooking: tiny pearl onions, small white or "boiling" onions, brilliant purple-red–colored onions, and yellow onions, which are the most common. Shallots are also a member of the vast onion family, but they are not widely used in Italian cooking.

In Italy, the best onions come from the Piedmont region in northern Italy. Classic Piedmontese preparations include onions stuffed with fontina cheese and sweet and sour onions.

The skins of large yellow onions should be peeled with a knife. White onions, with their thin, white, papery covering, can be most easily peeled if you plunge them into boiling water for about 20 seconds before peeling.

HOW TO CHOP AN ONION. Peel the onion and cut away the root end. Cut the onion in half lengthwise. Lay the flat sides of the onion halves on the cutting surface and make as many parallel slices as you can, very close together across each onion half. Make another horizontal slice about midway through the onion. Turn the onion one-quarter and make another series of slices at right angles to the first.

Peas

~ ~ ~

PISELLI

Fresh peas are enjoyed throughout Italy The most notable regional specialties are the classic Venetian dish *risi e bisi* (see page 119), a thick soup of rice and peas, and the Roman preparation of peas with mint.

Fresh peas, in order to be sweet and delicious, should be eaten as soon as possible after they are picked, because the natural sugar in the peas begins to turn to starch almost immediately. Therefore, if very fresh peas are not available to you, frozen peas can be a good substitute for some dishes. Frozen peas should be defrosted but not cooked before using.

Peppers

~ ~ ~

PEPERONI

Peppers were brought to Italy from the New World. Although almost all peppers belong to the same species (*Capsicum annuum*), there are two general groups of peppers: sweet (*peperoni*) and hot (*peperoncini*).

Sweet peppers—red, yellow, orange, brown, and green—all have a similar sweet flavor and crisp texture and are popular throughout Italy. Hot peppers, on the other hand, vary a lot and are used almost exclusively in southern Italian cooking.

There are dozens of preparations for peppers in Italian cuisine. Every region has its own specialties. Some of the classic preparations include *peperoni arrostiti* (roasted peppers, pages 81–82), *peperonata* (stewed peppers, pages 82–83), and *peperoni piemontesi* (stuffed peppers, page 83–84).

The Vegetables of Italy

Potatoes

PATATE

The humble potato, which has been a staple of entire nations for centuries, came to Italy relatively late in history and has not had a far-reaching impact on the cuisine. Potatoes are eaten mostly in the northern regions, where they are turned into gnocchi (potato dumplings, see pages 210–11), or *torte*, or served as an accompaniment to roasted meat. They have also become a common ingredient in Italian vegetable soups. Italy grows several different types of potatoes—red-, white-, or brown-skinned—just as we do in the United States.

Pumpkin or Winter Squash

ZUCCA

Italian pumpkins, with their tough green skin and bright orange-yellow pulp, are more like a combination of several varieties of our own winter squash than our pumpkins. For the recipes in this book, you can use pumpkin or Hubbard squash with equally good results.

Pumpkins are most closely associated with northern Italian cuisine. In Mantua, an agricultural center in Lombardy, the pumpkin is the city's symbol, and the dish *tortelli alla zucca*, pasta filled with pumpkin (see pages 172–73), comes from there. And throughout Lombardy *zucca* is used as an ingredient in risotto.

Spinach

SPINACI

Spinach is one of the most recent additions to Italian cuisine. In the late eighteenth century Vincenzo Corrado brought spinach and some recipes with him to Italy from Spain. Many of those recipes have been integrated into the classic repertoire of Italian cooking. One such early recipe, *spinaci in budin,* or spinach pudding, has become the classic preparation *sformato di spinaci,* or spinach custard (see variation with arugula on pages 61–62).

Spinach, which is rich in iron and vitamins, is the basis for many contemporary recipes. It is one of the ingredients most used in pasta stuffings, as well as in the making of green pasta and green gnocchi in the north. Spinach is commonly used in *torte* (savory pies), most notably the *torta pasqualina,* which is a traditional Easter dish made with layers of spinach and artichokes and other green vegetables to help celebrate the spring holiday. Recipes with names that include *alla fiorentina* or Florentine usually have spinach in them as well, since the Florentines have always had a special fondness for spinach.

Most of the spinach available in our markets is Savoy, or curly-leaf spinach, which is packed into 10–ounce plastic bags. Occasionally you can find flatleaf spinach in neat bunches, which I find easier to cook with because you can cut away the stems efficiently in one quick slice. There is no discernable difference in taste between the two varieties of spinach.

Spinach must be carefully and thoroughly washed before cooking because it is almost always sandy or gritty. The stems, which can be tough, should be broken or cut off and discarded.

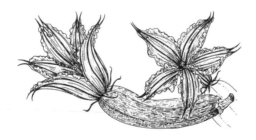

Squash Blossoms

~ ~ ~

FIORI DI ZUCCA

The tender yellow-orange flower of the zucchini and yellow summer squash is one of the great delicacies of Italian vegetable cooking. Picked when they are in full bloom, these flowers have a deliciously mild, subtle flavor that is reminiscent of the squash it bears.

Traditional preparations include coating them whole in batter and deep-frying or chopping and adding them to a risotto or pasta with spring vegetables (see page 175).

Squash blossoms are available in markets in Italy, but rarely in markets in the United States. In order to find them, you must grow your own zucchini or summer squash, or implore a friend or neighbor who grows them to give you their blooms. Fresh squash blossoms should be harvested and used the same day. Remove the stems and pistils and rinse and pat dry before using.

Tomatoes

~ ~ ~

POMODORI

It is hard to imagine Italian cooking today without tomatoes. They are in so many dishes, including soups, salads, antipasti, pasta, risotto, and on and on. But until the discovery of the New World, there were no tomatoes in Italian cuisine. Once they arrived, in the late sixteenth century, and were named *pomodoro*, or golden apple, tomatoes were accepted only gradually.

Tomatoes found a place first in southern Italian cooking because they grew so well in the warm, dry regions of Campania, Abruzzi, and Reggio-Calabria. The earliest recipes from that area show that tomatoes were usually stuffed (with anchovies, garlic, parsley, and oregano) and baked, or they were made into a sauce or *ragù*. It wasn't until the nineteenth century that tomatoes were cultivated for large-scale processing—making them available beyond the southern regions—and fully incorporated into the regional cuisines throughout Italy.

For recipes that call for the tomatoes to be cooked, I prefer to use fresh plum tomatoes that have been peeled and seeded. I always look for the smallest, reddest, ripest plum or pear-shaped tomatoes in the market. There are usually about 6 plum tomatoes in a pound. Even when they are not at their summertime best, the small plum tomatoes lend a fresh taste and quality to a dish that cannot be duplicated with canned tomatoes.

For recipes that call for uncooked tomatoes—salads, bruschetta, pasta sauce—I like to use juicy eating tomatoes. In general, I prepare these dishes only in the summer when tomatoes are at their best.

When tomatoes are cooked into a soup or other dishes to the point where they have lost their fresh-tasting quality, I prefer the convenience of canned tomatoes and usually buy imported cans of peeled Italian plum tomatoes that have been packed in their own juice with basil. For recipes that call for chopped tomatoes, I use canned tomatoes that have been "ground peeled."

In addition to canning tomatoes, Italians have other methods for preserving and extending the life of fresh tomatoes. Tomatoes are turned into tomato paste, *concentrato*, by cooking them for a long time to reduce their acidity. Tubes of *concentrato di pomodoro* are widely available in Italy and the United States. Tomatoes are also dried for future use, principally in Liguria, where farmers salt tomatoes, leave them to dry in the sun, and pack them in bags or in jars with oil. Sun-dried tomatoes have a strong, piquant flavor and should be used sparingly. I store sun-dried tomatoes in the refrigerator to prevent the oil they're packed in from turning rancid, but allow them to come to room temperature before using.

HOW TO PEEL TOMATOES. Bring 2 quarts of water to a boil in a large saucepan on top of the stove. Place 5 or 6 tomatoes at a time in the boiling water. Wait 1 minute, then using a slotted spoon or strainer, remove the tomatoes from the water. Place them in a colander to cool slightly. Add more tomatoes to the boiling water and repeat the process until all the tomatoes have been treated to the boiling water.

With a sharp paring knife, cut away the stem end of the tomato and peel off the skin. The skin should slip off easily; if it does not, place the tomato back in the boiling water for 30 seconds longer. Holding the peeled tomato in one hand, cut around the inside core with the knife and gently squeeze the core and seeds out. Hold the tomato under cold water to flush out any seeds. Set aside. Continue this process with all the tomatoes. Cut the tomatoes into quarters or chop them according to the recipe directions.

The Vegetables of Italy

Zucchini
~ ~ ~
ZUCCHINE

Zucchini grows in every part of Italy. Like tomatoes, they were introduced to Italian cuisine after the discovery of the Americas, in the seventeenth century, and similarly have become closely associated with Italian cooking. In the United States, the Italian name *zucchine*, but spelled "zucchini," has become the accepted name for this squash, although in England and France it is called *courgettes*.

There are many preparations for zucchini. My preference tends toward the simplest ones—steamed or sautéed with a hefty helping of garlic—that seem best able to bring out the zucchini's flavor. Ligurian stuffed, baked zucchini are also delicious.

When buying, look for zucchini with the shiniest green skins and smallest size, 1 to 2 inches in diameter. The younger, smaller, and fresher the zucchini, the more and better flavor they will have.

Chapter Five

~ ~ ~

Antipasti

THE ANCIENT ROMAN aristocrats left us some of the earliest protocols for meals of several different courses. Following reasoning they adapted from the Greeks about how different foods were best digested, they set about giving each food its place in elaborate, and even excessive, feasts. The place for vegetables and fruits, they decided, was at the beginning of the meal, or *antipasto*. *Antipasto* means "before the meal," and not before the pasta as is often misconstrued.

Even though vegetables have since found their way into virtually every course and aspect of Italian cuisine, the most characteristic place for vegetables is still at the antipasto table, where they are treated to a vast array of different preparations. In the recipes that follow, you will find vegetables that have been grilled, roasted, marinated, fried, sautéed, baked, and braised.

Vegetable antipasti are often served in combinations. This is particularly evident in southern Italy, where vegetables play a more prominent role in the cuisine and where the antipasto table is a fixture of most restaurants and the selections are numerous. There it's not uncommon for diners to indulge in an *antipasto misto*, which may include as many as six or eight different antipasti preparations. Many restaurants offer at least one *secondo piatto vegetariano* (vegetable second course), which can be just a larger serving of an antipasto dish. Traditionally, the midday meal was heavier and more substantial than the evening meal, when it was common to eat *pasta in brodo* (pasta in broth), eggs, or cold meats. Today Italians eat much the way we do in America, with lunch being the lighter meal and vegetable dishes from the antipasto table taken as the main course.

Antipasti can be served as a first course, as an accompaniment to a main course dish, or as the main course dish itself. A combination of two or three—marinated carrots, Roman-style artichokes, and roasted eggplant with sun-dried tomatoes—make a wonderful first course that will bring to mind a sense of the abundance of the antipasti table. Roasted vegetables—asparagus, peppers, and onions—are a versatile accompaniment for fish, chicken, or meat.

There are probably thousands of different antipasti recipes. I have tried to give you a selection that represents the range of what's available.

Artichokes Roman Style

~ ~ ~

CARCIOFI ALLA ROMANA

These artichokes, seasoned with garlic and salt and stewed in oil, are the most tender artichokes you'll ever taste. Every Roman restaurant seems to have them on its antipasto table in the fall. This version substitutes parsley for the mint that's called for in many traditional recipes.

1 small bunch fresh parsley, rinsed and thoroughly dried
1 large clove garlic, peeled and quartered
1 teaspoon salt
6 medium-size artichokes, about 4 inches high, prepared for cooking according to the directions on page 32
1 cup pure olive oil

1. In a food processor, combine the parsley, garlic, and salt. Process for about 30 seconds, or until the mixture is finely chopped. If you are

using a knife, not a food processor, finely chop the parsley and garlic and combine them with the salt in a small mixing bowl, stirring to combine.

2. Hold each artichoke upside down by the stem and press the head firmly into the countertop or other hard surface to force the leaves to open slightly. Spoon some of the parsley mixture into the leaves of each artichoke.

3. Place all the artichokes, stems pointing up, in a deep saucepan just large enough to hold all the artichokes in a single layer so they remain upright during cooking. Add the oil and enough cold water so that the liquid reaches the bases of the artichokes' stems.

4. Cover the saucepan, place over medium-high heat, and bring to a boil. Place the cover askew, reduce the heat to medium, and continue cooking for about 45 minutes, or until the artichokes are tender when pierced with a sharp knife. Most of the water should have cooked away.

5. Transfer the artichokes to a serving platter. Cool to room temperature before serving.

MAKES 6 SERVINGS

Venetian-Style Artichokes Cooked in Olive Oil and Lemon Juice

~ ~ ~

CARCIOFI ALLA VENEZIANA

This recipe is a specialty of the region around Venice where they typically use purple artichokes. The texture of the artichokes is similar to the preceding *carciofi alla romana*, but the lemon lends a slightly piquant flavor.

24 very small artichokes (carciofini), 2 to 3 inches high (see note below)
6 cups water
Juice of 1 lemon
1 tablespoon kosher salt
⅓ cup pure olive oil

1. After the artichokes are trimmed, drop them into a small non-aluminum casserole containing the water, lemon juice, and salt. When all the artichokes are in the pot, pour the olive oil over them.

2. Cover the casserole, place it over high heat, and bring to a boil. Set the cover askew, reduce the heat to medium, and continue cooking for 45 minutes to 1 hour, or until the artichokes are tender when pierced with a sharp knife and almost all of the liquid has cooked away.

3. Transfer the artichokes to a serving platter. Allow them to reach room temperature before serving.

MAKES 6 TO 8 SERVINGS

Note: These small artichokes need only the dark outer leaves removed and the stems trimmed. If you use large artichokes, cut out the chokes before cooking.

Fried Artichokes, Jewish Style

~ ~ ~

CARCIOFI ALLA GIUDIA

These artichokes are fried until they are delicately crisp on the outside and deliciously tender inside and fanned open like a bronze chrysanthemum. This recipe was originated by the Jews of the ghetto in Rome, therefore the name, and are still prepared this way in many Roman restaurants. It is difficult to duplicate the Italian recipe with American artichokes, which have tougher leaves. You'll get excellent results if you partially steam-cook the artichokes before frying. Serve them as soon as they're cooked with the stems up and the crisp leaves fanned out on the plate like a flower.

2 *cups water*

6 *medium-size artichokes, about 4 inches high, prepared for cooking according to the directions on page 32*

Vegetable oil for deep frying

1. Bring the water to a boil in a vegetable steamer. Place the artichokes in the steamer basket, cover, and steam for about 15 minutes, until barely tender when pierced with a knife. Be careful not to overcook the artichokes. (You can also microwave-steam the artichokes—place them in individual

resealable plastic bags and cook each one on high for 2 [...] the artichokes on a cutting board, stem end up. Use your [...] press down on the artichokes to loosen the leaves and force [...] to open slightly.

2. Pour oil into a deep saucepan to a depth of 3 to 5 [...] the oil over medium-high heat to about 325°F.

3. When the oil is hot, using a pair of long-handled kitchen tongs, place the artichokes into the oil with the stems pointing up. Turn the artichokes around in the oil so that they cook evenly. After 5 to 7 minutes, when the artichokes have turned golden brown, turn the artichokes so that the stems are pointing up again and press down on the stems so that the leaves spread open. Stand back and carefully sprinkle a few drops of water over the oil (this will cause a great amount of splattering, but it makes the outer leaves very crisp). Cook for about 2 minutes longer. Transfer to paper towels and let drain. Serve immediately.

MAKES 6 SERVINGS

Arugula Custard Mold

~ ~ ~

SFORMATI DI RUCOLA

Sformati are savory puddings that have the consistency of a quiche filling. They are typically served as an appetizer, although they can also easily be an entree when served with a salad and bread. I first tasted this updated version of the classic *sformato di spinaci* at Da Noi, one of Florence's nouvelle-style restaurants, where it was served with a smooth tomato sauce. The sharp flavor of the arugula made this dish memorable. *Sformati* are easy to prepare in the oven or microwave.

2 bunches fresh arugula, root ends and thick stems removed (about 4 cups leaves)

3 large eggs, lightly beaten

¾ cup heavy cream

⅓ cup freshly grated Parmesan cheese

Salt and freshly ground black pepper to taste

.. Preheat the oven to 350°F. Rinse the arugula well in several changes cold water. Do not dry. Blanch the arugula by dropping into a large saucepan of briskly boiling water. Leave for 1 minute and drain thoroughly.

2. Place the cooked arugula in a food processor fitted with the double-edge steel blade and process for about 30 seconds, until it is finely chopped but not pureed. While the machine is running, add the eggs, one at a time, and the cream and process for 1 minute. Add the cheese, pulsing the machine on and off to incorporate it into the arugula mixture. Season with the salt and pepper. Pour the mixture into six lightly buttered 4–ounce custard cups or ramekins, filling each about three-quarters.

3. Place the filled ramekins in a baking pan large enough to hold them comfortably. Pour in enough hot water to come about halfway up the sides of the ramekins. Bake in the preheated oven for about 35 minutes, or until the centers are firm and you can pierce the custard with a sharp knife and it will come out clean. Remove from the oven and allow to cool slightly before unmolding.

4. To unmold the *sformato*, run a sharp knife along the edge of the ramekin to loosen it. Invert the ramekin onto a serving plate and tap it firmly. Serve warm or at room temperature with Fresh Tomato Sauce (see pages 152–53).

MAKES 6 SERVINGS

CAULIFLOWER CUSTARD MOLD/*SFORMATI DI CAVOLFIORE.* Substitute 1 cup of cauliflower florets, precooked according to the directions on page 39, for the arugula, and reduce the Parmesan to ¼ cup. Begin with step 2.

MICROWAVE TECHNIQUE: Follow steps 1, 2, and 3 but do not butter the ramekins. Cover each ramekin with microwave-safe plastic wrap. Place the ramekins in the microwave in a circle. Cook on high power for 3 minutes and 30 seconds. Remove from the oven, pierce the plastic, and uncover the ramekins. Allow to cool slightly before unmolding. Proceed with step 4 before serving.

Asparagus Baked with Butter and Parmesan

~ ~ ~

ASPARAGI ALLA PARMIGIANA

Here fresh asparagus is lightly steamed and baked with a rich coating of butter and Parmesan cheese. Serve it as a first course before a pasta entree. Use the fatter asparagus spears.

2 pounds fresh asparagus, prepared for cooking according to the directions
on page 34 and steamed or boiled for 5 minutes
3 tablespoons unsalted butter, melted
Salt and freshly ground black pepper to taste
⅓ cup freshly grated Parmesan cheese

1. Preheat the oven to 400°F.
2. Place the cooked asparagus in an oval or rectangular baking dish just large enough to hold the spears in a single layer. Pour the melted butter over the spears and gently turn them so that they are evenly coated. Season with the salt and pepper and sprinkle with the Parmesan cheese.
3. Place the asparagus in the preheated oven on the topmost shelf. Bake until the cheese is melted and lightly browned, 7 to 10 minutes. Serve at once.

MAKES 4 SERVINGS

Roasted Asparagus

~ ~ ~

ASPARAGI AL FORNO

Johanne Killeen of the restaurant Al Forno in Providence, Rhode Island, first told me about cooking asparagus this way. Roasting at high heat really intensifies the flavor of the asparagus. Once you taste asparagus cooked this way, you'll never want to cook it any other way.

2 pounds fresh asparagus, preferably ½ inch thick or more, prepared for
    cooking according to the directions on page 34
¼ cup pure olive oil
Kosher salt

1. Prepeat the oven to 500°F.
2. Place the asparagus in a single layer in a heavy roasting pan. Pour
the olive oil over the asparagus and turn the spears around to be sure they
are completely coated. Especially coat the asparagus tips. Lightly sprinkle
with salt.
3. Roast the asparagus for 15 minutes, until they are just starting to
brown. When you pick up a spear it should bend but not droop. Transfer
to a serving dish and serve immediately or at room temperature.

MAKES 6 SERVINGS

Roasted Beets

~ ~ ~

BARBABIETOLE AL FORNO

The Italian way to cook beets is to roast them in the oven until they
are tender and intensely flavorful. I like to serve roasted beets on a bed of
dressed salad greens or in combination with other roasted vegetables to
make a colorful plate.

2 bunches beets (4 to 6 beets per bunch), the greens cut away and discarded,
    and the beets rinsed in cold water
2 tablespoons extra virgin olive oil
Salt and freshly ground black pepper to taste
1 tablespoon chopped fresh parsley or mint

1. Preheat the oven to 400°F.
2. Wrap the beets together in two layers of aluminum foil and bake
in the preheated oven for 2 to 2½ hours, until they are black and tender
when pierced with a knife. Remove from oven, unwrap, and allow to cool.
3. When the beets are cool enough to handle, peel away the black

skin with your fingers or use a knife. Slice the beets as thinly as possible and arrange on a serving plate.

4. Drizzle the oil over the sliced beets. Sprinkle with the salt, pepper, and parsley and serve immediately.

MAKES 6 SERVINGS

Marinated Carrots

~ ~ ~

CAROTE ALL'ACETO

This is my mother's recipe which she learned from an Italian friend in Washington, D.C. Carrots prepared this way have a marvelous texture and a tangy taste. Serve them as part of a mixed plate of antipasti or as an accompaniment to a cold summer buffet. These carrots can keep for weeks in your refrigerator without losing any of their flavor.

2 pounds carrots (do not use "baby" carrots), scraped and cut into
   ½-inch-thick rounds
½ cup white or cider vinegar
½ teaspoon salt
1 small clove garlic, crushed or finely minced
¼ cup extra virgin olive oil
1 tablespoon fresh oregano leaves

1. Place the sliced carrots in a 3–quart nonaluminum saucepan with the vinegar, salt, and enough cold water to just cover the carrots.

2. Bring to a boil and cook at a steady boil over medium-high heat for 15 minutes, or until the carrots are tender and can be pierced easily with a knife. Drain in a colander and transfer to a bowl.

3. Add the garlic and olive oil and stir to combine. Allow to cool, uncovered, to room temperature. Taste the carrots. Add the oregano, and more salt if necessary. Mix well, cover, and refrigerate for several hours or overnight.

4. Remove the carrots from the refrigerator at least 30 minutes before serving. Toss gently with a spoon and transfer the carrots to a serving platter or bowl.

MAKES 8 SERVINGS

Grilled Eggplant with Sun-Dried Tomatoes

~ ~ ~

MELANZANE AI POMODORI SECCHI

A Cambridge friend introduced this dish to me years ago; I tasted it again in Positano on a recent trip to Italy. The sharp distinctive taste of the sun-dried tomatoes is the perfect complement to eggplant. This dish makes a marvelous first course, but it is also an excellent accompaniment to a pasta or risotto main course.

2 medium-size eggplants (about 1 pound each), stem ends cut away, cut
lengthwise or crosswise into 1-inch-thick slices
Salt
12 oil-packed sun-dried tomato halves
2 tablespoons of the oil from the tomatoes
8 sprigs fresh parsley, washed and dried well
½ cup pure olive oil or more as needed for basting the eggplants

1. Place the eggplant slices in a colander, sprinkle liberally with salt, toss, and leave them to drain for at least 30 minutes, or until the eggplants begin to release their water.

2. Meanwhile, combine the tomatoes, the tomato oil, and the parsley in a food processor. Process for about 30 seconds, or until the mixture forms a coarse paste. If you are chopping by hand, finely chop the tomatoes and the parsley separately and combine with the oil in a small bowl. Set aside. Preheat the broiler in your oven.

3. Dry the eggplant slices with paper towels and arrange them in a single layer in a greased, flameproof baking dish (do not use glass because it will break under the broiler). Brush the eggplant with the olive oil. Place the pan directly under the broiler. Broil for about 5 minutes, or until the eggplant begins to brown. Turn the slices over with a spatula, brush with more olive oil, and return the pan to the broiler. Cook for another 5 minutes, or until the tops begin to brown. Remove the pan from the oven and turn off the broiler. Set the oven to bake at 325°F.

4. Using a teaspoon, spread some of the tomato-and-parsley mixture over each slice of eggplant. The slices need only a thin covering—if you put too much on, the saltiness of the tomatoes will be overpowering.

5. Return the pan to the oven and bake for 30 minutes. Transfer the eggplant slices to a serving dish and serve at room temperature.

MAKES 6 SERVINGS

Eggplant with Pine Nuts and Parsley

~ ~ ~

MELANZANE CON PIGNOLI

The pine nuts add a delicious richness to the eggplants.

2 medium-size eggplants, or 4 small eggplants (about 2 pounds total), stem
ends cut away, sliced into ½-inch rounds
Salt
Pure olive oil
2 tablespoons pine nuts
¼ cup chopped fresh parsley

1. Place the eggplant in a large colander, sprinkle liberally with salt, toss, and allow to stand for at least 30 minutes, or until the eggplant begins to release its water. Dry on paper towels. Preheat the broiler.

2. Pour enough olive oil into a large flameproof baking pan to barely cover the bottom. One at a time, place each piece of eggplant into the pan and turn it over so that both sides are coated with oil. The eggplant slices should lie in a single layer. If you have too many pieces, cook them in two batches. Place the pan directly under the broiler and cook until the top is evenly browned but not burned. Turn the eggplant slices over and broil again until the top is brown. Transfer to a serving dish and arrange the eggplant slices in an overlapping fashion.

3. Place the pine nuts in a small sauté pan over medium-high heat. Stirring almost constantly, cook until the nuts are lightly browned, 3 to 5 minutes. Watch closely since the nuts will burn easily.

4. Pour the nuts over the eggplant slices, sprinkle with the parsley, and serve at room temperature.

MAKES 6 SERVINGS

Breaded and Fried Eggplant

~ ~ ~

MELANZANE FRITTE

This is a classic southern Italian way to prepare eggplant, and it makes a wonderful main course when served with a green salad. If you're concerned about cholesterol, use egg whites in place of the whole egg.

2 medium-size eggplants (about 1 pound each), cut crosswise into 1-inch-thick
    rounds
Salt
½ cup all-purpose flour

Freshly ground black pepper to taste

1 large egg, lightly beaten with 2 tablespoons water, or 2 large egg whites, lightly beaten with 2 tablespoons water

2 cups plain bread crumbs

Vegetable oil for frying (use corn, safflower, olive, or canola oil, or any combination)

¼ cup chopped fresh parsley

1. Place the eggplant slices in a colander, sprinkle liberally with salt, toss, and allow to drain for at least 30 minutes, or until the eggplant begins to release its water. Pat the eggplant slices dry with paper towels.

2. Combine the flour with the black pepper in a shallow dish. Pour the beaten egg and water together into another dish, and the bread crumbs into a third dish.

3. Dredge each eggplant slice in the flour-and-pepper mixture. Turn it around to be sure it is completely covered, then pat it briskly between your hands to remove as much excess flour as possible. Next, place the eggplant slice into the egg-and-water mixture and turn it once to be sure the slice is completely coated. Remove the eggplant with a fork or pair of tongs and allow any excess egg to drip from it for about 10 seconds. Finally, place the eggplant into the dish with the bread crumbs, making sure the slice is completely covered. Transfer it to a sheet of waxed paper. Repeat this process until all the slices have been coated.

4. Meanwhile, place about 1 inch of oil in a deep, heavy frying pan over medium-high heat. Sprinkle some bread crumbs into the oil to test the heat. When the bread crumbs sizzle, the oil is hot enough. Put the eggplant slices into the pan in one layer. Cook until the bottom side is golden brown but not burned, about 7 minutes. Turn the eggplant slices over and cook until that side is evenly browned. Remove and drain on paper towels. Repeat this until all the slices have been fried. If necessary, add more oil to the pan, but wait for it to become hot before adding more eggplant. Garnish the fried eggplant with the chopped parsley and serve immediately.

MAKES 6 SERVINGS

Eggplant Baked with Tomato Sauce, Mozzarella, and Parmesan Cheese

~ ~ ~

MELANZANE ALLA PARMIGIANA

This dish is served all over southern Italy and is as standard on menus as spaghetti. I created this version, made with broiled eggplant slices and a sparing amount of fresh tomato sauce and mozzarella, and it is surprisingly light and delicate.

2 medium-size eggplants (about 1 pound each), stem ends cut away and cut crosswise into 1-inch-thick rounds
Salt
¼ cup pure olive oil
1 cup Fresh Tomato Sauce (see pages 152–53)
¼ cup freshly grated Parmesan cheese
4 ounces mozzarella, grated

1. Preheat the oven broiler. Place the eggplant in a colander, sprinkle liberally with salt, toss, and leave to stand for at least 30 minutes, or until the eggplant begins to release its water. Pat dry with paper towels.

2. Pour the oil into a flameproof baking pan. One at a time, place each piece of eggplant into the pan and turn it over so that both sides are coated with oil. Arrange the eggplant slices in a single layer in the pan; if necessary, do two batches. Place the eggplant directly under the broiler. Broil for 5 minutes, or until lightly browned on top. Turn the eggplant slices over and continue broiling until that side is lightly browned. (Repeat this until all the eggplant slices have been broiled.) Heat the oven to 400°F.

3. Lightly oil a baking dish approximately 9 × 13 inches and arrange the broiled eggplant slices in the pan in a single layer. Spoon about a teaspoon of the tomato sauce onto each slice and spread it to just barely cover. Sprinkle each slice with some Parmesan cheese and top with a hefty pinch of the grated mozzarella.

4. Place the baking dish in the oven and bake for about 10 minutes, until the cheese on top is melted and the sauce is bubbling. Serve hot.

MAKES 6 SERVINGS

Eggplant and Olive Stew

~ ~ ~

CAPONATA

Caponata is a classic Sicilian dish that has become popular well beyond Sicily. Because *caponata* has a good amount of vinegar in it, this dish will keep well for at least a week in the refrigerator. This recipe was inspired by Mary Taylor Simeti's book, *Pomp and Sustenance*.

1 large eggplant (about 1½ pounds), stem ends cut away and cut into
    1-inch cubes
Salt
½ cup pure olive oil
1 medium-size onion, chopped
2 ribs celery, thinly sliced
½ cup pitted small green Sicilian or Spanish olives
¼ cup capers, drained well
1 cup coarsely chopped canned tomatoes with their juice
¼ cup white wine vinegar
1 tablespoon sugar
1 tablespoon unsweetened cocoa

1. Place the eggplant in a colander, sprinkle liberally with salt, toss, and allow to stand for at least 30 minutes, or until the eggplant begins to release its water. Rinse well.

2. Place the oil in a deep, medium-size, nonaluminum casserole over medium-high heat. When the oil is hot, add the onion and celery and cook, stirring frequently, for 2 to 3 minutes, or until the onion begins to soften. Add the eggplant and cook and stir a few more minutes.

3. Add the olives, capers, tomatoes, vinegar, sugar, and cocoa. Stir well to combine. Reduce the heat to low and simmer for 45 minutes, stirring occasionally. Season with salt and remove from the heat.

4. When the *caponata* has cooled, transfer to a storage container with a tight-fitting lid and refrigerate for at least 24 hours. Allow the *caponata* to come to room temperature before serving.

MAKES 6 SERVINGS

Roasted Fresh Fennel

~ ~ ~

FINOCCHIO AL FORNO

This is one of the best ways to eat fresh fennel when it's in season during the fall and winter months. This dish is particularly nice to mix with other roasted vegetables.

3 fennel bulbs (about 2 pounds)
2 tablespoons pure olive oil
Kosher salt

1. Preheat the oven to 500°F. Cut away the leafy stalks and root ends from the fennel bulbs and save for another use or discard. Using a vegetable peeler or sharp knife, scrape or cut away any browned spots from the outside of the fennel bulbs. Slice each bulb lengthwise two or three times into three or four ½-inch-thick slices.

2. Coat a large baking pan with the olive oil and place the fennel in the pan. Brush the top sides of the fennel slices with some additional oil and sprinkle lightly with salt.

3. Bake for about 15 minutes, until the bottom is well browned but not burned. Turn the slices over and return to the oven. Continue roasting until the fennel slices are fully browned and tender when pierced with a sharp knife, about 10 minutes longer. Transfer to a serving plate and serve immediately or at room temperature.

MAKES 6 SERVINGS

Baked Fennel

~ ~ ~

FINOCCHIO AL LATTE

This dish is a regular feature on the vast antipasti table at the New York City trattoria Da Umberto. Blanching the fennel in milk gives it a mild, almost creamy flavor.

2 fennel bulbs (about 1½ pounds)

2 to 3 cups milk (you can use low-fat, skim, or whole)

2 tablespoons pure olive oil

3 tablespoons freshly grated Parmesan cheese

Salt and freshly ground black pepper to taste

1. Preheat the oven to 475°F. Cut away the leafy stalks and root ends from the fennel bulbs and save for another use or discard. Using a vegetable peeler or sharp knife, scrape or cut away any browned spots from the outside of the fennel bulbs. Slice each bulb lengthwise three times into four ½-inch-thick slices.

2. Place the fennel, cut side up, in a large saucepan so that all the pieces fit snugly in one layer. Pour the milk over the fennel to just cover. Bring the milk to a low boil over medium-high heat. Reduce the heat to medium and simmer for 10 to 15 minutes, until the fennel can be pierced easily with a sharp knife.

3. Remove the fennel with a slotted spoon and lay on paper towels. Pat them dry. Place the fennel in a small baking dish, cut sides up, and pour the olive oil over them. Sprinkle with the Parmesan cheese and salt and pepper.

4. Bake the fennel for 20 to 25 minutes, or until the cheese is lightly browned. Remove from the oven and serve at room temperature.

MAKES 6 SERVINGS

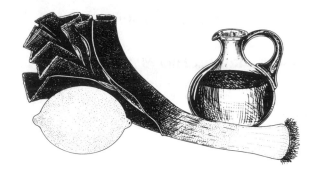

Leeks with Lemon Vinaigrette

PORRI AL LIMONE

The lemon brings out the best in the leeks.

6 large leeks, cleaned (see page 47) and sliced in half lengthwise
Salt to taste
¼ cup extra virgin olive oil
2 tablespoons fresh lemon juice
Freshly ground black pepper to taste

1. Place the leeks in a steamer basket or tray over boiling water, cover, and cook for 5 minutes. (If you want to use a microwave oven, place the leeks in a single layer on a microwave-safe dish in a circular pattern like the spokes of a wheel. Cover securely with microwave-safe plastic wrap and place in the microwave oven. Cook on high power for 5 minutes. Remove from the oven and allow to stand, covered, for 3 to 5 minutes.)

2. Transfer the leeks to a serving dish and arrange them so that their cut sides are all facing up. Sprinkle with salt.

3. In a small nonaluminum bowl, combine the olive oil and lemon juice, then pour over the leeks. Top with a few grinds of black pepper. Serve at room temperature.

MAKES 6 SERVINGS

Roasted Leeks

~ ~ ~

PORRI AL FORNO

Roasting intensifies the flavor of the leeks and leaves the outside crisp and brown and the inside deliciously tender.

12 small- to medium-size leeks, cleaned (see page 47) and left whole
1/4 cup pure olive oil
Kosher salt

1. Preheat the oven to 500°F. Place the leeks side by side in a baking dish just large enough to hold them in a single layer. Pour the olive oil over the leeks and turn them around to be sure that they are evenly coated. Lightly sprinkle with salt.

2. Place the leeks in the top third of the oven and roast for about 10 minutes. Turn the leeks (they should be browned on the bottom but not burned) and return to the oven. Roast for 7 to 10 minutes longer. Remove from the oven, transfer to a serving platter, and serve at once or at room temperature.

MAKES 6 SERVINGS

Leeks with a Green Caper Sauce

~ ~ ~

PORRI CON SALSA VERDE

The mild leeks are just a foil for this zesty, piquant green sauce that's usually served with bollito misto (mixed boiled meats).

6 large leeks, cleaned (see page 47) and sliced in half lengthwise
1 tablespoon chopped capers
1/2 cup finely chopped dill pickles (preferably French cornichons)
1/4 cup finely chopped fresh parsley
1/2 cup pure olive oil
3 tablespoons red wine vinegar
Freshly ground black pepper to taste

1. Place the leeks in a steamer basket or tray over boiling water, cover, and cook for 5 minutes. (If you are using a microwave oven, place the leeks in a single layer on a microwave-safe dish in a circular pattern like the spokes of a wheel. Cover securely with microwave-safe plastic wrap and place in the microwave oven. Cook on high power for 5 minutes. Remove from the oven and allow to stand, covered, for 3 to 5 minutes.)

2. In a small bowl, combine the capers, pickles, and parsley. Whisk in the olive oil and vinegar. Pour the mixture over the warm leeks and top with a few grinds of black pepper. Serve at room temperature.

MAKES 6 SERVINGS

Sautéed Mushrooms with Garlic and Parsley

~ ~ ~

FUNGHI TRIFOLATI

Trifolato means thinly sliced and can apply to zucchini as well as mushrooms. Serve these savory mushrooms with some fresh crusty bread.

⅓ cup pure olive oil
1 pound fresh wild mushrooms (crimini, portobello, shiitake, or oyster), stems
     removed and caps sliced as thinly as possible
Salt and freshly ground black pepper to taste
1 large clove garlic, finely minced or pressed
¼ cup finely chopped fresh parsley

1. Place the oil in a large sauté pan over medium-high heat. Add the mushrooms, salt, and pepper. Cook for 2 to 3 minutes, until the mushrooms begin to give off their liquid.

2. Lower the heat to medium and continue cooking, while stirring, until the mushrooms are completely tender and slightly browned, about 10 minutes. Add the garlic and cook, stirring, for 1 to 2 minutes longer. Stir in the parsley and serve immediately.

MAKES 6 SERVINGS

Marinated Mushrooms
~ ~ ~
FUNGHI MARINATI

Lots of garlic and rosemary make these mushrooms wonderfully tasty. Serve them as part of an *antipasto misto*. The mushrooms take on so many good flavors from the marinade that you can even use little white mushrooms.

1 pound fresh mushrooms (preferably crimini or white cultivated varieties of
    a uniform size), stems removed and caps thickly sliced
¼ cup pure olive oil
1 large clove garlic, minced or pressed
1 tablespoon fresh rosemary leaves
1 cup dry white wine
Salt and freshly ground black pepper to taste

1. Place the sliced mushrooms in a large mixing bowl.
2. Place the oil in a small nonaluminum saucepan over medium-high heat. Add the garlic, rosemary, and wine and bring the mixture to a boil. Boil for 3 full minutes, then add salt and pepper.
3. Pour the mixture over the mushrooms. Mix well and allow to stand until cool, mixing occasionally. Transfer to a covered container and refrigerate overnight. Serve at room temperature.

MAKES 6 SERVINGS

Grilled Whole Fresh Porcini Mushrooms
~ ~ ~
FUNGHI PORCINI ALLA GRIGLIA

Fresh porcini, which are the *Boletus edulis* variety of mushroom, are not widely available, although they can sometimes be found growing wild (you shouldn't forage for wild mushrooms unless you know the different varieties well) and occasionally specialty stores in some of the large cities

will import fresh porcini from Italy. When you can find them, grilling is absolutely the best way to prepare them. Porcini have an incredibly silky, smooth texture and incomparable woodsy flavor. You can also prepare this recipe with large portobello mushrooms.

1½ pounds fresh porcini or portobello mushrooms
½ cup extra virgin olive oil
Salt and freshly ground black pepper to taste
1 tablespoon finely chopped fresh parsley

1. Light the charcoal in your grill outside.
2. Trim away any brown spots on the mushrooms. Cut off the stems and reserve. Clean the mushroom caps with a damp paper towel; do not run them under water. Cut the mushroom caps into halves or thirds, depending on how many you have, how big the mushrooms are, and how many people you are serving.
3. Brush the undersides of the mushrooms with olive oil. Place the mushroom pieces, top side up, on a grilling rack 6 to 8 inches away from the heat. Cook for about 7 minutes, or until the mushrooms begin to turn golden brown.
4. Brush the tops with more olive oil, turn the mushroom pieces over, and return them to the heat. Cook for an additional 5 minutes, or until the mushrooms seem tender when pierced with a sharp knife.
5. Transfer the mushrooms to a serving platter (cap pieces should be top side up) and season with salt and pepper. Drizzle the remaining olive oil over the top. Sprinkle with the parsley and serve immediately.

MAKES 6 SERVINGS

Marinated Olives

~ ~ ~

OLIVE MARINATE

These spicy olives are a great accompaniment to *focaccia* (see pages 132–133) or plain crostini (see page 121) when served with a glass of wine before dinner. They're also a tasty condiment to serve with a meal. The best olives for this recipe are green Sicilian, also called Spanish olives, or Ligurian black Gaeta olives. You can use either one, or a combination. Avoid oil-cured black and Greek Calamata olives, which will be too salty, and American pitted black or stuffed green olives, which won't give the right flavor.

¾ cup extra virgin olive oil, approximately

2 heaping tablespoons fresh rosemary leaves

¼ teaspoon crushed red pepper

3 long strips lemon zest

2 cups Italian green or black olives, drained

1. Place ½ cup of the olive oil in a small saucepan over medium heat. Add the rosemary, crushed red pepper, and lemon zest and simmer for 3 minutes.

2. Place the olives in a nonreactive container (glass or heat-resistant plastic) with a lid. Pour the oil-and-pepper mixture over the olives and add remaining olive oil to cover the olives. Cover the container and allow to stand for several hours or overnight before serving.

MAKES 6 SERVINGS

Sweet and Sour Roasted White Onions with Balsamic Vinegar

~ ~ ~

CIPOLLINE AGRODOLCE AL BALSAMICO

This is a wonderful version of a classic recipe. Onions are naturally sweet and when they're roasted at high heat the sweetness intensifies. The balsamic vinegar lends just the right amount of sour taste.

2 pounds small white boiling onions, of uniform size, peeled (see pages 50–51)

3 to 4 tablespoons pure olive oil

Kosher salt

¼ cup balsamic vinegar

1. Preheat the oven to 450°F. Place the onions in a flameproof nonaluminum baking pan (such as enameled cast iron) large enough to hold them in a single layer. Spoon some olive oil over the tops of the onions, then turn them around once so they are completely coated. Lightly sprinkle with salt.

2. Place the onions in the oven, on the topmost shelf, and roast for about 15 minutes. The underside of the onions should be well browned. Turn the onions so the brown side is up. Return the onions to the oven and roast for an additional 10 to 15 minutes, or until the onions are completely browned and tender when pierced with a sharp knife. Carefully transfer to a serving dish.

3. Place the roasting pan over medium heat on a stove burner. Add the balsamic vinegar and, using a wooden spoon, scrape all the browned bits from the pan while stirring to combine them with the vinegar. When the vinegar mixture is reduced by about half and is thick and syrupy, turn off the heat and pour the mixture over the onions. Swirl them around in the liquid so they are well coated. Serve at once or at room temperature.

MAKES 6 SERVINGS

Note: This recipe is also wonderful when prepared with either yellow or red onions, which I usually cut in half before roasting and place, cut side down, in the pan. Cooking times will vary, depending on the size of the onion pieces.

Roasted Peppers I

~ ~ ~

PEPERONI ARROSTITI I

This is the traditional preparation for roasted peppers. Use sweet bell peppers—red, yellow, orange, green, and mix them for a colorful effect. You can roast the peppers under your oven broiler or on a charcoal grill, which leaves a nice flavor.

3 large bell peppers, cored, halved lengthwise, and seeded
Salt and freshly ground black pepper to taste
3 tablespoons extra virgin olive oil

1. Preheat the oven broiler or light the charcoal. If you are cooking indoors, place the peppers, cut side down, in a baking pan lined with aluminum foil and set them directly under the oven broiler. If you are cooking outside on a grill, place the peppers, cut side up, on a grill rack about 6 inches from the heat source. Allow the peppers to cook for 8 to 10 minutes, or until the side closest to the heat becomes completely blackened and blistered and the peppers begin to soften.

2. Place the peppers in a heavy plastic or brown paper grocery bag, turn the top down or tie to close the bag, and allow the peppers to stand for 10 minutes. Remove the peppers from the bag. Under cool running water, peel away the blackened skin of the peppers by gently rubbing with your fingers. The skins should peel away easily.

3. Cut the peppers into strips ¼ inch thick and arrange them on a serving platter. Sprinkle with salt and pepper and drizzle the olive oil over the peppers. Serve at room temperature.

MAKES 6 SERVINGS

Note: Peppers roasted this way will keep for several weeks. After peeling off the skins, place the pepper pieces in a jar with a tight-fitting lid. Pour enough olive oil over them to completely cover. Store in the refrigerator.

Roasted Peppers II

~ ~ ~

PEPERONI ARROSTITI II

In this recipe peppers are roasted with olive oil and salt until they are browned but not burned, and served with their skins on, which gives more roasted flavor. Peppers prepared this way won't keep for more than a couple of days. They are usually consumed quickly anyway.

5 tablespoons pure olive oil

3 large bell peppers (1 red, 1 yellow, 1 orange, or any combination of the
     three), cored, halved lengthwise, seeded, and each half cut into thirds

Kosher salt

1. Preheat the oven to 450°F.
2. Pour 3 tablespoons of the olive oil into a large baking pan and tilt it around to completely coat the bottom. Arrange the pepper slices in a single layer in the pan, skin side down. Pour the remaining oil over the pepper pieces. Lightly sprinkle with salt.
3. Place the peppers in the upper third of the oven. Roast for about 15 minutes, or until the undersides are well browned. Turn each piece of pepper over so that the skin sides are up and return the peppers to the oven. Roast for about 10 minutes longer, or until the pieces are completely tender and well browned. Transfer to a serving dish. Serve at room temperature.

MAKES 6 SERVINGS

Pepper Stew

~ ~ ~

PEPERONATA

This is a great way to cook up garden-fresh summer peppers and tomatoes. Serve *peperonata* as part of an *antipasto misto*, with grilled eggplant, marinated carrots, and roasted asparagus, or as an accompaniment to pasta or with crostini (see page 121).

1/4 cup pure olive oil

1 medium-size onion, thinly sliced

2 cloves garlic, finely minced or pressed

6 large red and yellow bell peppers (about 2 pounds), cored, seeded, and sliced
    into 1-inch-thick strips

Salt and freshly ground black pepper to taste

3 tablespoons red wine vinegar

6 fresh plum tomatoes (about 1 pound), peeled, cored, seeded, and coarsely
    chopped, or 1 cup chopped canned tomatoes with their juice

1/4 cup chopped fresh parsley

1. Place the oil in a large sauté pan that has a cover over medium-high heat. Add the onion and garlic and cook, stirring, for 5 minutes, until the onion begins to soften. Add the peppers, season with salt and pepper, and cook for a few minutes more. Add the vinegar. Reduce the heat to medium, cover the pan, and cook, stirring occasionally, for about 30 minutes.

2. When the peppers are tender, add the tomatoes and cook for about 15 minutes longer. Taste and add more salt if necessary. Stir in the parsley. Serve at room temperature.

MAKES 6 SERVINGS

Peppers Baked with Garlic and Tomato

~ ~ ~

PEPERONI PIEMONTESI

Fresh, ripe tomatoes and garlic give these peppers a sensational flavor. They are striking to look at, too.

2 large red bell peppers, cored, seeded, and quartered lengthwise

2 large yellow bell peppers, cored, seeded, and quartered lengthwise

2 cloves garlic, crushed

½ pound fresh Italian plum tomatoes, peeled, cored, seeded, and coarsely chopped

Pure olive oil

Salt and freshly ground black pepper to taste

1. Preheat the oven to 400°F. Place the peppers, skin side down, in an oiled baking dish. Put some of the crushed garlic, tomato, and ½ teaspoon olive oil inside each piece of pepper. Season with salt and pepper.

2. Bake for about 30 minutes, or until the peppers are tender and the undersides are lightly browned. Transfer to a serving platter. Serve at room temperature.

MAKES 6 SERVINGS

Potato-Leek Croquette

~ ~ ~

CROCCHETTE DI PATATE

One big potato pancake that's wonderfully crisp on the outside and moist and tender inside. Although traditional Sicilian recipes for this dish call for eggs, I find you can use only potatoes and leeks—potatoes have enough starch to hold this oversize pancake together. Use a pan with a nonstick coating on the surface for foolproof results. This antipasto can also be served as an entree with a green salad or as an accompaniment to a hearty main course.

1½ pounds Idaho potatoes (2 to 3), unpeeled and coarsely grated

1 medium-size leek, white part only, cleaned (see page 47) and cut into fine julienne strips

⅓ cup vegetable oil

Salt and freshly ground black pepper to taste

¼ cup chopped fresh parsley

1. Mix together the grated potatoes and leek in a large bowl.

2. Place the oil in a 10- or 11-inch sauté or omelette pan with a nonstick surface over medium-high heat. When the oil is hot, place the grated potatoes and leek in the pan in an even, thick layer. Season with salt and pepper. Using a spatula, push the mixture down, away from the sides, to make a neat edge on the potatoes and to flatten the mixture as much as possible.

3. Turn the heat to medium and cook the croquette for about 15 minutes, until the underside is well browned and holds together in a single piece when you try to lift it with a large spatula. Using two spatulas, turn the croquette over: place one spatula under the croquette and one over, and *carefully* ease it up and over. (Another way to flip the potato croquette is to place a large platter, inverted, over the pan; holding the platter, invert the pan and transfer the croquette to the platter, then slide the croquette back into the pan. Make sure you've loosened the croquette on the bottom with a spatula before doing this. This second method may require some additional oil in the pan.) Continue cooking until the bottom is golden brown, about 15 minutes longer. Transfer to a serving platter, sprinkle with the parsley, and serve immediately.

MAKES 6 SERVINGS

Potato and Mushroom Cake

~ ~ ~

TORTA ALLE PATATE

I first tasted this dish at the restaurant Evangelista in Rome, where it was offered as a main course. With lots of great-tasting mushrooms and garlic, it is very satisfying and wonderfully flavorful.

2 large baking potatoes (Idaho or russet), about 6 ounces each

1 tablespoon pure olive oil

3 tablespoons unsalted butter

1 pound wild mushrooms, preferably portobello, crimini, or shiitake, stems removed and caps very thinly sliced

Salt and freshly ground black pepper to taste

1 large clove garlic, finely minced or pressed

¼ cup chopped fresh parsley

1 cup (about) freshly grated Parmesan cheese

¼ cup plain bread crumbs

1. Preheat the oven to 425°F.

2. Peel the potatoes and slice them as thinly as possible, preferably in a food processor or on a mandoline. Place them in a bowl with enough cold water to cover until you are ready to use them (it prevents them from browning).

3. Place the oil with 2 tablespoons of the butter in a large sauté pan over medium-high heat. Add the mushrooms and season with salt and pepper. Cook, stirring, until the mushrooms begin to soften and give up their liquid. Stir in the garlic and the parsley. Turn off the heat.

4. Lightly butter a 9–inch glass or ceramic pie plate. Drain the potato slices and pat them dry with paper towels. Make a layer of the potato slices, in a neat overlapping fashion, in the bottom of the plate. Spread half of the sautéed mushrooms over the layer of potato slices. Sprinkle ⅓ cup of the Parmesan cheese over the mushrooms. Make another neat layer of potatoes and cover that with the remaining mushrooms. Sprinkle with another ⅓ cup of cheese. Top the *torta* with a final layer of potatoes. Melt the remaining tablespoon of butter and pour it evenly over the top. Sprinkle the remaining Parmesan cheese and the bread crumbs over the top.

5. Cover with aluminum foil and bake for 45 minutes. Uncover and bake for about 15 minutes longer, or until the top is well browned and the potatoes are tender when pierced with a sharp knife. Serve at once.

MAKES 6 SERVINGS

Grilled Radicchio

~ ~ ~

RADICCHIO ALLA GRIGLIA

Delicately bitter radicchio takes on a different dimension of flavor when it's grilled.

3 small heads radicchio
Pure olive oil
Kosher salt

1. Preheat the oven broiler.
2. Pull the outer leaves off the radicchio if they are browned or wilted, and discard. Cut the heads into quarters lengthwise from the root end. Set the radicchio pieces on a flameproof baking sheet and brush liberally with olive oil. Lightly sprinkle with salt.
3. Place the radicchio under the broiler, about 6 inches from the heat. Broil for about 3 to 5 minutes, or just until the top starts to brown but does not burn. Turn the oven to 500°F and bake for 10 minutes longer, or until the radicchio is tender when pierced with a sharp knife. Serve hot or at room temperature.

MAKES 6 SERVINGS

Note: You can grill radicchio on an outside grill. Brush the radicchio with olive oil and place, cut side down, on the grill. Grill for 7 to 10 minutes, until brown. Turn and grill until bottom side is browned, about 5 minutes longer.

Spinach with Oil and Lemon

SPINACI ALL'OLIO E LIMONE

When vegetables are served as a side dish in Italy, they are served like this, just lightly steamed with some olive oil and lemon juice. Serve this spinach as an accompaniment to a pasta or risotto dish.

Two 10-ounce packages fresh spinach, stems removed
2 tablespoons extra virgin olive oil
Salt and freshly ground black pepper to taste
Juice of ½ lemon

1. Wash the spinach in several changes of cold water but do not drain. Place the wet spinach in a large saucepan or small stockpot over medium-high heat. Cover and cook for about 5 minutes, until the spinach is completely wilted and greatly reduced in bulk.
2. Using a fork, transfer the spinach to a serving plate. Drizzle the olive oil over the spinach and season with salt and pepper. Gently toss the spinach to combine. Just before serving, squeeze the lemon juice over the spinach. Serve at room temperature.

MAKES 6 SERVINGS

Spinach with Raisins and Pine Nuts

SPINACI ALLA ROMANA

This classic Roman dish dates back thousands of years. The pine nuts and raisins serve as a nice contrast to the flavor of the spinach. Fresh spinach makes a big difference in this dish, but if it's not available you can use frozen spinach.

2 tablespoons raisins
¼ cup pure olive oil

1 clove garlic, cut in half

3 tablespoons pine nuts

Two 10-ounce packages fresh spinach, stems removed, washed thoroughly, and
   patted dry

Salt to taste

1. Place the raisins in a 1–cup glass measuring cup and cover with boiling water. Allow to stand for 15 minutes.

2. Drain the raisins and squeeze as much water out of them as possible. Place the oil in a large sauté pan over medium heat. Add the garlic and cook for 2 to 3 minutes, stirring, to flavor the oil, being careful to brown but not to burn it. Remove the garlic from the oil, add the raisins and pine nuts, and cook for about a minute longer, stirring frequently, until the pine nuts are brown. Watch carefully because they will burn quickly. Put half the spinach in the pan and continue cooking, while tossing, for about 3 minutes, until all the ingredients are well combined and the spinach is cooked. Transfer to a serving dish. Put the remaining spinach in the pan and cook for about 3 minutes, until it is fully cooked. Add to the serving dish and toss to combine. Season with salt. Serve at room temperature with a little additional olive oil drizzled over the spinach.

MAKES 6 SERVINGS

String Beans with Tomato Sauce

~ ~ ~

FAGIOLINI AL POMODORO

String beans lightly cooked with fresh tomatoes become deliciously flavorful. Be careful not to overcook the beans; they should be tender but firm.

1 pound fresh green beans, stem ends trimmed

3 tablespoons pure olive oil

1 pound fresh, ripe plum tomatoes (about 6), peeled, cored, seeded, and
   coarsely chopped

1 large clove garlic, finely minced or pressed

Salt and freshly ground black pepper to taste

1. Place the green beans in a steamer basket or tray over boiling water. Cover and cook for 4 minutes. They should be barely tender. Refresh under cold running water to stop the cooking process.

2. Place the oil in a medium-size sauté pan over medium-high heat. Add the tomatoes and garlic and cook for about 10 minutes, until the tomatoes become a thick sauce. Add the green beans and cook for about 5 minutes longer, until the beans are tender but firm. Season with salt and pepper. Serve immediately.

MAKES 6 SERVINGS

Baked Tomatoes with Bread Crumbs, Garlic, and Herbs

~ ~ ~

POMODORI GENOVESI

Use really ripe, big, and juicy summer-fresh tomatoes for the best flavor. These are a perfect main course for lunch.

6 large, firm, ripe tomatoes

3 tablespoons pure olive oil

1 clove garlic, finely minced or pressed

⅓ cup plain bread crumbs

1 tablespoon chopped fresh herbs (marjoram, oregano, parsley, and/or basil)

¼ cup freshly grated Parmesan cheese

1. Preheat the oven to 350°F.

2. Cut the top half-inch off the tomatoes and gently squeeze to remove the seeds. Place the tomatoes in a baking dish, cut side up, so that they are not touching one another.

3. Place the oil in a small sauté pan over medium heat. Add the garlic and cook, stirring, for 1 minute. Turn off the heat and add the bread crumbs and herbs. Using a wooden spoon, mix the bread crumbs with the oil. Stir in the Parmesan cheese. Spoon about 1 heaping tablespoon of the bread-crumb mixture over the top of each tomato, gently pressing it down into the seed cavities and completely covering the tops. Add about ½ cup of water mixed with 1 teaspoon olive oil to the baking pan.

4. Bake for about 30 minutes, or until the tomatoes are tender when pierced with a sharp knife and the bread crumbs are lightly browned. Allow to cool slightly before serving.

MAKES 6 SERVINGS

Zucchini with Garlic and Parsley

~ ~ ~

ZUCCHINE AL FUNGHETTO

Green and garlicky, this zucchini is deliciously fresh tasting.

1½ pounds fresh zucchini (6 small- to medium-size), sliced into ½-inch-thick rounds and ends discarded
Salt
3 tablespoons extra virgin olive oil
2 cloves garlic, thinly sliced lengthwise
3 scallions, both white and green parts, trimmed, sliced in half lengthwise, then thinly sliced crosswise
⅓ cup chopped fresh parsley
Freshly ground black pepper to taste

1. Place the zucchini in a colander, sprinkle liberally with salt, toss, and allow to stand for at least 30 minutes. Shake the colander with the zucchini at least once while it is standing.

2. Place the oil in a medium-size sauté pan over medium-high heat.

Add the garlic, and when it just begins to sizzle but is not brown, add the zucchini. Reduce the heat to medium and cook, stirring frequently, for 5 to 7 minutes, until the zucchini is light brown and tender. Turn off the heat.

3. Add the scallions, parsley, and pepper. Stir to combine and turn out onto a platter. Serve hot or at room temperature.

MAKES 6 SERVINGS

Genoa-Style Stuffed Zucchini

~ ~ ~

ZUCCHINE ALLA GENOVESE

Prepare zucchini this way in the summer, when they are so plentiful and very fresh. Use the smallest zucchini that are firm and shiny for the best flavor.

6 small zucchini, about 6 inches long by 1 inch around, trimmed and cut in
    half lengthwise

2 tablespoons pure olive oil

1 clove garlic, finely minced or pressed

Salt and freshly ground black pepper to taste

⅓ cup plain bread crumbs

1 teaspoon minced fresh oregano or ¼ teaspoon dried

2 tablespoons freshly grated Parmesan cheese

1. Preheat the oven to 375°F.

2. Using an apple or zucchini corer, scoop out the top ½ inch of the zucchini pulp, being careful not to break the skin. Arrange the cored zucchini in a single layer in a baking dish. Chop the pulp finely.

3. Place the oil in a medium-size sauté pan over medium-high heat. Add the zucchini pulp, garlic, salt, and pepper and sauté for about 3 minutes, until the zucchini is cooked. Turn off the heat and stir in the bread crumbs, oregano, and Parmesan. With a teaspoon, fill the cored zucchini with the bread-crumb stuffing. Try to keep the stuffing confined to the cavities. Do not pack the zucchini tightly.

4. Pour about ½ cup water mixed with 1 teaspoon olive oil into the bottom of the baking dish, being careful not to spill the water on the zucchini. Place the dish in the oven and bake for 25 to 30 minutes, or until the bread crumbs are just beginning to turn brown. Remove from the oven and serve at once or allow to cool to room temperature.

MAKES 6 SERVINGS

Fried Zucchini

~ ~ ~

ZUCCHINI FRITTI

Long strips of zucchini are light and crisp. It's important to use a large pot with enough oil so that the zucchini can float. If it's crowded while cooking you'll get soggy, greasy results.

1 to 2 quarts vegetable oil
½ cup all-purpose flour
Salt and freshly ground black pepper to taste
6 small zucchini, trimmed and cut into fine julienne strips

1. Heat enough oil to fill a large saucepan or deep fryer three-quarters full to about 325°F over medium-high. Test the oil by dropping a pinch of flour into the oil. If it sizzles, it's hot enough.

2. Combine the flour, salt, and pepper in a large mixing bowl, then add the zucchini. Toss to dredge the zucchini. Place the zucchini and flour in a wire-mesh colander, then shake it to remove as much excess flour as possible.

3. Immediately transfer the floured zucchini to the oil and cook for about 5 minutes. When the zucchini is golden brown, quickly remove it from the oil with a slotted spoon. Drain on paper towels, season with salt to taste, and serve.

MAKES 6 SERVINGS

Mixed Vegetable Antipasto
~ ~ ~

The antipasti table is a place where you traditionally mix and match different dishes. There remain, however, a few vegetable antipasti that are mixed from the start and bound together by a sauce, a dip, or a marinade.

Garlic Dip
~ ~ ~

BAGNA CAUDA

This is one of Italy's best-known mixed vegetable antipasti. *Bagna cauda*, which literally means "hot bath," is a garlicky hot dip from the northern region of Piedmont. This traditional version includes anchovies, but you can omit them if you like. For dipping, use fresh raw vegetables such as celery, red bell pepper, fennel, carrots, and endive. If you can find them, cardoons—a relative of the artichoke—are a staple of the *bagna cauda* platter. The dip should have a thin consistency and be served warm.

4 tablespoons (½ stick) unsalted butter

4 cloves garlic, mashed

5 anchovy fillets, finely minced

1 cup pure olive oil

Salt and freshly ground black pepper to taste

Melt the butter in a small saucepan over medium-low heat. Add the garlic and anchovies and stir until the anchovies are blended into the butter. Slowly whisk in the olive oil in a steady stream and simmer for about 10 minutes. Season with salt and pepper. Serve warm with fresh raw vegetables.

MAKES ABOUT 1¼ CUPS

Assorted Fried Vegetables

~ ~ ~

FRITTO MISTO

As the name implies, this dish is a "mixed fry," and you can use any combination of vegetables that you like. Vegetables prepared in a *fritto misto* are usually lightly cooked first, dredged in flour, and then dipped in batter before they are fried. Cut the vegetables into pieces of uniform size or thickness so that they will cook evenly. Use enough oil and a large pot so that the vegetables can float and are not crowded while they cook; otherwise you will have soggy results.

8 cups vegetable pieces (artichoke hearts, asparagus, carrots, cauliflower,
   zucchini)
2¼ cups all-purpose flour
1 teaspoon salt
1 cup cold water
1 large egg, lightly beaten
2 tablespoons unsalted butter, melted
Vegetable oil

1. Blanch the vegetables (see page 17). Drain well and pat dry.
2. In a large mixing bowl, combine 1¼ cups of the flour with the salt. Combine the water with the egg and add to the flour and salt while stirring vigorously with a wire whisk. Pour in the melted butter and stir well to combine. Cover and refrigerate the batter for at least 15 minutes.
3. Heat the oil in a deep saucepan or deep fryer to 350°F over medium-high. While the oil is heating, toss half the vegetables with the remaining cup of flour. Working quickly so that the flour does not become sticky, take the vegetables from the flour, place them in a strainer, and shake over the sink to remove any excess flour. Transfer the flour-coated vegetables to the bowl with the batter. Using two forks, turn each piece of vegetable around in the batter, then transfer it to the oil. The vegetables will cook quickly. When they are lightly brown all over, remove them with a slotted spoon to paper towels to drain. Repeat with the remaining vegetables. Serve at once.

MAKES 6 SERVINGS

Fresh Vegetables with Olive Oil

~ ~ ~

PINZIMONIO

This is a wonderful way to enjoy deliciously fresh raw vegetables—served with a dip that is nothing more than the best extra virgin olive oil lightly flavored with lemon juice, salt, and freshly ground black pepper.

1 large red bell pepper, cored, seeded, and sliced into ½-inch-thick strips

1 head endive, separated into individual leaves

2 Kirby cucumbers or other small-seeded variety, peeled and sliced into strips

1 small fennel bulb, stalks and leaves removed and sliced into ½-inch-thick strips

2 medium-size carrots, peeled and cut into 2- to 3-inch-long strips

2 ribs celery, cut into 2- to 3-inch-long strips

½ cup extra virgin olive oil

1 teaspoon fresh lemon juice

Salt and freshly ground black pepper to taste

1. Arrange the vegetables in a decorative manner, such as alternating different vegetables of different colors in a circular, overlapping fashion on a large serving platter. Leave space in the middle of the platter for a small dish in which you can put the dipping mixture. You can refrigerate this dish for up to several hours before serving.

2. When you are ready to serve, combine the olive oil with the lemon juice, salt, and pepper and pour into a small dish on the serving platter.

MAKES 4 TO 6 SERVINGS

Pickled Vegetables
~ ~ ~
GIARDINIERA

Vegetables prepared this way will keep for months in your refrigerator. They are a perfect accompaniment to many dishes. Store them in an attractive canning jar with a tight-fitting lid which can be used for serving as well as storing.

1 cup white wine vinegar

¾ cup pure olive oil

2 tablespoons sugar

1½ teaspoons salt

1 tablespoon fresh oregano leaves or ½ teaspoon dried

¼ teaspoon freshly ground black pepper

1 small head cauliflower, cut into florets

4 medium-size carrots, peeled and sliced into 2-inch strips

2 medium-size red bell peppers, cored, seeded, and cut into ½-inch strips

1 cup pitted green olives

1. In a large saucepan, combine the vinegar, oil, sugar, salt, oregano, and pepper and place over medium-high heat. When the mixture begins to boil, add the vegetables. Reduce the heat to medium-low and simmer for 5 minutes. Stir in the olives.

2. Transfer the vegetables to a glass or other nonreactive storage container with a tight-fitting lid and allow to cool. Cover and refrigerate until ready to serve.

MAKES 1 QUART, OR 6 SERVINGS

Chapter Six

~ ~ ~

Soups

Zuppe e Minestra

WHAT MANY ITALIAN SOUPS have in common, throughout all the regions of the Italian peninsula, is that they are overwhelmingly made with vegetables, dried legumes, and a robust broth as a base.

There are two basic types of Italian soups: a *zuppa* is a thick soup, a hearty combination of fresh vegetables and/or dried legumes, with pasta, rice or other grains, and seasonings; a *minestra* is a soup in which the ingredients—vegetables, pasta, rice, beans, etc.—are separate and distinguishable from the broth. But within these two categories there is great diversity.

Meat broth is the base of most Italian soups. You should feel free, however, to use whatever type of broth—meat, chicken, vegetable, or plain water—that you like to prepare your soups.

A lot of the variety in Italian soups comes from regional differences. In the north, soups might be enriched with butter; in the central and southern regions, soups are prepared only with olive oil. In Tuscany, there is a long tradition of bread soups in which the soup is cooked with or ladled over pieces of crusty bread, or crostini. In Genoa, fresh pesto is often added to flavor soup, and in Abruzzi *peperoncino* (hot pepper flakes) is typically used to enliven a pot. And what may be called *minestrone* or *pasta e fagioli* can be totally different from city to city.

Historically, Italian soups were generally eaten by the poor, the peasants and the farmers who would prepare soup to stretch whatever ingredients were on hand. The use of bread in Tuscan soups came from a desire to use—and not waste—day-old bread that was no longer fresh.

Soups are served in a traditional Italian meal as a *primo piatto* (first course) in place of pasta or risotto. Since so many Italian soups are hearty, they can also be served as a main course at lunch or even dinner with some antipasti or a salad on the side and some crusty bread. For most of the year, soups are served hot, with a sprinkling of freshly grated Parmesan cheese. In the summer, the same soups are often served cold or at room temperature, with a drizzle of good olive oil and Parmesan cheese.

Spinach, Escarole, and Rice Soup

~ ~ ~

ZUPPA DI SPINACI, SCAROLE E RISO

I first tasted this soup in Milan. The sharp flavor of the escarole and spinach is the perfect contrast to the smoothness of the rice.

4 tablespoons (½ stick) unsalted butter

1 small onion, finely chopped

One 10-ounce package fresh spinach, stems removed and thoroughly washed,
    or one 10-ounce package frozen chopped spinach, defrosted

1 bunch escarole, roughly chopped

4 cups broth (see pages 10–13) or water

½ cup uncooked short-grain Italian rice, preferably Arborio

Salt and freshly ground black pepper to taste

Freshly grated Parmesan cheese

1. Melt the butter in a medium-size flameproof casserole or large saucepan over medium-high heat. Add the onion and cook, stirring, for 2 to 3 minutes, until the onion begins to soften. Add the spinach and cook, stirring, for about 5 minutes, until the spinach is wilted or, if you are using frozen spinach, heated through. Stir in the escarole and cook for 3 to 5 minutes, until soft.

2. Add the broth, turn the heat to high, and bring the soup to a boil. Add the rice, lower the heat to medium, and cook, covered, for 20 minutes, or until the rice is tender but still firm. Season with salt and pepper, ladle into bowls, and serve with Parmesan cheese.

MAKES 6 SERVINGS

Celery Soup

~ ~ ~

MINESTRA DI SEDANO

Celery soup is popular in Italian homes—you probably won't find it on restaurant menus—and there are as many variations as there are cooks who prepare it. This one makes a thick and very tasty and filling soup.

¼ cup pure olive oil

1 medium-size onion, chopped

1 large bunch celery, trimmed and thinly sliced

1 large Idaho or russet potato, peeled and diced

4 cups broth (see pages 10–13) or water

12 Basic Crostini Toasts (see page 121)

½ cup freshly grated Parmesan cheese

1. Place the oil in a medium-size flameproof casserole or a large saucepan over medium-high heat. Add the onion and cook, stirring, for 2 to 3 minutes, until the onion begins to soften. Add the celery and potato and cook, stirring, for about 5 minutes longer, until the celery softens.

2. Add the broth and bring to a boil. Reduce the heat to medium-low and simmer, covered, for about 1 hour.

3. Transfer about 3 cups of the soup to a food processor fitted with the steel blade or to a blender and process for about 30 seconds until smooth. Pour the blended soup back into the pot, stir well, and heat through.

4. Ladle into bowls and top each serving with 2 crostini and Parmesan cheese.

MAKES 6 SERVINGS

Fennel and Broccoli Soup

~ ~ ~

ZUPPA DI FINOCCHIO E BROCCOLI

The strong anise flavor of fennel becomes mild and creamy when it's cooked, and complements the broccoli to perfection.

1 bunch broccoli (about 2 pounds), cut into florets and the thick bottom stalks
　discarded
1 tablespoon unsalted butter
2 tablespoons pure olive oil
1 medium-size onion, chopped
1 large fennel bulb (about 1 pound), long stalks discarded, leaves reserved, and
　the bulb thinly sliced
Salt and freshly ground black pepper to taste
4 cups chicken broth (see pages 11–12) or water

1. Place the broccoli florets in a large bowl with cold water to cover and allow to stand for 30 minutes.

2. Combine the butter and olive oil in a large saucepan or medium-size flameproof casserole over medium-high heat. Add the onion and cook, stirring, for about 3 minutes, until the onion begins to soften. Drain the broccoli and add with the fennel to the pot. Reduce the heat to medium-low, season with salt and pepper, and cook, stirring, for about 5 minutes longer.

3. Add the broth, raise the heat to high, and bring the soup to a boil. Reduce again to medium-low and simmer, covered, for about 45 minutes, or until the fennel and broccoli are fork tender.

4. Transfer the soup in batches to a food mill, food processor, or blender and process for about 30 seconds, until smooth. Return to the pot and heat through. Garnish with fennel leaves and serve immediately.

MAKES 6 SERVINGS

Puree of Asparagus Soup
~ ~ ~
PASSATO DI ASPARAGI

This is one of my favorite soups. The asparagus is cooked with potatoes, onion, and broth and run through a food mill for a creamy consistency. If you use your food processor instead, the asparagus spears should be peeled first; otherwise the tough skins will mar the texture of the soup.

4 tablespoons (½ stick) unsalted butter

2 medium-size onions, chopped

1½ pounds asparagus, tough bottoms discarded, tips reserved, and spears cut into 1-inch pieces

1 medium-size potato, peeled and diced

3 to 4 cups chicken broth (see pages 11–12) or water

Salt and freshly ground black pepper to taste

1. Melt the butter in a medium-size flameproof casserole or large saucepan over medium-high heat. Add the onions and cook, stirring, for 2 to 3 minutes, until the onion begins to soften. Add the asparagus, potato, and broth and bring to a boil. Reduce the heat to medium-low, cover, and simmer for 30 minutes, until the asparagus is very tender.

2. Strain the soup through a wire-mesh sieve. Place the solids in a food mill, food processor, or blender and pour the liquid back into the pot. Process the solids for about 30 seconds, until smooth. Transfer the puree back to the pot and stir well to incorporate with the liquid. Add the asparagus tips and turn the heat to medium. Simmer for 5 to 7 minutes, or until the tips are tender. Season with salt and pepper and serve.

MAKES 6 SERVINGS

Fresh Tomato Soup

~ ~ ~

ZUPPA DI POMODORO

Many traditional Italian soups are made with water and no broth and are called *aquacotta*. This is a light-tasting and refreshing soup that you should make in the late summer and early fall when fresh tomatoes are at their peak. No broth is added to this soup—all the liquid comes from the tomatoes.

½ cup pure olive oil

1 large carrot, peeled and finely chopped

1 medium-size onion, finely chopped

2 ribs celery, finely chopped

3 pounds fresh, ripe Italian plum tomatoes, peeled, cored, seeded, and coarsely chopped

1 cup packed fresh basil leaves, coarsely chopped

Salt and freshly ground black pepper to taste

Freshly grated Parmesan cheese

1. Place the oil in a large saucepan or medium-size flameproof casserole over medium-high heat. Add the carrot, onion, and celery and cook, stirring, for about 5 minutes, until the onion begins to soften.

2. Add the tomatoes and basil, season with salt and pepper, and stir to combine the ingredients. When the liquid in the pot begins to boil, turn the heat down to medium-low, cover the pot, and simmer for about 30 minutes, stirring occasionally, until the vegetables are tender. Add more salt, if necessary. If you find the soup is too thick, add a little water for a thinner texture and heat through. Ladle into bowls and serve with freshly grated Parmesan cheese.

MAKES 6 SERVINGS

Mushroom Tomato Soup

~ ~ ~

MINESTRA DI FUNGHI

This is a wonderfully rich and aromatic soup with an intense mush-roomy taste. Try to use wild mushrooms of any variety for the most flavor.

¼ cup pure olive oil

2 cloves garlic, finely minced or pressed

1 pound fresh wild mushrooms (preferably a mixture of portobello, crimini, shiitake, and oyster mushrooms), stems removed, thinly sliced

1 cup canned Italian plum tomatoes, with their juice, chopped

4 cups broth (see pages 10–13) or water

Salt and freshly ground black pepper to taste

½ cup packed fresh basil leaves, chopped

12 Basic Crostini Toasts (see page 121)

Place the oil in a medium-size flameproof casserole or large saucepan over medium-high heat. Add the garlic and cook briefly, stirring, being careful not to brown it. Add the mushrooms and tomatoes, reduce the heat to medium-low, and simmer for 15 minutes. Add the broth, season with salt and pepper, raise the heat to medium-high, and bring the soup to a boil. Reduce the heat again to medium-low and simmer, covered, for about 15 minutes longer. Stir in the basil and serve the soup with the crostini on the side.

MAKES 6 SERVINGS

Sweet Yellow Pepper Soup

~ ~ ~

ZUPPA DI PEPERONI

This is a soup you're likely to find in some of Italy's newer and less traditional restaurants, such as Cibreo in Florence where I first tasted it.

5 large yellow bell peppers

2 tablespoons unsalted butter

1 tablespoon pure olive oil

1 medium-size onion, chopped

1 small potato (about 4 ounces), peeled and sliced

¼ teaspoon crushed red pepper

Salt and freshly ground black pepper to taste

3 to 4 cups broth (see pages 10–13) or water

Extra virgin olive oil

1. Cut 4 of the peppers in half lengthwise, remove the seeds and stems, and coarsely chop. Combine the butter and pure olive oil in a large saucepan over medium-high heat. Add the onion and cook, stirring, for 2 to 3 minutes, until it begins to soften. Add the peppers, potato, and crushed red pepper, season with salt and pepper, and cook for 5 minutes longer. Add enough broth to cover. Turn the heat to high and bring the soup to a boil, then reduce the heat to medium-low and simmer, partially covered, for about 30 minutes, or until the vegetables are tender.

2. While the soup is cooking, preheat the oven broiler. Cut the remaining pepper in half lengthwise, remove the core and seeds, and place it on a piece of aluminum foil, cut side down, directly under the broiler until it turns completely black, about 7 minutes. Put the charred pepper in a paper bag, turn the top down to seal it, and allow to stand for 10 minutes. Under cold running water, use your fingers to peel the blackened skin from the pepper. Slice the roasted pepper into thin strips, place in a bowl, and cover with olive oil.

3. When the soup is cooked, transfer it in batches to a food processor or blender and process for about 30 seconds, until smooth. Return the soup to the pot and heat through. Serve the soup in individual bowls garnished with a few slices of roasted pepper.

MAKES 6 SERVINGS

Note: This soup can also be made with sweet red bell peppers. For the best color, do not mix red and yellow peppers together.

Zucchini Soup

~ ~ ~

ZUPPA DI ZUCCHINE

This is my mother's recipe. It is a quick, easy soup to make and is very low in fat and calories. You can serve it hot or cold.

4 small zucchini, trimmed and cut into 1-inch pieces

1 small onion, sliced

4 cups (about) chicken broth (see pages 11–12)

¼ cup chopped fresh basil, chives, or scallion greens

12 Basic Crostini Toasts (see page 121)

1. In a medium-size flameproof casserole or large saucepan, place the zucchini with the onion and enough chicken broth to cover over medium-high heat.

2. Bring the broth to a boil, cover, reduce the heat to medium-low, and simmer for about 20 minutes, until the zucchini is quite tender.

3. Transfer the soup to a food processor fitted with the double-edge steel blade, a blender, or a food mill and process until completely smooth. (You may have to do this in batches.) The soup will be quite thick. Stir in the basil. Ladle into bowls and top each serving with 2 crostini toasts.

MAKES 6 SERVINGS

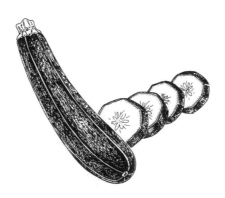

Minestrone

~ ~ ~

Minestrone means "big soup," and it is the name for a thick soup made with a variety of vegetables. It is usually prepared with seasonal vegetables and rice, beans, or pasta. What distinguishes one minestrone from another are the particular ingredients, which vary from Italian region to region. Minestrone is always best served with a sprinkling of freshly grated Parmesan cheese. You can also serve leftover minestrone at room temperature in the summer with a drizzle of good olive oil.

Vegetable Soup Milan Style

~ ~ ~

MINESTRONE ALLA MILANESE

This traditional minestrone from Milan, which I learned there, is made with northern Italian Arborio rice and is hearty enough to serve as a main course with a green salad and some crusty peasant bread.

⅓ cup pure olive oil

2 tablespoons unsalted butter

1 medium-size onion, chopped

1 medium-size carrot, peeled and chopped

2 ribs celery, diced

1 small Idaho potato, peeled and diced

1 medium-size zucchini, diced

1 cup 1-inch green bean pieces

½ head green cabbage (preferably savoy), shredded (about 4 cups)

Salt and freshly ground black pepper to taste

8 cups broth (see pages 10–13)

One 16-ounce can cannellini beans, drained and rinsed

1 cup canned Italian plum tomatoes with their juice

½ cup uncooked short-grain Italian rice, preferably Arborio

⅓ cup freshly grated Parmesan cheese

1. Place the olive oil and butter in a large flameproof casserole or stockpot over medium-high heat. Add the onion, carrot, and celery and cook, stirring, for 2 to 3 minutes, or until the onion begins to soften. Add the potato, zucchini, and green beans and continue cooking a few minutes longer. Stir occasionally. Add the cabbage, salt, and pepper and cook for about 10 minutes, until the cabbage is wilted.

2. Add the broth, beans, and tomatoes, turn up the heat to high, and bring the soup to a boil. Lower the heat and simmer, partially covered, for about 30 minutes. Add the rice, reduce the heat to medium, and cook for 20 minutes longer, or until the rice is tender. If the soup seems too thick, add more broth and heat through. Serve the soup immediately with a sprinkling of grated Parmesan cheese.

MAKES 8 SERVINGS

Vegetable Soup Genoa Style

~ ~ ~

MINESTRONE ALLA GENOVESE

Typical Ligurian vegetables such as eggplant, spinach, and zucchini and some pesto give this minestrone its special character.

1 medium-size eggplant (about 1½ to 2 pounds), stemmed and cut into 1-inch cubes

Salt

⅓ cup pure olive oil

1 small onion, finely chopped

1 medium-size carrot, peeled and finely chopped

1 rib celery, finely chopped

1 medium-size zucchini, diced

1 small Idaho potato, peeled and diced

One 10-ounce package spinach, stems removed, washed thoroughly, and roughly chopped, or one 10-ounce box frozen chopped spinach, cooked and well drained

8 cups broth (see pages 10–13) or water, or a combination

2 cups canned Italian plum tomatoes with their juice

¼ cup packed chopped fresh basil

½ pound small elbow macaroni, cooked al dente and drained

One 16-ounce can cannellini beans, drained and rinsed

Salt and freshly ground black pepper to taste

2 tablespoons Pesto (see pages 154–55)

Freshly grated Parmesan cheese

1. Place the cubed eggplant in a colander, sprinkle liberally with salt, and allow to stand for at least 30 minutes, or until it begins to release its water.

2. Place the oil in a large flameproof casserole or stockpot over medium heat. Add the onion, carrot, and celery and cook, stirring, for about 3 minutes, until the onion begins to soften. Add the eggplant, zucchini, and potato and cook, stirring occasionally, for about 5 minutes longer. Add the spinach and cook, stirring, until it is wilted, or heated through if you're using frozen. Add the broth, tomatoes, and basil, turn the heat to medium-high, and bring the soup to a boil. Reduce the heat to medium-low, cover, and simmer for about 1 hour.

3. Add the cooked macaroni to the pot of soup. Stir in the beans and heat through. If the soup seems too thick, add more broth. Season with the salt and pepper.

4. Ladle the soup into bowls and top each serving with a teaspoon of pesto and a sprinkling of cheese.

MAKES 8 SERVINGS

Bread Soups

~ ~ ~

Many traditional soups from Tuscany are cooked with bread, which thickens and flavors them.

Vegetable and Bread Soup

~ ~ ~

RIBOLLITA

I tasted many versions of *ribollita*—which means "boiled again"—throughout Tuscany. Ideally, Tuscan cooks say, you should start cooking it one day and finish it the next. It's meant to be cooked for a long time, and to be thick and very flavorful.

⅓ *cup pure olive oil*

1 medium-size onion, finely chopped

2 ribs celery, finely chopped

2 medium-size carrots, coarsely chopped

2 cloves garlic, minced

1 large Idaho or russet potato, peeled and diced

4 cups shredded cabbage

1 large bunch Swiss chard, roughly chopped, or 1 pound fresh spinach leaves, stems removed, washed thoroughly, and roughly chopped

2 cups canned Italian plum tomatoes with their juice

8 cups broth (see pages 10–13)

Salt and freshly ground black pepper to taste

One 16-ounce can cannellini beans, or 2 cups cooked white beans, drained and rinsed

½ *pound stale Italian bread, thickly sliced*

Freshly grated Parmesan cheese

1. Place the oil in a large flameproof casserole or heavy stockpot over medium heat. Add the onion, celery, carrots, and garlic and cook, stirring, for about 3 minutes, until the onion is softened. Add the potato and cabbage

and cook, stirring, about 5 minutes longer, until the cabbage is wilted. Add the Swiss chard and cook an additional 5 minutes, stirring frequently.

2. Add the tomatoes and broth, season with salt and pepper, and bring the soup to a boil. Turn the heat down to medium-low, cover, and simmer for about 2 hours, or until all the vegetables are very tender. Stir in the beans and let heat through. For best results, take the soup off the stove and allow it to cool to room temperature before proceeding or refrigerate overnight.

3. Transfer about two-thirds of the soup from the pot to a large bowl. Place three of the bread slices over the soup left in the pot. Ladle half the soup in the bowl back into the pot over the bread slices. Continue alternating slices of bread and soup until each is used up. Place the pot over medium-low heat, cover, and bring the soup to a simmer. Once the soup begins to boil, stir frequently to be sure the bottom does not burn. Keep the pot covered while cooking. Cook for 1 to 1½ hours longer, or until all the bread is completely dissolved into the soup. Add more salt and pepper, if necessary. Ladle the soup into individual bowls and serve with Parmesan cheese.

MAKES 8 SERVINGS

Tomato and Bread Soup

~ ~ ~

PAPPA AL POMODORO

This classic Tuscan soup is very simple to prepare because the tomatoes require no peeling. Make it in the summer and early fall when fresh tomatoes are plentiful and at their peak flavor. This soup is meant to be very thick and served at room temperature.

⅓ cup homemade plain bread crumbs or 2 cups stale bread, cut into cubes

⅓ cup pure olive oil

2 cloves garlic, finely chopped or pressed

3 pounds fresh, ripe Italian plum tomatoes, cored and quartered

Salt and freshly ground black pepper to taste

1 cup packed fresh basil leaves, coarsely chopped

Extra virgin olive oil to taste

1. Place the bread crumbs in a small mixing bowl with just enough cold water to cover and allow it to stand while you prepare the soup.

2. Place the olive oil in a large flameproof casserole or stockpot over high heat. Add the garlic, tomatoes, salt, and pepper and cook, stirring occasionally, for about 5 minutes, until the tomatoes begin to soften and give up their juice. Add the basil and reduce the heat to medium-low. Simmer for 10 to 15 minutes, until the tomatoes cook into a thick sauce.

3. Pour the water off the bread crumbs, which will be about doubled in volume, and combine the bread crumbs with the tomatoes and basil. Stir well to combine. Allow to cool to room temperature. Ladle into bowls and serve with a drizzle of your best olive oil.

MAKES 6 SERVINGS

Bean Soups

~ ~ ~

An enormous variety of bean soups are prepared in Italy, where dried beans are a staple. To prepare these soups you can use dried beans (directions for cooking dried beans can be found on pages 216–17) or you can use cooked beans from a can. Bean soups, which are naturally high in protein, can become a whole meal when served with a salad and good crusty bread.

White Bean Soup
~ ~ ~
ZUPPA DI FAGIOLI

This is a wonderfully rich and flavorful soup that will warm any heart or soul on a cold winter night.

⅓ cup pure olive oil

1 medium-size onion, finely chopped

2 cloves garlic, finely chopped or pressed

Two 16-ounce cans cannellini beans, drained and rinsed, or 2 cups dried white beans, cooked according to the directions on pages 216–17 and drained

¼ cup chopped fresh parsley, plus extra for serving

2 cups broth (see pages 10–13)

Salt and freshly ground black pepper to taste

Extra virgin olive oil to taste

1. Place the olive oil in a medium-size flameproof casserole or large saucepan over medium-high heat. Add the onion and garlic and cook, stirring, for 2 to 3 minutes, until the onion begins to soften.

2. Add the beans, parsley, and broth and bring the soup to a boil. Reduce the heat to medium-low and simmer, covered, for about 30 minutes, or until the soup is thick.

3. Transfer 2 cups of the soup to a food processor or blender and process for about 15 seconds, until smooth. Pour the pureed soup back into the pot, season with salt and pepper, and add more broth or water if the soup seems too thick; heat through. Ladle soup into bowls and top each serving with some parsley and a drizzle of your best olive oil.

MAKES 6 SERVINGS

Soup of Pasta and Beans

~ ~ ~

PASTA E FAGIOLI

This is a quick and easy version of one of Italy's most classic soups. It's meant to be very thick.

⅓ cup pure olive oil

1 medium-size onion, chopped

Two 16-ounce cans cannellini beans, drained and rinsed, or 2 cups dried white
    kidney beans, cooked according to the directions on pages 216–17 and
    drained

½ cup dry white wine

1 tablespoon fresh rosemary leaves or ½ teaspoon dried

¼ teaspoon crushed red pepper

1 cup canned Italian plum tomatoes with their juice

6 to 8 cups broth (see pages 10–13)

½ pound uncooked small tubular dry pasta, such as elbow macaroni or tubetti

Salt and freshly ground black pepper to taste

Freshly grated Parmesan cheese

1. Place the olive oil in a medium-size flameproof casserole or large saucepan over medium-high heat. Add the onion and cook, stirring, for 2 to 3 minutes, until the onion begins to soften. Add the beans and, using a wooden spoon, mash some of them against the side of the pot. Add the wine, rosemary, and red pepper and cook, stirring occasionally, until the wine is mostly evaporated, about 5 minutes. Add the tomatoes and stir well to combine.

2. Add 6 cups of the broth, raise the heat slightly, and bring to a boil. Reduce the heat to medium-low and simmer, partially covered, for 30 minutes. Add the pasta and cook for 10 minutes longer, or until tender. Season with salt and pepper. Ladle the soup into bowls and top each serving with Parmesan cheese.

MAKES 6 SERVINGS

Note: This soup will thicken as it stands. Add more broth as needed before reheating.

Lentil Soup

~ ~ ~

ZUPPA DI LENTICCHIE

One of my family's favorites. This lentil soup from Umbria has a rich, full flavor.

⅓ cup pure olive oil
1 medium-size onion, finely chopped
1 rib celery, finely chopped
2 cloves garlic, minced or pressed
2 cups dried lentils, rinsed and picked over
One 16-ounce can Italian plum tomatoes with their juice, chopped (about
    2 cups)
8 cups broth (see pages 10–13) or water
Salt and freshly ground black pepper to taste
Freshly grated Parmesan cheese

1. Place the oil in a large casserole or saucepan over medium-high heat. Add the onion, celery, and garlic and cook, stirring, for 2 to 3 minutes, until the onion begins to soften. Add the lentils, then stir in the tomatoes and broth.

2. Bring the liquid to a boil, reduce the heat to medium-low, cover, and simmer for 45 minutes, or until the lentils are tender and the soup is thick. Season with salt and pepper and serve with Parmesan cheese.

MAKES 6 TO 8 SERVINGS

PRESSURE COOKER METHOD: This soup can be prepared quickly in the pressure cooker. Follow step 1, placing all the ingredients in the pressure cooker, then close the pressure cooker according to the manufacturer's directions. Bring the pressure up to full over a high heat. When the pressure is up, turn the heat down to medium-low and cook at full pressure for 15 minutes. Turn off the heat and allow the pressure to drop on its own. Open the cooker according to the manufacturer's directions. Add salt and pepper to taste, and serve with Parmesan cheese.

Mushroom and Bean Soup
~ ~ ~
ZUPPA DI FAGIOLI E PORCINI

The woodsy aroma and flavor of the dried mushrooms star in this soup.

½ ounce dried porcini mushrooms

1 cup boiling water

⅓ cup pure olive oil

1 medium-size onion, finely chopped

Two 16-ounce cans cannellini beans, drained and rinsed, or 2 cups dried white kidney or Great Northern beans, cooked according to the directions on pages 216–17 and drained

1 cup canned Italian plum tomatoes with their juice

4 cups broth (see pages 10–13) or water

Salt and freshly ground black pepper to taste

2 tablespoons chopped fresh parsley

1. Put the mushrooms in a heatproof glass measuring cup with the water and allow to stand for 30 minutes. Strain the mixture through a double thickness of cheesecloth, reserve the liquid, and coarsely chop the mushrooms.

2. Place the olive oil in a flameproof medium-size casserole or large saucepan over medium-high heat. Add the onion and cook, stirring, for 2 to 3 minutes, until the onion begins to soften.

3. Add the beans, mashing some of them against the side of the pot,

the tomatoes, the mushrooms with their soaking liquid, and the broth. Turn the heat to high and bring the soup to a boil. Reduce the heat to medium-low and simmer, partially covered, for about 30 minutes, until the soup is thick. Season with salt and pepper. Ladle the soup into bowls and top each serving with parsley.

MAKES 6 SERVINGS

Chickpea Soup

~ ~ ~

ZUPPA DI CECI

I tasted this soup on my first trip to Sicily. Coarsely textured and highly seasoned, it could almost be a stew. For a more refined soup, puree the cooked chickpeas first in a blender or food processor.

⅓ cup pure olive oil

2 cloves garlic, finely minced or pressed

1 tablespoon fresh rosemary leaves or ¼ teaspoon dried

1 cup canned Italian plum tomatoes with their juice, coarsely chopped

Two 16-ounce cans chickpeas, drained and rinsed, or 2 cups dried chickpeas, cooked according to the directions on pages 216–17 and drained

3 cups broth (see pages 10–13) or water

Salt and freshly ground black pepper to taste

Pinch of crushed red pepper

1. Place the oil in a medium-size flameproof casserole or large saucepan over medium-high heat. Add the garlic and cook 1 minute, until lightly browned. Add the rosemary and tomatoes and cook, stirring, about 10 minutes, until the tomato juice is evaporated and the mixture is thick.

2. Add half the chickpeas and cook for about 5 minutes, stirring and mashing to combine them with the tomatoes. Add 2 cups of the broth, turn the heat to high, and boil briskly, stirring occasionally to prevent it from sticking, for 20 minutes longer, or until the soup is thick. Add the remaining chickpeas and broth and cook until they are heated through. Season with salt, pepper and crushed red pepper and serve.

MAKES 6 SERVINGS

Bean and Barley Soup

~ ~ ~

ZUPPA AL FARRO

Little trattorias in Tuscany serve up wonderful versions of this soup. I first tasted *zuppa al farro* in Lucca where it was made with barley—purists prefer emmer.

⅓ *cup pure olive oil*

1 large onion, chopped

1 clove garlic, minced or pressed

Two 16-ounce cans red kidney beans, drained and rinsed, or 2 cups dried red kidney beans, cooked according to the directions on pages 216–17 and drained

4 cups broth (see pages 10–13) or water

1 cup emmer (see note below) or barley

Salt and freshly ground black pepper to taste

Extra virgin olive oil

1. Place the oil in a 4-quart flameproof casserole or large saucepan over medium heat. Add the onion and garlic and cook for 2 to 3 minutes, until the onion begins to soften. Add the kidney beans and broth. Cover and cook for 10 minutes.

2. Using a slotted spoon, transfer the beans and onions from the soup to a food processor fitted with the steel blade or a blender and process until smooth, about 30 seconds. Pour the beans back into the soup and stir well to combine. Raise the heat to medium-high and bring to a boil. Add the emmer, reduce the heat to medium-low, cover, and simmer for 45 minutes or longer, until the emmer has expanded and is tender. Stir frequently because the emmer tends to stick to the bottom of the pot. Season with salt and pepper, and serve with a drizzle of your best olive oil.

MAKES 6 TO 8 SERVINGS

Note: Emmer is similar to wheat berries, which are available in health food stores.

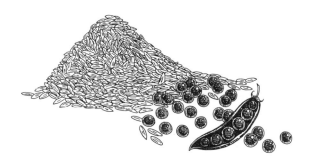

Soup of Rice and Peas
~ ~ ~
RISI E BISI

Risi e bisi is a specialty of Venice, where it has been served for centuries. Hundreds of years ago it was the dish the ruling Doges ate at the feast celebrating their patron saint, Saint Mark. Traditional recipes call for the peas to cook for a long time. I like to add the peas in the last few minutes of cooking so they keep their fresh flavor and bright green color.

3 tablespoons unsalted butter

1 tablespoon pure olive oil

1 medium-size onion, finely chopped

6 cups broth (see pages 10–13) or water

1 cup uncooked short-grain Italian rice, preferably Arborio

3 cups shelled fresh peas, or one 10-ounce package frozen peas, defrosted but
   not cooked

Salt and freshly ground black pepper to taste

½ cup freshly grated Parmesan cheese

1. Place the butter and olive oil in a medium-size flameproof casserole or large saucepan over medium-high heat. Add the onion and cook, stirring, for 2 to 3 minutes, until the onion begins to soften.

2. Add the broth and bring to a boil. Add the rice, lower the heat to medium, cover, and simmer for about 20 minutes, until the rice is tender. Add the peas and cook for 5 minutes longer. Season with salt and pepper, ladle into bowls, and serve with Parmesan cheese.

MAKES 6 SERVINGS

Chapter Seven

~ ~ ~

Crostini, Bruschetta, and Pizza

IN TUSCANY, where bread is the primary starch, rather than pasta or rice, crostini and bruschetta (or *fett'unta* as it is called by the Florentines) are everywhere. You can hardly sit down to a meal without at least considering if not consuming one of these similar but definitely different dishes.

Crostini and bruschetta, both toasted bread, were originally created as a solution for using up day-old bread. Crostini means, simply, "little toasts," and they are just that: small thin pieces of bread lightly brushed with olive oil and then toasted. They are most typically served as an appetizer topped with flavorful pureed spreads, though they can also be served plain, as croutons for soup. Bruschetta, which means "brushed," is usually a bigger, thicker piece of toasted or grilled bread that is more likely to be toasted dry and then rubbed or brushed with garlic and olive oil. It is usually served with a coarsely assembled topping that could be a salad or even large pieces of grilled vegetables. My own favorite is bruschetta with grilled eggplant.

In Italy, crostini are brought to the table with their topping already added, but I find that at home it is easier and better—because the toast doesn't get soft or soggy—to put out a platter or basket of the toasts with one or two ramekins of the toppings and let my friends have the pleasure of making their own while we have a glass of wine before dinner. Heartier bruschetta is more of a first course and should be served at the table, assembled.

For both crostini and bruschetta, you should use a dense, crusty, coarsely textured bread. I like to use baguettes for crostini, sliced on the diagonal for neat oval-shaped toasts, and large round loaves, approximately 8 to 10 inches in diameter, for bruschetta. You can use a round loaf for crostini as well; just cut the slices thinner and then crosswise into smaller pieces. If a baguette or round loaf is unavailable, rectangular loaves of bread can be sliced, then cut from corner to corner to make two triangles. Bread for bruschetta and crostini does not have to be at its freshest. In fact, bread that is a day or two old, provided it's been kept in an airtight bag or container, can work just as well. Once you prepare the toasts you can turn your attention to preparing the toppings.

Crostini toasts and their spreads can be prepared in advance (toasts will keep for two days in an airtight container). Bruschetta toasts should be prepared just before serving.

Crostini are ideal for entertaining, as hors d'oeuvres or as a first course. They can be served warm or at room temperature, which makes them ideal spring and summer fare. Bruschetta can be the featured attraction or main course at lunch as well as a first course at dinner.

Basic Crostini Toasts

~ ~ ~

1 baguette (or other) loaf white bread, preferably a crusty, coarsely textured Italian bread
About ½ cup olive oil

1. Preheat the oven to 300°F.
2. Slice the bread on an exaggerated diagonal to make long oval pieces, then lightly brush the bread slices on both sides with olive oil. Arrange in a single layer on a baking sheet.
3. Bake on the lowest rack until the tops have begun to turn golden brown, about 15 minutes. Turn the slices of bread over and bake for 5 to 10 minutes longer, until evenly brown. Allow the toasts to cool to room temperature before serving with a prepared topping.

MAKES 6 SERVINGS

Crostini with Cannellini Beans

~ ~ ~

CROSTINI AI FAGIOLI

I make these crostini regularly because they're so simple and are always a hit with guests. Serve the beans warm in a bowl and let everyone make their own.

2 tablespoons pure olive oil

1 small onion, minced

1 clove garlic, minced or pressed

2 small, fresh, ripe Italian plum tomatoes, peeled, cored, seeded and coarsely chopped

One 15-ounce can cannellini beans, drained and rinsed

Salt and freshly ground black pepper to taste

1 recipe Basic Crostini Toasts (see preceding recipe)

1. Place the olive oil in a large skillet over medium-high heat. Add the onion and cook, stirring, until softened, about 2 minutes. Add the garlic and cook, stirring, for about 1 minute longer.

2. Stir in the tomatoes and beans. Reduce the heat to low and simmer, while crushing the beans with a wooden spoon, until heated through, about 5 minutes. Season generously with salt and pepper. Cool to room temperature before serving with crostini toasts.

MAKES 6 SERVINGS

Crostini with Mushrooms

~ ~ ~

CROSTINI AI FUNGHI

A gutsy topping with a wonderfully woodsy taste.

½ cup olive oil

2 cloves garlic, very finely minced or pressed

2 small, fresh, ripe Italian plum tomatoes, peeled, cored, seeded, and finely chopped

1 pound fresh wild mushrooms (shiitake, portobello, or crimini), stems removed,
   caps minced

Salt and freshly ground black pepper to taste

2 tablespoons chopped fresh marjoram or 1 teaspoon dried

1 recipe Basic Crostini Toasts (see page 121)

1. Place the oil in a large skillet over medium-high heat. Add the garlic and tomatoes and cook, stirring, for about 1 minute. Add the mushrooms and stir well to combine. Season with salt and pepper. Turn the heat to medium-low and cook, stirring, until the mushrooms begin to soften and give up their juices. Add the marjoram and cook for about 5 minutes longer. Allow to cool slightly before serving with crostini toasts.

MAKES 6 SERVINGS

Crostini with Pâté of Black Olives

~ ~ ~

CROSTINI ALL'OLIVATA

This is a traditional Ligurian specialty that you can find packed in jars in many specialty stores. Homemade is much better—a lot less salty and more enjoyable to eat. An olive/cherry pitter is a big help.

1 cup Gaeta or oil-cured black olives (do not use Calamata or California black
   olives), pitted

1 tablespoon pure olive oil

1 teaspoon red wine vinegar

½ teaspoon fresh lemon juice

1 recipe Basic Crostini Toasts (see page 121)

Place the olives in a food processor fitted with the steel blade or a blender. Process for about 15 seconds. With the machine running, slowly add the oil, vinegar, and lemon juice. Stop the machine, scrape down the sides of the bowl, and process for about 10 seconds longer. Store in an airtight container in the refrigerator until ready to serve with crostini toasts. This will keep for up to 2 months in the refrigerator.

MAKES ABOUT ½ CUP, OR 6 SERVINGS

Crostini with Herb-Flavored Goat Cheese Spread

~ ~ ~

CROSTINI ALL'AGLIATA E CAPRINO

Garlic, basil, parsley, and lemon juice are combined with goat cheese, olive oil, and Parmesan cheese to make a deliciously sharp-tasting spread.

¼ cup chopped fresh parsley

¼ cup chopped fresh basil

1 clove garlic

¼ cup pure olive oil

1 teaspoon fresh lemon juice

1 tablespoon freshly grated Parmesan cheese

4 ounces mild goat cheese, at room temperature

1 recipe Basic Crostini Toasts (see page 121)

1. Combine the parsley, basil, and garlic in a food processor fitted with the steel blade or a blender. Process for about 15 seconds, or until

the herbs and garlic are finely chopped. With the mach
add the oil and lemon juice. When the oil is incorp<
machine and add the Parmesan cheese. Pulse the mact
or three times to combine the cheese with the herb m

slowly ad
the to
sp

2. Put the goat cheese in a small mixing bowl a
a wooden spoon. Add the herb mixture to the cheese ;
until the cheese is smooth and well combined with
Refrigerate until ready to serve with crostini toasts. This will keep for
several days in the refrigerator.

MAKES 6 SERVINGS

Eggplant Caviar and Sun-Dried Tomatoes

~ ~ ~

CAVIALE DI MELANZANE E POMODORI SECCHI

Eggplant caviar is an old family favorite. I find that the sun-dried
tomatoes add the perfect sharp contrast to the eggplant. Use only sun-
dried tomatoes that have been packed in oil.

1 medium-size eggplant (about 1 to 1½ pounds)
8 oil-packed sun-dried tomato halves
½ cup packed fresh parsley leaves
1 small clove garlic
¼ cup pure olive oil
1 recipe Basic Crostini Toasts (see page 121)

1. Preheat the oven to 350°F.
2. Wrap the eggplant in aluminum foil and place on a baking sheet in
the oven. Bake for 1½ to 2 hours, until completely tender. Unwrap, slice
the eggplant in half, and carefully pour off any liquid. Using a soup spoon,
scrape the eggplant flesh from the skin and place in a small mixing bowl.
3. In a food processor fitted with the steel blade or a blender, combine
the sun-dried tomatoes, parsley, and garlic and process for about 15 seconds, until the tomatoes are finely chopped. With the machine running,

the oil until it is fully incorporated into the tomatoes. Transfer mato mixture to the mixing bowl with the eggplant and use a wooden on to beat the eggplant until it is almost smooth (you want the mixture to have some texture). Serve with crostini toasts. This will keep in the refrigerator for up to a week.

MAKES 6 SERVINGS

Basic Bruschetta Toast

~ ~ ~

1 round loaf crusty white bread
1/3 cup pure olive oil
1 clove garlic, finely minced or pressed

1. Preheat the oven broiler.
2. Cut the loaf of bread in half down the middle. Place the cut side down, and cut each half-loaf into 1-inch-thick slices. Place the slices on an ungreased baking sheet under the oven broiler, about 6 inches from the heat source. (You can also grill the bread on a charcoal grill.) When the bread begins to turn light brown, turn the pieces over and brown the other side.
3. Combine the olive oil with the garlic in a small mixing bowl or glass measuring cup. When the bread is toasted, lightly brush it with the oil and garlic mixture while still warm.

MAKES 6 SERVINGS

Bruschetta with Grilled Eggplant

~ ~ ~

BRUSCHETTA ALLE MELANZANE ALLA GRIGLIA

I learned this recipe in the kitchen at Da Ganino, a wonderful trattoria in Florence. For the best flavor, grill the eggplant on an outdoor barbecue or a stove-top cast iron grill. This is a hearty first course dish.

2 medium-size eggplants (about 1 to 1½ pounds each), stems removed and
   cut crosswise into 1-inch slices
Salt
Pure olive oil
¼ cup chopped fresh parsley
1 recipe Basic Bruschetta Toast (see preceding recipe), without the oil
   and garlic

1. Place the eggplant slices in a colander and sprinkle liberally with salt. Allow to stand for at least 30 minutes, or until they begin to release water. Pat the eggplant slices dry with paper towels.

2. Light the outdoor barbecue or preheat the stove-top grill. Brush the eggplant on both sides with olive oil and place on the grill. Grill for about 5 minutes on each side, until tender when pierced with a sharp knife. Transfer the eggplant to a deep glass or ceramic dish, piling the pieces on top of one another as necessary. Sprinkle with the parsley and pour enough olive oil over the eggplant to cover it. Allow to stand for at least 3 hours. Using a fork, move the pieces around in the olive oil from time to time.

3. Serve with bruschetta toast, 2 to 3 pieces of eggplant per slice of bruschetta.

MAKES 6 SERVINGS

Bruschetta with Tomatoes and Fresh Arugula

~ ~ ~

BRUSCHETTA AL POMODORO E RUCOLA

3 large, fresh, ripe eating tomatoes, cut in half lengthwise, cored, seeded,
   and diced
¼ cup chopped arugula
2 tablespoons extra virgin olive oil
1 teaspoon red wine vinegar
Salt and freshly ground black pepper to taste
1 recipe Basic Bruschetta Toast (see page 126)

1. Place the tomatoes in a small nonaluminum mixing bowl and combine with the arugula, olive oil, vinegar, salt, and pepper.

2. Prepare the bruschetta and pile some of the tomato mixture onto each slice.

MAKES 6 SERVINGS

Bruschetta with Red and Yellow Pepper Topping
~ ~ ~
BRUSCHETTA AI PEPERONI

3 tablespoons pure olive oil

2 large red bell peppers, cored, seeded, and cut into ½-inch strips

1 large yellow bell pepper, cored, seeded, and cut into ½-inch strips

Salt to taste

1 clove garlic, mashed (optional)

1 recipe Basic Bruschetta Toast (see page 126)

1. Place 1 tablespoon of the olive oil in a large cast iron or other heavy skillet over medium-high heat. Add the peppers and cook, stirring, for 7 to 10 minutes, until the edges of the pepper strips begin to turn brown and the peppers are tender and soft but not limp.

2. Transfer the peppers to a mixing bowl. Add the remaining olive oil, the salt, and garlic. Stir well to combine. Allow the peppers to reach room temperature before serving with bruschetta toast.

MAKES 6 SERVINGS

Pizza

~ ~ ~

Pizza is one of the best-known Italian foods in the world, and one of the oldest. Its origins date back to the Greeks, who occupied southern Italy from around 700 to 100 B.C. and flavored their flat breads before baking them. The ancient Romans took the concept further, adding olive oil and herbs and eventually cheeses, seafood, and vegetables as toppings. In the eighteenth century, after the tomato had arrived and taken hold in southern Italy, the pizza as we know it today was finally born. Focaccia— an herb-flavored flat bread—is still available to happily remind us of pizza's predecessors.

Pizza has always been a snack food in Italy, originally sold from stalls along the streets of Naples. More recently it has been taken inside to small special pizza establishments, *pizzerie*. Pizza remains—and usually with only the most basic toppings—the foremost Italian fast food, from Sicily in the south to Venice in the north, where it can be found in espresso bars, bakeries, and anywhere people stop to refresh and sustain themselves. Pizza is rarely if ever prepared or eaten in Italian homes or fine restaurants.

We in America, on the other hand, have made pizza much more than a snack food. It can be found in the freezer sections of most supermarkets, in pizzerias, and as the delicate, thin-crusted *pizzetti* on the menus of the finest Italian restaurants. And it is often eaten at home. Although most of the pizza eaten is still of the frozen or take-out variety, more and more cooks are making their own because it is so easy to do and can provide a healthful, delicious meal for the entire family. Preparing pizza at home is not difficult or particularly time-consuming. If you know the basic technique and have a few special ingredients and tools, you can produce great pizza.

EQUIPMENT

~ ~ ~

Making pizza doesn't require special equipment, but some items will improve the final product. You can bake pizza in a jelly roll pan or on a cookie sheet, but you'll get a crisper crust if you use a special pizza pan with a perforated bottom or a pizza stone. If you use a pizza stone you'll need a peel, a large wooden spatula for transferring the assembled unbaked pizza to the hot stone. The only other really useful tool is a pizza cutter with a circular rotating knife blade. It does wonders for cutting the pizza without pulling the baked toppings apart.

INGREDIENTS

~ ~ ~

FLOUR. I recommend using durum flour for making pizza dough. It will give you the best crust—crusty on the outside and tender, but not doughy, inside. Durum flour, finely ground from hard durum (also called winter) wheat, has a powdery texture. It can usually be bought in Italian specialty food stores and some health food stores (see pages 295–96 for sources).

Do not confuse durum flour with semolina, which is also called pasta flour. It is coarsely ground from the same hard durum wheat, but has a granular texture and resembles cornmeal. It is used in making pizza, but only for dusting the baking sheet or pizza stone.

You can also use all-purpose or unbleached white flour in the preparation of pizza dough, but I don't find the flavor or the texture of the finished crust as good as the crust you make with durum flour.

YEAST. You can use any dry yeast you find in packages in the supermarket. Be sure to check the date on the package to see that it is not expired. You can also use fresh cakes of yeast to prepare the dough. You'll need only about half as much fresh yeast as the amount of dry yeast that's called for. All the recipes that follow call for dry yeast.

OIL. Pizza dough calls for a small quantity of oil. I like to use olive oil because I like the flavor it imparts to the crust. You can also use other mildly flavored vegetable oils such as corn oil, oil blends, or safflower oil.

SALT. The dough gets most of its flavor from the salt that's added. If you are on a sodium-restricted diet, you can reduce the quantity of salt or omit it altogether. *Never* add sugar to the dough. Although many recipes I've seen call for some sugar to be added to the yeast to get it started rising, pizza dough should never have a sweet taste. If anything, it should taste slightly sour.

PREPARATION

~ ~ ~

Pizza dough can be made in a food processor or electric mixer, or by hand (the last is my preference, since you can gauge exactly how much water to add). The taste and texture of machine-made dough won't differ from that of the handmade.

Whatever technique you choose, pizza dough requires little in the way of kneading. You want to knead the dough just enough to make it smooth and elastic, 2 to 3 minutes; you don't want to make it too light and airy. Once you've prepared the dough, allow it to rise for at least 1½ hours, or until it is doubled in bulk. At that point, turn the dough out onto a floured work surface, divide it into two pieces, and lightly knead each piece before rolling or stretching it out.

Pizza dough can be refrigerated, after it has risen, for up to 3 days, or frozen for as long as several months. If you refrigerate it, allow it to come to room temperature before rolling or stretching and baking it. If you freeze the dough, defrost it in the refrigerator, then allow it to reach room temperature before proceeding. Refrigerate or freeze dough in securely covered plastic containers.

When you roll or stretch out the dough, keep the work surface and the rolling pin well floured to prevent the dough from sticking. For a thicker crust, roll the dough out to a diameter of 10 inches. For a thinner crust, roll the dough to about 12 inches.

TOPPINGS

~ ~ ~

After you roll out the dough, you are ready to put the toppings on your pizza. Always place the dough in the pan you intend to bake it in (or on the pizza peel) before adding any toppings since once the toppings are in place the dough is difficult to move or handle.

There are countless toppings for pizza—almost any combination of herbs, vegetables, and cheeses can be used. But while you can put whatever you like on top of your pizza, my experience is that the simplest combinations with a light hand are the best. If you overdo it, the crust doesn't have a chance to bake evenly and can end up underbaked and soggy.

The recipes given here are a mix of traditional Italian and my own up-dated variations. I always use Fresh Tomato Sauce (see pages 152–53) or fresh sliced tomatoes on my pizzas. In Italy they might use canned tomatoes. You can substitute whatever tomato sauce you like or have on hand. I also like to use fresh mozzarella cheese, which is readily available where I live, instead of the packaged mozzarella from the supermarket because it is creamier. You can use any mozzarella cheese available to you or you can substitute other good melting cheeses, which include fontina, Bel Paese, and Taleggio. Goat cheese is a pungently flavorful and creamy addition to pizza, but it doesn't melt particularly well. As a rule, vegetables that are added as toppings to pizzas are cooked—steamed, sautéed, or roasted—first. This maximizes their flavor, cooks away any water that might make the crust soggy, and ensures they will be fully cooked after baking.

BAKING

~ ~ ~

Pizza should be baked on the topmost shelf in a preheated 450°F oven. If you are using a pizza stone or baking tiles, they should also be preheated. Bake the pizza for 15 to 20 minutes, or until the crust is golden brown and the cheeses on top are melted. As soon as the pizza is finished baking, remove it from the oven, slice, and serve it.

A NOTE ABOUT CALZONE AND FOCACCIA

~ ~ ~

Calzone, which literally means "trouser leg," is essentially a closed pizza: the dough is rolled out to the desired size and the topping, which becomes the filling of a calzone, is spread over half the circle of dough. The dough is folded over the filling and sealed closed by moistening the two edges of the dough that meet and crimping the edge. An air vent or two in the dough prevents the calzone from bursting while baking. All of the pizza recipes that follow are suitable for calzone. The baking time for calzone is about 25 to 30 minutes.

Focaccia is a flat bread that, like pizza, is also a descendant of the earliest breads. And also like pizza, focaccia is a snack food in Italy, although it is now widely served as a bread at tables in Italian restaurants in the United States. Focaccia gets its name from the Latin *focus*, which means "hearth." Although there are places in Italy where focaccia is still baked on an open hearth, most is baked in ovens like bread. Focaccia is usually prepared with a special dough that is heavily enriched with olive oil, but you can make a wonderful focaccia with the pizza dough recipe that follows. When making focaccia, roll out the dough as for pizza, dimple the top by pressing your fingertips into the dough, drizzle some good olive oil over it, and season with a sprinkling of salt and/or fresh herbs over the top. Bake according to the directions for pizza.

Basic Pizza Dough

~ ~ ~

Great pizza depends on really good crust: not too thick or thin, slightly crisp on the outside, and tender inside. I have tried many recipes for pizza crust, but this one, from my good friend Rob Robinson in Washington, D.C., which calls for using only finely ground durum flour, is my favorite.

1½ *cups warm water*

1 *package (1 tablespoon) active dry yeast*

2 *tablespoons pure olive oil*

4 *cups finely ground durum flour*

1 *tablespoon salt*

Vegetable oil

Cornmeal or coarse semolina for dusting

1. Combine the water and yeast in a glass measuring cup and allow to stand for 15 minutes. Add the oil to the water and stir with a teaspoon until the yeast is dissolved in the water.

2. Combine the flour and salt in a large mixing bowl. Gradually add the yeast mixture. Mix with a wooden spoon until all the ingredients are well combined. Add more water, a tablespoon at a time, if the dough seems too dry. It's better if the dough is slightly sticky. Turn the dough

out onto a well-floured work surface and knead for about 5 minutes, or just until the dough is smooth and elastic. Lightly grease the mixing bowl with some vegetable oil and place the dough in the bowl, cover with a clean dish towel, and place in a warm spot to rise for 1½ to 2 hours, or until doubled in bulk.

3. Turn the dough out onto a lightly floured work surface, pull it apart into two even pieces, and knead each piece for a minute or two, until it becomes smooth. Form two even balls. The dough should roll or stretch out quite easily. You can use your hands—gently pulling on the dough while turning it so that it becomes bigger, evenly, the way a professional pizza baker does it—or use a rolling pin on a well-floured surface and roll out the dough to a diameter of approximately 10 inches. If you like a thinner crust, stretch or roll the dough to 12 inches.

MAKES TWO 10– TO 12-INCH PIZZAS

TO PREPARE THE DOUGH IN A FOOD PROCESSOR: Combine the flour and salt in a food processor with the metal blade in place. With the processor running, slowly add the yeast mixture. Process for about 2 minutes, or until the dough forms a ball on the metal blade. Take out and knead for about 5 minutes before setting out to rise.

Pizza with Fresh Tomato Sauce, Mozzarella, and Basil

~ ~ ~

PIZZA MARGHERITA

This is classic pizza at its best. Named in honor of Queen Margherita of Italy, who visited Naples in the late 1800s, it bears the colors of the Italian flag: red, white, and green.

1 recipe Basic Pizza Dough (see preceding recipe), rolled out into 2 rounds
Semolina or cornmeal for dusting
2 cups Fresh Tomato Sauce (see pages 152–53)
8 ounces mozzarella cheese, thinly sliced
¼ cup packed fresh basil leaves, coarsely chopped
Olive oil

1. Preheat the oven to 450°F.

2. Prepare one pizza at a time. Place the dough on a cookie sheet, in a pizza pan, or on a peel that has been dusted with semolina or cornmeal. Spoon 1 cup of the tomato sauce onto each pizza and spread it around the dough, leaving about 1 inch of dough around the edge uncovered. Arrange the cheese over the tomato sauce, sprinkle the basil on top, and drizzle the olive oil all over.

3. Bake the pizza on the topmost shelf of the oven for about 15 minutes, or until the cheese is melted and the crust is lightly browned. Remove the pizza from the oven, transfer to a cutting board or serving plate, and cut into 6 pieces.

MAKES TWO 10- TO 12-INCH PIZZAS

Pizza with Fresh Tomatoes and Fontina

~ ~ ~

PIZZA CON POMODORO E FONTINA

Sliced fresh tomatoes are marinated in fruity olive oil with garlic and parsley to give them an exceptionally flavorful taste. This recipe was given to me by Rebecca Mattarazzi, a chef who lives and works in California. Use only Italian fontina cheese.

1 pound fresh, ripe Italian plum tomatoes, stems removed and sliced
   ½ inch thick

1 clove garlic, minced or pressed

¼ cup pure olive oil

Salt and freshly ground black pepper to taste

2 tablespoons chopped fresh parsley

1 recipe Basic Pizza Dough (see pages 133–34), rolled out into 2 rounds

Semolina or cornmeal for dusting

6 ounces Italian fontina cheese, rind removed and grated

1. Preheat the oven to 450°F.

2. Place the tomatoes in a medium-size mixing bowl. Add the garlic, oil, salt, pepper, and parsley, stir to combine, and set aside.

3. Prepare one pizza at a time. Place the dough on a cookie sheet, pizza pan, or peel that has been dusted with semolina or cornmeal. Arrange half the slices of tomato on the pizza dough as close together as possible without overlapping them, leaving about an inch of dough uncovered around the edge of the pizza. Sprinkle half the cheese over the tomato slices.

4. Bake the pizza on the topmost shelf of the oven for about 15 to 20 minutes, or until the cheese is melted and the crust is lightly browned. Transfer to a cutting board and cut into 6 slices and serve.

MAKES TWO 10- TO 12-INCH PIZZAS, OR 6 SERVINGS

Pizza with Fresh Tomatoes, Olives, and Mozzarella Cheese

~ ~ ~

PIZZA CON POMODORO, OLIVE, E MOZZARELLA

For best results, use olives that aren't too salty—preferably Gaeta olives.

1 pound fresh, ripe Italian plum tomatoes, stems removed and sliced
   ½ inch thick

1 clove garlic, minced or pressed

¼ cup olive oil

Salt and freshly ground black pepper to taste

2 tablespoons chopped fresh parsley

1 recipe Basic Pizza Dough (see pages 133–34), rolled out into 2 rounds

Semolina or cornmeal for dusting

1 cup Gaeta olives, pitted

8 ounces mozzarella cheese, grated

1. Preheat the oven to 450°F.

2. Place the tomatoes in a medium-size mixing bowl. Add the garlic, oil, salt, pepper, and parsley, stir to combine, and set aside.

3. Prepare one pizza at a time. Place the dough on a cookie sheet, pizza pan, or peel that has been dusted with semolina or cornmeal. Arrange half the tomato slices on the pizza dough as close together as possible without overlapping them, leaving about an inch of dough uncovered around the edge of the pizza. Sprinkle half the olives over the tomatoes and top with half the cheese.

4. Bake the pizza on the topmost shelf of the oven for 15 to 20 minutes, or until the cheese is melted and the crust is lightly browned. Transfer to a cutting board and cut into 6 slices and serve.

MAKES TWO 10- TO 12-INCH PIZZAS, OR 6 SERVINGS

Pizza with Artichokes

~ ~ ~

PIZZA AI CARCIOFI

This is a light, delicate—even elegant—pizza. It becomes an easy pizza to make when you use ready-to-cook artichoke hearts.

One 10-ounce package frozen artichoke hearts (cooked according to the directions on the box), or 4 medium-size artichokes trimmed according to the directions on page 32, chokes removed, thickly sliced, and steamed until tender (about 10 minutes)

1 clove garlic, minced or pressed

¼ cup pure olive oil

Salt and freshly ground black pepper to taste

2 tablespoons chopped fresh parsley

1 recipe Basic Pizza Dough (see pages 133–34), rolled out into 2 rounds

Semolina or cornmeal for dusting

8 ounces mozzarella cheese, grated

1. Preheat the oven to 450°F.

2. Place the cooked artichoke hearts in a small mixing bowl. Add the garlic, oil, salt, pepper, and parsley and stir to combine.

3. Prepare one pizza at a time. Place the dough on a cookie sheet, pizza pan, or peel that has been dusted with semolina or cornmeal. Arrange half the artichoke hearts over the dough in a single layer, leaving about an inch of dough uncovered around the edge of the pizza. Sprinkle half the cheese over the artichoke hearts.

4. Bake the pizza on the topmost shelf of the oven for 15 to 20 minutes, or until the cheese is melted and the crust is lightly browned. Transfer to a cutting board or serving dish and cut into 6 slices and serve.

MAKES TWO 10- TO 12-INCH PIZZAS, OR 6 SERVINGS

Pizza with Fresh Tomato Sauce, Mushrooms, and Fontina

~ ~ ~

PIZZA AL BOSCO

The mushrooms add a wonderful earthy flavor to this pizza.

3 tablespoons pure olive oil

1 clove garlic, minced or pressed

½ pound mushrooms (preferably crimini), stems removed and caps thinly sliced

Salt and freshly ground black pepper to taste

1 recipe Basic Pizza Dough (see pages 133–34), rolled out into 2 rounds

Semolina or cornmeal for dusting

2 cups Fresh Tomato Sauce (see pages 152–53)

2 tablespoons chopped fresh marjoram or 2 teaspoons dried

8 ounces Italian fontina cheese, rind removed and coarsely grated

1. Preheat the oven to 450°F.
2. Place the oil in a medium-size skillet over medium-high heat. Add the garlic and mushrooms, season with salt and pepper, and cook, stirring, for about 5 minutes, until the mushrooms are tender. Turn off the heat and set aside.
3. Prepare one pizza at a time. Place the dough on a cookie sheet, pizza pan, or peel that has been dusted with semolina or cornmeal. Spoon 1 cup of the tomato sauce over the dough, leaving about an inch uncovered around the edge of the pizza. Arrange half the mushrooms, in a single layer, over the tomato sauce, sprinkle half the marjoram over the mushrooms, and top with half the cheese.
4. Bake the pizza on the topmost shelf of the oven for 15 to 20 minutes, or until the cheese is melted and the crust is lightly browned. Transfer to a cutting board or serving dish and cut into 6 slices and serve.

MAKES TWO 10- TO 12-INCH PIZZAS, OR 6 SERVINGS

Pizza with Mushrooms, Broccoli, Zucchini, and Artichoke Hearts

~ ~ ~

PIZZA QUATTRO STAGIONI

This is a hearty pizza with a variety of deliciously well-seasoned vegetables. Have fun arranging them decoratively on the dough.

1 medium-size zucchini, thinly sliced

Salt

½ cup plus 1 tablespoon pure olive oil

3 cloves garlic, minced or pressed

½ pound mushrooms (preferably crimini), stems removed and caps thinly sliced

Freshly ground black pepper to taste

4 cups broccoli florets

One 10-ounce package frozen artichoke hearts, cooked according to the directions on the package and drained

2 tablespoons chopped fresh parsley

1 recipe Basic Pizza Dough (see pages 133–34), rolled out into 2 rounds

Semolina or cornmeal for dusting

2 cups Fresh Tomato Sauce (see pages 152–53)

8 ounces mozzarella cheese, grated

1. Preheat the oven to 450°F.

2. Place the zucchini in a colander, sprinkle liberally with salt, and allow to stand for 30 minutes, or until it begins to release water. Meanwhile, place 3 tablespoons of the oil in a medium-size skillet over medium-high heat. Add a third of the garlic and all the mushrooms, season with salt and pepper, and cook, stirring, for about 5 minutes, until the mushrooms are tender. Transfer to a small bowl and set aside. Steam the broccoli over boiling water over medium-high heat for 5 minutes. Refresh under cold water and drain very well. Heat 1 tablespoon of the oil in the skillet. Add the broccoli and cook for about 5 minutes, stirring occasionally, until it begins to brown. Transfer to a small bowl and set aside. Place the cooked artichoke hearts in a small mixing bowl with half of the remaining garlic,

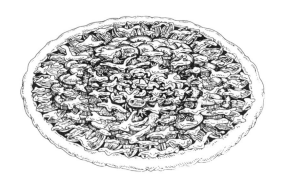

3 tablespoons of the olive oil, salt, pepper, and the parsley and stir well to combine. Place the remaining olive oil in the skillet over medium-high heat. Add the remaining garlic and the zucchini and cook, stirring, for about 5 minutes, until tender.

3. Prepare one pizza at a time. Place the dough on a cookie sheet, pizza pan, or peel that has been dusted with semolina or cornmeal. Spoon 1 cup of the tomato sauce over the dough, leaving about an inch uncovered around the edge of the pizza. Arrange half the cooked mushrooms in the center of the pizza. Arrange half the cooked broccoli in a ring around the mushrooms, half the cooked zucchini around the broccoli, and half the artichoke hearts around the zucchini, so that the tomato sauce is covered and there is about an inch of dough uncovered around the edge of the pizza. Sprinkle half the cheese over the vegetables.

4. Bake the pizza on the topmost shelf of the oven for 15 to 20 minutes, or until the cheese is melted and the crust is lightly browned. Transfer to a cutting board or serving dish and cut into 6 slices and serve.

MAKES TWO 10- TO 12-INCH PIZZAS, OR 6 SERVINGS

Pizza with Fresh Tomato Sauce, Roasted Eggplant, Smoked Mozzarella, and Basil

~ ~ ~

PIZZA CON LE MELANZANE

This is a robust pizza that makes a perfect main course. I first tasted this combination at the restaurant Michela's in Cambridge, Massachusetts.

The smoked mozzarella lends a distinctive flavor—you can also use plain mozzarella.

2 very small eggplants (about ¼ pound each), sliced ½ inch thick
Salt
½ cup pure olive oil
1 recipe Basic Pizza Dough (see pages 133–34), rolled out into 2 rounds
Semolina or cornmeal for dusting
2 cups Fresh Tomato Sauce (see pages 152–53)
8 ounces smoked mozzarella cheese, coarsely chopped
2 tablespoons chopped fresh basil

1. Preheat the oven to 450°F.

2. Place the eggplant in a colander, sprinkle liberally with salt, and allow to stand for about 30 minutes, or until they begin to release water. Pat dry with paper towels.

3. Preheat the oven broiler. Pour the oil into a roasting pan and turn the pan to distribute the oil evenly. Lay the eggplant slices in the pan in a single layer, turning them once to coat both sides with the oil. Place the pan on the topmost shelf under the broiler and broil the eggplant for 3 to 5 minutes on each side, or until evenly browned. Transfer to a platter.

4. Prepare one pizza at a time. Place the dough on a cookie sheet, pizza pan, or peel that has been dusted with semolina or cornmeal. Spoon 1 cup of the tomato sauce over the dough, leaving about an inch uncovered around the edge of the pizza. Arrange half the eggplant slices over the tomato sauce in a single layer. Sprinkle half the cheese over the eggplant and top with half the chopped basil.

5. Bake the pizza on the topmost shelf of the oven for 15 to 20 minutes, or until the cheese is melted and the crust is lightly browned. Transfer to a cutting board or serving dish and cut into 6 slices and serve.

MAKES TWO 10- TO 12-INCH PIZZAS, OR 6 SERVINGS

Pizza with Fresh Tomatoes, Roasted Red and Yellow Peppers, Fontina, and Crushed Red Pepper

~ ~ ~

PIZZA AI PEPERONI E PEPERONCINO

This pizza has a nice contrast in flavors. The sweetness of the peppers is offset by the tanginess of the tomatoes and cheese.

½ cup pure olive oil
2 large red bell peppers, cored, seeded, and sliced into ½-inch strips
1 large yellow bell pepper, cored, seeded, and sliced into ½-inch strips
Kosher salt
1 pound fresh, ripe Italian plum tomatoes, stems removed and sliced ½ inch thick
1 clove garlic, minced or pressed
Salt and freshly ground black pepper to taste
2 tablespoons chopped fresh parsley
1 recipe Basic Pizza Dough (see pages 133–34), rolled out into 2 rounds
Semolina or cornmeal for dusting
1 teaspoon crushed red pepper
8 ounces Italian fontina cheese, rind removed and coarsely grated

1. Preheat the oven to 450°F.
2. Pour half the oil into the roasting pan and tilt the pan to distribute the oil evenly. Lay the pepper slices, skin sides down, in a single layer in the pan. Lightly sprinkle with kosher salt, place the pan on the topmost shelf of the oven, and roast for 15 to 20 minutes, until the pepper slices begin to brown on the bottom and are tender when pierced with a sharp knife. Transfer the pepper slices to a platter.
3. While the peppers are roasting, place the tomatoes in a medium-size mixing bowl with the remaining oil, the garlic, salt, pepper, and parsley. Stir to combine and set aside.
4. Prepare one pizza at a time. Place the dough on a cookie sheet, pizza pan, or peel that has been dusted with semolina or cornmeal. Arrange half the tomatoes on the dough in a single layer as close together as possible

without overlapping them, leaving about an inch uncovered around the edge of the pizza. Arrange half the roasted peppers over the tomatoes, alternating the red and yellow strips. Sprinkle half of the crushed red pepper over the pepper slices and top with half of the cheese.

5. Bake the pizza on the topmost shelf of the oven for 15 to 20 minutes, or until the cheese is melted and the crust is lightly browned. Transfer to a cutting board or serving dish. Cut into 6 slices and serve.

MAKES TWO 10- TO 12-INCH PIZZAS, OR 6 SERVINGS

Pizza with Fresh Tomatoes, Sun-Dried Tomatoes, Goat Cheese, and Mozzarella

~ ~ ~

PIZZA AI POMODORI SECCHI E CAPRINO

The goat cheese and sun-dried tomatoes give this pizza a deliciously tangy flavor.

1 pound fresh, ripe Italian plum tomatoes, stems removed and sliced ½ inch thick

1 clove garlic, minced or pressed

¼ cup pure olive oil

Salt and freshly ground black pepper to taste

2 tablespoons chopped fresh parsley

1 recipe Basic Pizza Dough (see pages 133–34), rolled out into 2 rounds

Semolina or cornmeal for dusting

½ cup chopped, oil-packed sun-dried tomatoes, with 2 tablespoons of the oil reserved

4 ounces goat cheese, crumbled

4 ounces fresh mozzarella cheese, thinly sliced

1. Preheat the oven to 450°F.

2. Place the sliced tomatoes in a medium-size mixing bowl and add the garlic, olive oil, salt, pepper, and parsley. Stir to combine and set aside.

3. Prepare one pizza at a time. Place the dough on a cookie sheet, pizza pan, or peel that has been dusted with semolina or cornmeal. Arrange

half the tomato slices on the pizza dough as close together as possible without overlapping them, leaving about an inch of dough uncovered around the edge of the pizza. Sprinkle half the sun-dried tomatoes over the fresh tomatoes and drizzle a tablespoon of the reserved oil over the top. Distribute half the cheeses over the tomatoes.

4. Bake the pizza on the topmost shelf of the oven for 15 to 20 minutes, or until the cheese is melted and the crust is lightly browned. Transfer to a cutting board or serving dish. Cut into 6 slices and serve.

MAKES TWO 10- TO 12-INCH PIZZAS, OR 6 SERVINGS

Pizza with Roasted Onions, Rosemary, and Taleggio

~ ~ ~

PIZZA ALLE CIPOLLE, ROSMARINO, E TALEGGIO

A little rosemary goes a long way on this pizza.

¼ cup pure olive oil

2 large red onions, cut in half lengthwise and sliced lengthwise ¼ inch thick

Kosher salt

1 recipe Basic Pizza Dough (see pages 133–34), rolled out into 2 rounds

Semolina or cornmeal

2 tablespoons fresh rosemary leaves

8 ounces Taleggio cheese, coarsely grated

1. Preheat the oven to 450°F.

2. Pour the oil into a roasting pan and tilt the pan to distribute the oil evenly. Lay the onion slices in the pan in a single layer, turning them once to coat both sides with the oil. Lightly sprinkle with salt, place the pan on the topmost shelf of the oven, and roast for 15 to 20 minutes, until the onion slices begin to brown. Transfer the onions to a platter.

3. Prepare one pizza at a time. Place the dough on a cookie sheet, pizza pan, or peel that has been dusted with semolina or cornmeal. Arrange half the onion slices on the dough, sprinkle half the rosemary over them, and top with half the cheese.

4. Bake the pizza on the topmost shelf of the oven for 15 to 20 minutes, or until the cheese is melted and the crust is lightly browned. Transfer to a cutting board or serving dish. Cut into 6 slices and serve.

MAKES TWO 10- TO 12-INCH PIZZAS, OR 6 SERVINGS

Pizza with Pesto and Three Cheeses
~ ~ ~
PIZZA AL PESTO E TRE FORMAGGI

This is a pizza for pesto lovers. The tangy goat cheese adds an exciting contrast to the flavor.

1 recipe Basic Pizza Dough (see pages 133–34), rolled out into 2 rounds
Semolina or cornmeal for dusting
½ cup Pesto (see pages 154–55)
⅓ cup freshly grated Parmesan cheese
8 ounces mozzarella cheese, grated
4 ounces goat cheese, crumbled

1. Preheat the oven to 450°F.
2. Prepare one pizza at a time. Place the dough on a cookie sheet, pizza pan, or peel that has been dusted with semolina or cornmeal. Spread half of the pesto sauce over the dough, leaving about an inch of dough uncovered around the edge of the pizza. Sprinkle half the Parmesan over

the pesto. Spread half the mozzarella over the pesto and half cheese over that.

3. Bake the pizza on the topmost shelf of the oven fo minutes, or until the cheese is melted and the crust is light' Transfer to a cutting board or serving dish. Cut into 6 slices and ser

MAKES TWO 10- TO 12-INCH PIZZAS, OR 6 SERVINGS

Olive's Pizza with Olive Pâté, Caramelized Onions, and Goat Cheese

~ ~ ~

PIZZA AL OLIVIE

Olive's is one of Boston's best restaurants and owners Tod and Olivia English serve this pizza every night. Made with an enriched dough, the result is truly outstanding.

1 recipe Basic Pizza Dough (see pages 133–34)

¼ pound (1 stick) unsalted butter, at room temperature

¼ cup pure olive oil

2 medium-size red onions, cut in half lengthwise and sliced lengthwise ¼ inch thick

Kosher salt

Semolina or cornmeal for dusting

6 tablespoons olive pâté (see pages 123–24) or from a jar

⅓ cup Gaeta olives, pitted

4 ounces goat cheese, crumbled

1. Prepare the pizza dough. After the dough has risen, punch it down, separate it into two equal pieces, and knead it lightly. Roll each piece into a rectangle about 8 × 6 inches. Spread half the butter over each piece of dough, leaving an inch all around the edge of the dough. Fold the dough into thirds, then roll it out again. Fold it

.nto thirds again, wrap it in plastic, and refrigerate for about 1 hour. Repeat the folding and rolling two more times.

2. Preheat the oven to 450°F.

3. Pour the olive oil into a baking pan and tilt the pan to evenly distribute the oil. Place the onion slices into the pan in a single layer, turning them once to coat both sides with the oil. Lightly sprinkle with the salt and place in the oven. Bake for about 20 minutes, until the edges of the onion begin to turn brown and the onions are tender.

4. Roll out the dough to make two rounds 10 to 12 inches in diameter. Prepare one pizza at a time. Place the dough on a cookie sheet, pizza pan, or peel that has been dusted with semolina or cornmeal. Spread half of the olive pâté over the dough, leaving about an inch of dough uncovered around the edge of the pizza. Arrange half the roasted onions over the olive pâté, distribute half the olives over the pizza, and sprinkle half the goat cheese over the top.

5. Bake the pizza on the topmost shelf of the oven for 15 to 20 minutes, or until the cheese is melted and the crust is lightly browned. Transfer to a cutting board or serving dish. Cut into 6 slices and serve.

MAKES TWO 10- TO 12-INCH PIZZAS, OR 6 SERVINGS

Chapter Eight

~ ~ ~

Pasta

PASTA HAS BEEN CONSUMED in Italy for centuries and has been traced back to the ancient Romans, the Etruscans, and even to the Greeks. But it wasn't until the fourteenth century, when pasta began to be sold commercially like bread in special shops, that it became an integral part of Italian life, first in southern Italy and then in the north. By the nineteenth century, pasta had become so popular that production was moved to large factories where the process—combining flour and water to make a dough, rolling and cutting the dough, and finally drying the pasta shapes—was expanded and completely mechanized. Today the region around Naples, the towns of Torre Annunziata and Gragnano, is the center of pasta manufacturing, where over six hundred different pasta shapes are produced.

Two basic types of pasta are eaten in Italy. The first, more prevalent, and popular type is dried pasta. Made only with hard wheat semolina flour and water, dried pasta is a manufactured product, sold in bags or boxes or in bulk in markets. When cooked it has a clean, almost nutty flavor. Traditionally when it is cooked it should retain a firm, chewy texture, *al dente* ("to the tooth") as it is called. The second type is fresh pasta. Generally made by hand, with all-purpose flour and whole eggs, it is most characteristic of northern Italian cooking. But both fresh and dried pasta can be found in many restaurants and in homes throughout Italy.

It is the type of pasta—dried or fresh—that ultimately determines what sauce will be used with it: olive oil-based sauces are typically served with dried pastas and butter-based sauces with fresh pasta. In addition, the pasta shape influences what the texture of the sauce should be. Ideally, you want a sauce that "fits" the type of pasta—one that clings to the ridges of rotini or stays on the strands of spaghetti.

A large part of the repertoire of pasta dishes with vegetables comes from the southern regions of Italy—Campania, Calabria, Abruzzo, and Sicily—where an abundance of vegetables grows and where meat is not as affordable. However, you also find a wonderful selection of pasta dishes served with vegetables in northern regions. Some of these may be more uncommon, such as *fettucine al tartufo bianco* (see page 179), pasta with white truffles, from Piedmont, while others are more familiar, such as pasta with pesto from Liguria.

When trying to figure quantities of pasta per serving, as a main course 2 to 3 ounces of fresh and 4 ounces of dried pasta are generally considered appropriate.

When pasta was introduced into Italy, it was customary to eat it with your fingers. Forks came into use during the Renaissance—at the time they were considered to be very elegant, and people would carry their own with them—and have remained the pasta implement of choice ever since.

Dried Pasta/Pasta Secca

~ ~ ~

Dried factory-made pasta comes in many forms, from shells and squiggles to quill shapes and strands. The best dried pasta—with the most flavor and firmest texture after it is cooked—is made only with hard wheat semolina flour. I find that the imported Italian semolina products—De-Cecco is my particular favorite brand—have the better qualities and I prefer to use them.

Cooking dried pasta doesn't require scientific precision, but it is useful to follow a few guidelines for optimum results.

- Cook pasta in a lot of water. An adequate quantity of water plus frequent stirring will help the pasta to cook evenly and prevent the strands or shapes from sticking together or to the bottom of the pot. Figure 6 to 8 quarts of water for every pound of pasta.
- When the water is boiling rapidly, just before you add the pasta, add 1 tablespoon of salt for every 6 quarts of water, if you don't have a sodium problem. The salt makes the pasta, even without any sauce, very flavorful.
- Add the pasta all at once to the boiling water, and keep the heat

high to bring the water back to the boil as quickly as possible. Cook the pasta, uncovered, at a lively boil.

- It is difficult to give exact cooking times since different shapes and thicknesses of pasta will take less or more time to cook. Most dry pasta will cook in 7 to 10 minutes. Angel hair, *capellini*, will cook in 3 to 5 minutes.
- Dried pasta is best when cooked *al dente*, tender but still quite firm to the bite. To be sure, bite into a piece of the pasta. You should be able to see a pindot of uncooked pasta at the core. It is always better to err on the side of undercooking than overcooking. Pasta will continue to cook and soften even after it has been taken from the water.
- Always drain pasta but never run it under cold or hot water. As soon as it is drained, remove it from the colander and place it in a preheated serving dish or in individual preheated bowls.
- Once the pasta is in the serving bowl, use a fork and spoon and quickly toss it with the sauce. Don't spend too much time tossing or the pasta will cool off before you eat it.
- Freshly grated Parmesan cheese is usually served with pasta and veg-etables (although there are some exceptions, such as pasta with mush-rooms, which is usually served without cheese because the strong flavor of the mushrooms conflicts with the distinctive flavor of the cheese). When Parmesan cheese is called for, you can either pass a bowl of freshly grated cheese around the table or put a chunk of cheese on a plate with a hand-grater for each diner to grate his or her own (see page 23).

Fresh Tomato Sauce

~ ~ ~

SUGO DI POMODORO

You will find tomato sauces in all the regions of Italy. The best tomato sauce is made with fresh, ripe Italian plum or pear-shaped tomatoes. The riper the tomatoes, the more flavorful and rich-tasting the sauce will be. These have a high flesh-to-core ratio, which makes a thick and not watery sauce. Plum tomatoes also tend to have a slightly thicker skin, compared to other tomatoes, which makes them easier to peel (see page 55 for directions on peeling tomatoes). If you have only large eating tomatoes, you can make a pasta sauce with them, but the sauce may require more cooking to eliminate excess watery liquid. As this recipe shows, a fresh tomato sauce needs very little in the way of ingredients for good flavor, but you can add more vegetables or seasonings to your taste.

Use a wide, flat-bottomed pan for best results. It helps the tomatoes to cook evenly.

This recipe makes a coarse, chunky sauce. (If you like an even-textured, smooth sauce, you can prepare this sauce with unpeeled tomatoes with their cores and seeds intact. Cook the sauce as directed below, and after cooking, put the sauce through a food mill to extract the seeds and skins.)

⅓ cup pure olive oil

1 large clove garlic, finely minced or pressed

3 pounds fresh, ripe Italian plum tomatoes, peeled, cored, and coarsely chopped

Salt to taste

¼ cup coarsely chopped fresh basil, or 2 tablespoons chopped fresh parsley

1. Place the oil in a large skillet over medium-high heat. Add the garlic and cook, stirring, for 1 minute, making sure it doesn't brown.

2. Add the tomatoes and stir them well to combine. Liberally season with salt. Turn the heat down to medium and cook for about 20 minutes, stirring occasionally, until the sauce is thick and the watery liquid in the tomatoes has cooked away. You should be able to still see some chunks of tomatoes in the sauce.

3. When the sauce has finished cooking, turn off the heat. Taste for salt and add more if necessary. Stir in the basil and toss with hot pasta.

MAKES ABOUT 3 CUPS, OR 6 SERVINGS

Spaghetti with Uncooked Fresh Tomato Sauce

~ ~ ~

SPAGHETTI AL SUGO DI POMODORO CRUDO

Prepare this sauce in the summer when fresh tomatoes are at their best. Serve it at room temperature for a refreshing main course.

1 pound uncooked dry spaghettini

⅓ cup extra virgin olive oil

6 large, ripe eating tomatoes (about 2 pounds), cut in half lengthwise, cored, squeezed gently to remove seeds, and diced

½ cup packed coarsely chopped fresh basil leaves

1 clove garlic, finely minced or pressed

Salt and freshly ground black pepper to taste

1. Bring a large pot of water to a boil over high heat. Add a tablespoon of salt and the spaghettini. Cook, stirring occasionally, for 7 to 10 minutes, until the pasta is tender but firm, *al dente*. Drain well and transfer to a large serving bowl. Drizzle a little of the olive oil over the pasta, toss well, and allow to stand until cool.

2. Place the tomatoes in a small mixing bowl and combine with the basil, remaining olive oil, garlic, and salt and pepper. Pour over the pasta, toss well, and serve.

MAKES 6 SERVINGS

Penne with Fresh Tomato Sauce and Fontina Cheese

~ ~ ~

PENNE AL POMODORO E FONTINA

The fontina gives this pasta a rich taste. I like to serve this to large gatherings of friends.

1 pound uncooked penne
2 cups Fresh Tomato Sauce (see preceding recipe)
4 ounces Italian fontina cheese, rind removed and finely chopped
¼ cup chopped fresh basil
Salt and freshly ground black pepper to taste
Freshly grated Parmesan cheese

1. Bring a large pot of water to a boil over high heat. Add the penne and 1 tablespoon of salt. Cook, stirring occasionally, for 7 to 10 minutes, until the pasta is tender but firm, *al dente*. Drain well.

2. Meanwhile, place the tomato sauce in a 4-quart casserole over medium heat. Add the cooked penne, fontina, and basil. Turn off the heat and stir until the cheese is melted and the pasta is combined with the tomato sauce and cheese. Season with salt and pepper and serve with Parmesan cheese.

MAKES 4 SERVINGS

Pesto

~ ~ ~

Lots of fresh basil gives pesto its characteristic flavor. One of the most popular and classic of all pasta sauces, pesto is originally a Ligurian invention—Liguria is the area of Italy that includes the Mediterranean coast known as the Italian Riviera and the hills to the north—where it is traditionally prepared by hand with a mortar and pestle. You'll find a food processor or blender will do the job with equally good results a lot more quickly. Pesto sauce is traditionally made with grated cheese—Parmesan and pecorino. Although it's unconventional, I have found that pasta with pesto has a fresher taste when the cheese is added to the pasta rather than the sauce. Leaving the cheese out of the pesto also makes it easier to freeze the sauce for months or refrigerate it, tightly covered, for several weeks. Pesto recipes can vary, with walnuts added in addition to the pine nuts. I like the simplicity of this recipe.

2 cups packed fresh basil leaves

2 tablespoons pine nuts

1 clove garlic

1 teaspoon salt

½ cup pure olive oil

Combine the basil leaves, pine nuts, garlic, and salt in a food processor or blender. Process for about 30 seconds, until the mixture is finely minced and just beginning to turn into a paste. Scrape the sides down. With the machine running, add the oil in a slow, steady stream. When all the oil has been added, stop the machine and scrape the sides down again. Continue processing for about 30 seconds longer, until the mixture is smooth.

MAKES 1 CUP

Linguine with Pesto and Green Beans
~ ~ ~
LINGUINE AL PESTO E FAGIOLINI

This dish was served to me by Lorenza de' Medici at her Tuscan estate, the Badia a Coltibuono.

½ pound fresh green beans, ends trimmed

1 pound uncooked dry linguine

⅓ cup freshly grated Parmesan cheese

1 recipe Pesto (see preceding recipe)

Freshly ground black pepper to taste

1. Place the beans on a steamer tray over boiling water, cover, and cook 8 minutes. Refresh under cold water and set aside.

2. Bring a large pot of water to a boil over high heat. Add the pasta and one tablespoon of salt and cook, stirring occasionally, for 7 to 10 minutes, until the pasta is tender but firm, *al dente*. Drain the pasta and immediately transfer it to a large preheated serving bowl. Add the green beans, cheese and pesto sauce and mix well to combine. Add pepper to taste. Serve at once.

MAKES 6 SERVINGS

Trenette with Potatoes

~ ~ ~

TRENETTE AL PESTO

In Liguria, pesto is often served with trenette (flat pasta that is similar to fettucine, but slightly narrower) over a layer of sliced boiled potatoes. Although pasta and potatoes may seem like more starch than you would want in this dish, the potatoes are used to line the serving bowl and absorb any excess pesto. When you finally get to eat the potatoes, when the pasta's all gone, they are a flavorful treat. Potatoes and pesto are a wonderful combination (see Potato Gnocchi with Pesto, page 212).

½ pound new red potatoes
1 tablespoon salt
1 pound uncooked dry trenette, linguine, or fettuccine
1 recipe Pesto (see pages 154–55)
⅓ cup freshly grated Parmesan cheese

1. Put the potatoes in a saucepan with water to cover and place over medium-high heat. Bring the water to a boil and cook for about 20 minutes, until the potatoes are tender when pierced with a sharp knife. Drain and allow to stand until cool enough to handle. Peel the potatoes, slice thinly, and arrange them in a single layer in six individual serving bowls. Set aside.

2. Bring a large pot of water to a boil over high heat. Add ⌐
and pasta and cook, stirring occasionally, for 7 to 10 minutes, u⌐
pasta is tender but firm, *al dente*. Drain and transfer to a large mixi⌐
Add the pesto and Parmesan and toss well to combine.

3. Divide the pasta with pesto evenly among the six serving bowls.
Serve immediately.

MAKES 6 SERVINGS

Spaghetti with Garlic, Oil, and Hot Red Pepper

~ ~ ~

PASTA AGLIO E OLIO E PEPERONCINO

This classic and simple pasta dish is standard fare in southern Italy.
You can adjust the amount of *peperoncino* (crushed red pepper) to your
taste.

1 pound uncooked dry spaghettini
Salt
¼ cup pure olive oil
1 large clove garlic, cut in half
¼ teaspoon crushed red pepper
¼ cup chopped fresh parsley
Freshly ground black pepper to taste
Freshly grated Parmesan cheese

1. Bring a large pot of water to a boil over high heat. Add a tablespoon of salt and the pasta and cook, stirring occasionally, for 7 to 10
minutes.

2. While the pasta is cooking, place the oil in a large skillet over medium-high heat. Add the garlic and cook for 2 to 3 minutes, stirring, until it turns golden. Remove the garlic from the pan and discard. Add the crushed red pepper to the oil. Turn off the heat and set aside.

3. When the pasta is tender but firm, *al dente*, drain and immediately transfer to the skillet with the oil and crushed red pepper. Add the parsley, salt, and pepper and toss well to combine. Serve in six individual bowls with Parmesan cheese.

MAKES 6 SERVINGS

Spaghettini with Herbs

~ ~ ~

SPAGHETTI ALLE ERBE

An assortment of fresh herbs gives this pasta sauce a delightful flavor and aroma. You can substitute different herbs, depending on what's fresh and available.

1 pound uncooked dry spaghettini
¼ cup pure olive oil
1 large clove garlic, cut in half
1 cup loosely packed chopped fresh herbs (basil, parsley, marjoram, chives)
Salt and freshly ground black pepper to taste
Freshly grated Parmesan cheese

1. Bring a large pot of water to a boil over high heat. Add a tablespoon of salt and the pasta and cook, stirring occasionally, for 7 to 10 minutes, until the pasta is tender but firm, *al dente*.

2. Meanwhile, place the oil in a large skillet over medium-high heat. Add the garlic and cook, stirring, for 2 to 3 minutes, until golden. Turn off the heat, remove the garlic from the pan, and discard. Add the herbs to the pan and set aside.

3. Drain the pasta and immediately transfer it to the skillet. Toss well until the herbs are evenly distributed. Season with salt and pepper. Serve at once with freshly grated Parmesan cheese.

MAKES 6 SERVINGS

Orecchiette with Artichoke Sauce
~ ~ ~
ORECCHIETTE AI CARCIOFI

Orecchiette, or "little ears," are a disk-shaped pasta with an indentation that is just perfect for holding sauce. I first tasted this pasta and sauce combination at Evangelista, a restaurant in Rome that had many wonderful ways to cook artichokes.

3 to 4 medium-size artichokes (1½ to 2 pounds total)
Juice of ½ lemon
4 teaspoons salt
1 pound uncooked dry orecchiette
1 cup pure olive oil
1 large clove garlic, finely minced or pressed
¼ cup chopped fresh parsley
Salt and freshly ground black pepper to taste
Freshly grated Parmesan cheese

1. Cut the dried ends from the artichoke stems and about 2 inches from the tops of the artichokes, and pull off all the tough outer green leaves until only the yellow-green leaves are visible. Cut the artichokes in quarters lengthwise, and, using a small paring knife, cut out the fuzzy choke and sharp, spiky leaves just above it. Place the artichokes in a saucepan with the lemon juice, enough water to cover, and 1 teaspoon of the salt. Bring to a boil over medium-high heat. Reduce the heat to medium-low and simmer, covered, for about 20 minutes, until the artichokes are completely tender. Drain and transfer the artichokes to a food processor and process, pulsing the machine on and off, until the artichokes are finely chopped but not pureed. If you don't have a food processor, chop the artichokes with a knife on a cutting board.

2. Bring a large pot of water to a boil over high heat. Add the remaining salt and the orecchiette and cook, stirring occasionally, for 7 to 10 minutes, until the pasta is tender but firm, *al dente.* Drain and place in a large serving bowl.

3. Meanwhile, place the oil in a medium-size skillet over medium-

high heat. Add the garlic and chopped artichokes. Using a wooden spoon, stir the mixture until the oil is incorporated into the artichokes and the sauce is heated through. Stir in the parsley and season with salt and pepper.

4. Pour the artichoke sauce over the pasta and toss well to combine. Serve with Parmesan cheese.

MAKES 6 SERVINGS

Capellini with Broccoli

~ ~ ~

CAPELLINI CON I BROCCOLETTI

The taste of the broccoli is made all that much better with garlic and pepper. This dish makes a perfect main course.

1 bunch broccoli (about 2 pounds), trimmed and cut into florets, large stems reserved for another use
¼ cup pure olive oil
1 clove garlic, finely minced or pressed
¼ teaspoon crushed red pepper
Salt and freshly ground black pepper to taste
½ pound uncooked dry imported capellini
Freshly ground Parmesan cheese

1. Place the broccoli in a large bowl with cold water to cover and allow to stand for 30 minutes to clean. Drain, place them in a steamer

basket or tray over boiling water, cover, and steam-cook for 5 m
or until tender when pierced with a sharp knife. Drain in a colar
refresh under cold water.

2. Bring a large pot of water to a boil over high heat.

3. Meanwhile, place the oil in a large sauté pan over medium-high
heat. When the oil is hot, add the garlic, crushed red pepper, and broccoli.
Season with salt and pepper. Cook, stirring or tossing frequently, until
the broccoli begins to brown.

4. When the water boils, add a tablespoon of salt and the capellini
and cook, stirring occasionally, for 3 to 5 minutes, until the pasta is tender
but firm, *al dente*. Drain and add the pasta to the sauté pan. Using a large
serving fork and spoon, toss the pasta with the broccoli. Serve in four
individual serving plates with Parmesan cheese.

MAKES 4 SERVINGS

Orecchiette and Cauliflower with a Spicy Tomato Sauce

~ ~ ~

ORECCHIETTE CON CAVOLFIORE ALL'ARRABBIATA

All'arrabbiata means "in an angry way," and it describes numerous dishes
from the southern region of Abruzzi that are made with spicy hot chili
peppers. This recipe is adapted from a dish that is served at the Providence,
Rhode Island, restaurant Al Forno.

¼ *teaspoon crushed red pepper*

1 *clove garlic, minced or pressed*

¼ *cup pure olive oil*

1 *cup canned Italian plum tomatoes in heavy puree, chopped*

2 *oil-packed sun-dried tomatoes, finely chopped*

1 *tablespoon chopped fresh parsley*

1 *medium-size head cauliflower (about 2 pounds), cut into florets, cooked
     according to the directions on page 39*

½ *pound uncooked dry orecchiette*

1. Preheat the oven to 500°F.

2. Combine the crushed red pepper, garlic, and olive oil in a large heavy skillet over medium-high heat. Cook the mixture, stirring, for about 2 minutes, until the garlic begins to brown. Add the tomatoes, with their puree, and bring to a boil. Reduce the heat to medium-low and simmer for 5 minutes. Add the chopped dried tomatoes and parsley and simmer for 5 minutes longer. Turn off the heat.

3. Arrange the cauliflower in a baking dish large enough to hold it in a single layer. Pour the sauce evenly over the cauliflower. Place it in the oven and bake for about 15 minutes, until it is bubbling.

4. Bring a large pot of water to a boil over high heat. Add a tablespoon of salt and orecchiette and cook, stirring occasionally, for 7 to 10 minutes, until it is tender but firm, al dente. Drain and transfer to a large serving dish. Add the baked cauliflower and tomato sauce, toss well with the pasta, and serve.

MAKES 4 SERVINGS

Penne with Asparagus

~ ~ ~

PENNE CON GLI ASPARAGI

The wonderful fresh, grassy flavor of the asparagus makes this dish a springtime favorite.

1 pound uncooked dry penne
¼ cup pure olive oil
1 clove garlic, finely minced or pressed
*1 pound skinny fresh asparagus spears, tough bottoms trimmed and cut
    diagonally into 2-inch pieces*
¼ cup chopped fresh parsley
Salt and freshly ground black pepper to taste
Freshly grated Parmesan cheese

1. Bring a large pot of water to a boil over high heat. Add a tablespoon of salt and penne and cook, stirring occasionally, for 7 to 10 minutes, until the pasta is tender but firm, al dente. Drain the pasta and transfer it to a large serving bowl.

2. Place the oil in a medium-size sauté pan over medium-high. Add the garlic and asparagus, lower the heat to medium, and cook, stirring, for 5 to 7 minutes, until the asparagus is tender. Pour the asparagus over the cooked penne, add the parsley, season with salt and pepper, and toss well to combine. Serve with Parmesan cheese.

MAKES 6 SERVINGS

Bow-Tie Pasta with Fresh Wild Mushrooms and Garlic

~ ~ ~

FARFALLE AI FUNGHI

The delectably golden and crisp mushrooms are the perfect complement to the frilly pasta.

¾ cup pure olive oil

2 cloves garlic, finely minced or pressed

1 pound shiitake mushrooms, stems removed and caps thinly sliced

Salt and freshly ground black pepper to taste

1 pound uncooked dry bow-tie pasta

2 tablespoons chopped fresh parsley

1. Bring a large pot of water to a boil over high heat.

2. Place the oil in a large sauté pan over medium-high heat. Add the garlic and mushrooms, season with salt and pepper, and cook, stirring, for about 20 minutes, until the edges of the mushroom slices turn golden brown. Turn off the heat and set aside.

3. When the water boils, add a tablespoon of salt and the pasta and cook, stirring occasionally, for 7 to 10 minutes, until the pasta is tender but firm, *al dente*. Drain and transfer to a large serving bowl. Add the mushrooms and parsley and toss well to combine.

MAKES 4 SERVINGS

Spaghetti with Roasted Vegetables

~ ~ ~

SPAGHETTI CON VERDURE AL FORNO

The roasted vegetables have a robust, concentrated flavor that makes this flavorful pasta a hearty dish.

½ cup pure olive oil

3 large, fresh, ripe Italian plum tomatoes, cored, quartered, and seeded

1 medium-size onion, thinly sliced

1 small zucchini, thinly sliced

1 small eggplant (about ½ pound), sliced into ¼-inch-thick rounds

1 large red bell pepper, cored, seeded, and sliced ½ inch thick

Kosher salt

1 pound uncooked dry imported spaghetti no. 12

1. Preheat the oven to 500°F. Bring a large pot of water to a boil over high heat.

2. Pour the oil into a large baking pan and tilt to distribute it evenly. Arrange the vegetables in the pan in one even layer. Lightly sprinkle with kosher salt. Place the pan on the topmost shelf of the oven and roast for 15 minutes. Using a spatula, stir the vegetables, then return the pan to the oven. Roast for 15 minutes longer, or until the peppers and onions begin to turn brown. Remove from the oven and set aside.

3. When the water boils, add a tablespoon of salt and spaghetti and cook, stirring occasionally, for 7 to 10 minutes, until the spaghetti is tender but firm, *al dente*. Drain and put in a large serving bowl.

4. Spoon the roasted vegetables over the spaghetti, getting as much of the oil from the pan as possible. Toss well and serve immediately.

MAKES 6 SERVINGS

Spaghetti with Zucchini

~ ~ ~

PASTA ALLE ZUCCHINE

This is a southern Italian specialty. This version comes from a chef in Positano, a beautiful resort town on the Amalfi coast.

4 medium-size zucchini (about 2 pounds), sliced as thinly as possible (use slicing disk of food processor or mandoline for best results)
Salt
⅓ cup pure olive oil
1 large clove garlic, finely minced or pressed
Freshly ground black pepper to taste
1 pound uncooked dry imported spaghetti no. 12
¼ cup chopped fresh parsley
Freshly grated Parmesan cheese

1. Bring a large pot of water to a boil over high heat.
2. Put the zucchini slices in a colander and sprinkle liberally with salt. Shake the colander a few times to distribute the salt and allow to stand at least 30 minutes, or until most of the liquid drains from the zucchini. Place the oil in a large skillet over medium-high heat. Add the

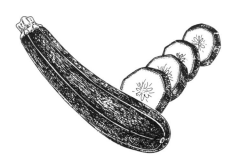

garlic and cook for about 1 minute, until it begins to sizzle but does not brown. Add the zucchini all at once and stir with a wooden spoon to combine. Reduce the heat to medium-low and cook for 5 to 10 minutes, while stirring, until the zucchini is tender. Season with several turns of the pepper mill and add more salt, if necessary. Turn off the heat and set aside.

3. When the water boils, add a tablespoon of salt and the spaghetti and cook, stirring occasionally, for 7 to 10 minutes, until the spaghetti is tender but firm, *al dente*. Drain and transfer to a preheated serving bowl. Add the zucchini to the spaghetti and, using a large fork and spoon, toss well. Add the parsley and serve with Parmesan cheese.

MAKES 6 SERVINGS

Rigatoni with Pepper Stew

~ ~ ~

RIGATONI ALLA PEPERONATA

The peppers are cooked with tomatoes and olive oil until they are very tender and flavorful—a perfect complement to the formidable rigatoni.

Salt
1 pound uncooked dry imported rigatoni
1 recipe Pepper Stew (see pages 82–83)
Freshly ground black pepper to taste
Freshly grated Parmesan cheese

Bring a large pot of water to a boil over high heat. Add a tablespoon of salt and rigatoni and cook, stirring occasionally, for 7 to 10 minutes, until the rigatoni is tender but firm, *al dente*. Drain and transfer to a large serving bowl. Add the *peperonata* and season with a few turns of the pepper mill and more salt, if necessary. Toss well to combine. Serve at once with Parmesan cheese.

MAKES 6 SERVINGS

Note: This dish may also be served cold. Cover tightly with plastic wrap and allow to reach room temperature before serving.

Fresh Pasta/Pasta Fresca

For those who have the time and inclination, homemade pasta has its rewards. Fresh, homemade pasta is extraordinarily tender and delicate, and almost melts in your mouth. What's more, you can cut it any way you want (in sheets for lasagna, thick strips for pappardelle, or squares for ravioli which are not available commercially) and sauce it or fill it with a mixture to your liking. For those recipes calling for fresh fettucine or linguine, you can buy commercially prepared fresh pasta, if you prefer.

Preparing fresh pasta is surprisingly easy and I wholeheartedly recommend it. You can either mix the dough by hand, which allows you to gauge just how much flour is needed, or you can make pasta dough in a food processor—although I have found that processor pasta dough isn't as tender as the pasta you make by hand. However you prepare the dough, the pasta is most easily kneaded and rolled in a hand-cranked pasta machine. (Before you start, check the section on pasta equipment, pages 25–26.)

Like dried pasta, fresh pasta should be cooked in a large quantity of briskly boiling salted water until it is tender but firm, *al dente.* It generally cooks faster than dry pasta.

Fresh Pasta Dough

PASTA FRESCA

Fresh pasta dough is made of a combination of eggs and all-purpose flour. I prefer to use unbleached flour, but it is not essential. Here is a basic recipe that can be increased if you want to prepare more or decreased for a smaller quantity. Variations for using your food processor and preparing colored and flavored pasta follow.

3 cups all-purpose flour
4 extra large eggs

MIXING THE DOUGH. Pile the flour onto a clean work surface. Make a well in the center and break the eggs into it. Using a fork, start to beat the eggs while gradually incorporating the flour into them as you beat. When you have a soft, malleable ball of dough, knead the dough with your hands on the floured work surface, incorporating more flour as needed. If you intend to roll the dough with a rolling pin, knead the dough for approximately 10 minutes. If you intend to roll the dough in a pasta machine, knead the dough for 5 minutes. Cover the dough with plastic wrap and allow it to rest, unrefrigerated, for about 15 minutes before rolling it out or running it through a pasta machine.

ROLLING THE DOUGH. To roll the dough with a rolling pin, place the ball of dough on a lightly floured work surface and flatten it down with the heel of your hand. Using a lightly floured rolling pin, roll it out to the desired degree of thinness. Pasta is usually rolled out to about 1/32 inch thick. As you roll, keep the work surface, the rolling pin, and the dough lightly floured so that it doesn't stick.

To roll the dough by machine, divide the dough into two or three pieces. Flatten each piece with your hand so that it is approximately ½ inch thick. Turn the gauge on the pasta machine's smooth roller to its widest (lowest) setting. Lightly flour the dough before feeding it through the rollers. Once the dough has come through the machine, fold it into thirds, lightly flour it again, and press it down with your fingers to remove as much air as possible. Run the dough through the machine again on the widest setting, feeding the open end in first. Repeat this three or four times until the dough is smooth. Reduce the setting on the gauge one notch. Lightly flour the dough and, without folding it, run it through the rollers. Continue to narrow the width of the rollers one notch after each pass of the dough until you reach the highest (narrowest) setting. Since pasta machines differ, you may not be able to roll the pasta out on the highest (narrowest) setting without breaking the dough. The strip of dough will become very long. Cut it in half if it is difficult to handle. Lightly flour the strip of dough each time before passing it through the machine.

CUTTING THE DOUGH. Once the dough has been rolled as thinly as possible, you can cut it to the desired shape. Most pasta machines offer at least two cutting dies with a wider and narrower width. I usually prefer to cut the pasta by hand. When cutting wider shapes—pappardelle, ravioli, lasagna—I simply place the long strips of dough on a cutting board that's been dusted with flour or semolina and cut the dough. To form long strands, I first fold the dough over repeatedly and then slice the dough into even widths. With the exception of lasagna and ravioli, cut pasta should be allowed to dry in the air before cooking. Ravioli should be filled and sealed (see below) while the pasta is soft and pliable.

Widths for pasta are as follows:

lasagna	3 inches
pappardelle	1 inch
tagliatelle	1/4 inch
fettucine	1/8 inch
linguine	1/16 inch
spaghetti	1/24 inch
capellini (angel hair)	threads

STORING THE DOUGH. Fresh, uncooked pasta dough can be refrigerated for up to 2 days. It should be frozen if you intend to use it after that. It will keep in the freezer for several months. To prevent strips of pasta dough from sticking together, lightly dust with semolina flour. Store the dough in a plastic container with a tight-fitting lid or securely wrapped in plastic wrap or waxed paper. Frozen pasta is best when it is cooked frozen and not defrosted.

MAKES 6 SERVINGS

FOOD PROCESSOR PASTA DOUGH/*PASTA FRESCA ALLA MACCHINA.* Place the flour in a food processor fitted with the double-edge steel blade. Pulse the machine on and off a couple of times to evenly distribute the flour in the bowl. Break the eggs into a separate small bowl and lightly beat them, just to combine the yolks and whites. With the machine running, add the eggs in a slow, steady stream until they are all incorporated into the flour. The dough should form a ball on the blade. If the dough is too sticky, add more flour, a tablespoon at a time, and, pulsing the machine on and off, process until the dough holds together in a ball. Take the dough from the machine, knead for 5 to 10 minutes (as directed above), cover, and allow it to rest, unrefrigerated, at least 15 minutes before rolling it out.

SPINACH PASTA/*PASTA VERDE.* Spinach can be added to the pasta dough to make green pasta. Wash and trim the stems from 1 cup packed fresh spinach. Place the wet spinach in a small saucepan, cover, and set over medium heat. Cook for about 5 minutes, until the spinach is wilted. Transfer the cooked spinach to a mesh strainer and, using a wooden spoon, thoroughly press any liquid from the spinach. Place the spinach on a cutting board and chop finely. Proceed with the recipe for fresh pasta, adding the spinach to the eggs and incorporating it into the dough as you mix in the flour with a fork. At first, the spinach in the dough will appear as green flecks, but as you proceed to knead and roll out the dough, the dough will become uniformly green in color.

BLACK PEPPER-FLAVORED PASTA/*PASTA AL PEPE.* Black pepper can be added to the pasta dough to make a spicy, sharp-tasting pasta. Proceed with the recipe for fresh pasta, above, and add 1 teaspoon of freshly ground black pepper to the eggs, incorporating it into the dough as you mix in the flour.

RED TOMATO-FLAVORED PASTA/*PASTA ROSSA.* Proceed with the recipe for fresh pasta, above, and add 2 tablespoons of tomato paste with the eggs, incorporating it into the dough as you mix in the flour.

Ravioli with Spinach and Ricotta Filling

~ ~ ~

RAVIOLI AGLI SPINACI E RICOTTA

Ravioli can also be called *tortelli, tordelli,* or *pansotti* depending on where you are in Italy. The shapes may vary but they are all similar: pockets of fresh pasta dough filled with a savory, flavorful mixture. (*Agnolotti,* another type of ravioli, typically have a meat filling.) The combination of spinach and ricotta cheese is probably the most popular variation of ravioli found in Italy.

1 recipe Fresh Pasta Dough (see pages 167–69)
One 10-ounce package fresh spinach, stems removed, thoroughly cleaned, steamed
    for 5 minutes, well drained, and chopped, or one 10-ounce package frozen
    chopped spinach, cooked according to the directions on the box and well
    drained
½ cup ricotta cheese
⅓ cup freshly grated Parmesan cheese, plus extra for serving
1 large egg
Salt
Freshly ground black pepper to taste
4 tablespoons (½ stick) unsalted butter
6 large basil leaves, cut crosswise into strips

1. Roll out the pasta dough as thinly as you can and cut it into 4-inch squares. Keep the dough covered so that it doesn't dry out.

2. Combine the spinach, ricotta, Parmesan, egg, salt, and pepper in a medium-size bowl and mix well to combine.

3. Place ½ teaspoon of the spinach-and-ricotta mixture in the center of a square of pasta. Fold the opposite corners of the pasta together to form a triangle. With your fingers, press firmly on the pasta and all around the mound of filling to remove any air trapped inside. Roll a pastry crimper along the two cut edges of the triangle, removing about ¹⁄₁₆ inch from each side, to seal it. Transfer the ravioli to a wire rack until ready to cook. Repeat until all the squares of pasta have been filled. These can be prepared ahead of time and refrigerated on racks for a day or frozen for several months. If the ravioli are frozen, do not defrost before cooking.

4. To cook the ravioli, bring a large pot of water to a boil over high heat. Add a tablespoon of salt and the ravioli and cook for 7 to 10 minutes, until the pasta is tender but firm, al dente. Drain.

5. Melt the butter in a large skillet over medium heat until it begins to bubble. Turn off the heat and add the ravioli. Shake the pan back and

forth to coat the ravioli evenly with the butter. Transfer to a large preheated serving platter and top with freshly ground black pepper and the basil. Serve with Parmesan cheese.

MAKES 6 SERVINGS

Ravioli with Pumpkin Filling

~ ~ ~

TORTELLI ALLA ZUCCA

This is a traditional dish from Mantua in northern Italy. The pumpkin filling is light and savory and very rich.

1 recipe Fresh Pasta Dough (see pages 167–69)

2 pounds fresh pumpkin, or Hubbard squash, peeled, seeded, and cut into pieces

⅓ cup ricotta cheese

¼ cup freshly grated Parmesan cheese, plus extra for serving

Pinch of ground nutmeg

Salt and freshly ground black pepper to taste

4 tablespoons (½ stick) unsalted butter

6 small fresh sage leaves

1. Roll out the pasta dough as thinly as you can and cut into 4-inch squares. Wrap in wax paper until ready to fill.

2. Place the pumpkin in a saucepan with water to cover and bring to a boil over medium-high heat. Reduce the heat to medium-low and simmer for about 20 minutes, until the pumpkin is tender when pierced with a sharp knife. Drain and place in a food processor fitted with the double-edge steel blade. Process for 15 to 30 seconds, until smooth. Add the ricotta, Parmesan, nutmeg, salt, and pepper and process for another 10 seconds.

3. Place a teaspoon of the pumpkin mixture in the center of a square of pasta. Fold the opposite corners of the pasta together to form a triangle. Using your fingers, press firmly on the pasta all around the mound of filling

to remove any air trapped inside. Roll a pastry crimper along the two cu
edges of the triangle, removing about ⅟₁₆ inch from each side, to seal it.
Transfer the ravioli to a wire rack until ready to cook. Repeat until all the
squares of pasta have been filled. These can be prepared ahead of time
and refrigerated for a day on racks or frozen for several months. If the
ravioli are frozen, do not defrost before cooking.

4. To cook the ravioli, bring a large pot of water to a boil over high
heat. Add a tablespoon of salt and the ravioli and cook for 7 to 10 minutes,
until the pasta is tender but firm, *al dente*. Drain.

5. Melt the butter in a large skillet over medium heat until it begins
to bubble. Turn off the heat and add the ravioli. Shake the pan back and
forth to coat the ravioli evenly with the butter. Transfer to a large preheated
serving platter and top with freshly ground black pepper and the sage.
Serve with Parmesan cheese.

MAKES 6 SERVINGS

en Ravioli with Basil and Goat Cheese Filling

~ ~ ~

.._VIOLI VERDI COL PESTO E FORMAGGIO CAPRINO

Green ravioli with pesto-flavored goat cheese filling is one of the best combinations there is.

1 recipe Spinach Pasta (see page 170)

8 ounces mild goat cheese, crumbled

½ cup Pesto (see pages 154–55)

¼ cup freshly grated Parmesan cheese, plus extra for serving

2 cups Fresh Tomato Sauce (see pages 152–53)

1. Roll out the pasta dough as thinly as possible and cut into 4-inch squares.

2. In a mixing bowl, combine the goat cheese with the pesto and Parmesan and beat briskly with a wooden spoon until smooth.

3. Place ½ teaspoon of the pesto-cheese mixture in the center of a square of pasta. Fold the opposite corners of the pasta together to form a triangle. With your fingers, press firmly on the pasta and all around the mound of filling to remove any air trapped inside. Roll a pastry crimper along the two cut edges of the triangle, removing about ¹⁄₁₆ inch from each side, to seal it. Transfer the ravioli to a floured baking sheet until ready to cook. Repeat until all the squares of pasta have been filled. These can be prepared ahead of time and refrigerated on racks for a day or frozen for several months. If the ravioli are frozen, do not defrost before cooking.

4. Bring a large pot of water to a boil over high heat. Add a tablespoon of salt, drop the ravioli into the boiling water, and cook for 7 to 10 minutes, until the pasta is tender but firm, *al dente*. Drain and arrange on preheated individual plates or on a large serving platter. Top with the tomato sauce and serve with Parmesan cheese.

MAKES 6 SERVINGS

Tagliatelle with Fresh Spring Vegetables

TAGLIATELLE ALLE VERDURE

This pasta sauce is the essence of spring. Tagliatelle are a slightly thinner version of fettucine and, for convenience, you can use store-bought pasta. There are a lot of variations of this dish. This version comes from the restaurant/inn La Chiusa in Montefollonico in Tuscany.

6 tablespoons (¾ stick) unsalted butter

1 tablespoon finely chopped scallion, white part only, or shallot

1 small zucchini, cut into fine julienne strips

1 small yellow squash, cut into fine julienne strips

1 cup packed fresh spinach leaves, thoroughly cleaned, drained, stems removed, and finely chopped

6 squash blossoms, shredded (see pages 53–54) (optional)

1 tablespoon chopped fresh basil

Salt and freshly ground black pepper to taste

½ recipe Fresh Pasta Dough (see pages 167–69), cut into tagliatelle, or one 10-ounce package prepared fresh fettucine

¼ cup chopped fresh chives

Freshly grated Parmesan cheese

1. Bring a large pot of water to a boil over high heat.
2. Melt the butter in a large skillet over medium-high heat. Add the scallion and cook, stirring, for 1 minute. Add the zucchini, squash, spinach, squash blossoms, and basil, season with salt and pepper, and cook, stirring, for 5 to 7 minutes, until the zucchini is tender.
3. When the water comes to a boil, add a tablespoon of salt and the pasta and cook, stirring occasionally, for about 5 minutes, until the pasta is tender but firm, *al dente*. Drain well and transfer to a large serving bowl. Pour the cooked vegetables over the pasta and toss well to combine. Garnish with the chives and serve with Parmesan cheese.

MAKES 4 SERVINGS

Spaghetti with Porcini Mushrooms
SPAGHETTI COI FUNGHI PORCINI SECCHI

A traditional recipe that's served wherever porcini are found. Porcini mushrooms have a forceful, woodsy flavor and aroma that dominates this rich-tasting pasta.

2 ounces dried porcini mushrooms

1 cup boiling water

4 tablespoons (½ stick) unsalted butter

Salt and freshly ground black pepper to taste

1 cup heavy cream

1 recipe Fresh Pasta Dough (see pages 167–69), cut into spaghetti, or one
    10-ounce package prepared fresh linguine

1. Bring a large pot of water to a boil over high heat.

2. Place the porcini in a heatproof glass measuring cup, cover with the boiling water, and allow to stand for 30 minutes. Drain and rinse the porcini to be sure any grit is washed away. Coarsely chop the mushrooms. Melt the butter in a medium-size skillet over medium-high heat. Add the porcini, season with salt and pepper, add the cream, and cook, stirring, until the cream thickens and is reduced by half, about 5 minutes. Turn off the heat and set aside.

3. When the water boils, add a tablespoon of salt and the pasta and cook, stirring occasionally, for about 5 minutes, until the pasta is tender but firm, al dente. Drain well and transfer to a large serving bowl. Add the mushroom cream sauce, toss well, and serve immediately.

MAKES 4 SERVINGS

Pappardelle with Fresh Wild Mushrooms

~ ~ ~

PAPPARDELLE AI FUNGHI

A grand pasta dish made with wide, flat pappardelle and a deliciously flavorful fine-textured mushroom sauce.

4 tablespoons (½ stick) unsalted butter

2 tablespoons pure olive oil

2 small, fresh, ripe Italian plum tomatoes, peeled, cored, seeded, and chopped

1 clove garlic, finely minced or pressed

1 pound fresh wild mushrooms (portobello, shiitake, or crimini), stems removed and caps finely chopped

Salt and freshly ground black pepper to taste

½ cup dry white wine

1 recipe Fresh Pasta Dough (see pages 167–69), cut into pappardelle

2 tablespoons chopped fresh parsley

1. Bring a large pot of water to a boil over high heat.
2. Place the butter and oil in a large skillet over medium-high heat. Add the tomatoes and garlic and cook for about 1 minute. Add the mushrooms, season with salt and pepper, and cook, stirring, for about 5 minutes, until the mushrooms have cooked down and given up most of their liquid. Add the wine and cook until most of it has evaporated.
3. When the water in the pot comes to a boil, add 1 tablespoon of salt and the pappardelle and cook for 3 to 5 minutes, until it is tender but firm, *al dente*. Drain well and transfer to a large serving bowl. Pour the mushroom mixture over the pappardelle, add the parsley, and toss well to combine. Serve immediately.

MAKES 6 SERVINGS

Tagliatelle with Walnut Sauce
~ ~ ~
TAGLIATELLE CON SALSA DI NOCE

Walnuts, cream, butter, and cheese combine to make this an incomparable dish. I first tasted this sauce at a Ligurian restaurant, Taverna Giulia, in Rome. This sauce is quite rich, so use it sparingly. You can also serve this sauce with spinach-and-ricotta ravioli (see pages 170–72)—it's a wonderful combination.

4 tablespoons (½ stick) unsalted butter
1 tablespoon pure olive oil
½ cup finely ground walnuts
1 cup heavy cream
Salt and freshly ground black pepper to taste
½ recipe Fresh Pasta Dough (see pages 167–69), cut into fettuccine, or one
*   10-ounce package fresh fettucine*
Freshly grated Parmesan cheese

1. Bring a large pot of water to a boil over high heat.
2. Place the butter and olive oil in a medium-size skillet over medium-high heat. Stir in the ground walnuts and add the heavy cream. Season with salt and pepper. Bring the cream to a boil, lower the heat to medium, and simmer for about 2 minutes, until the sauce has thickened. Turn off the heat and set aside.

3. When the water boils, add a tablespoon of salt and the pasta and cook, stirring occasionally, for about 5 minutes, until the pasta is tender but firm, *al dente*. Drain well and transfer to individual serving dishes. Top each serving with approximately ¼ cup of the sauce. Serve with Parmesan cheese.

MAKES 4 SERVINGS

Fettucine with White Truffles

~ ~ ~

FETTUCCINE AI TARTUFI BIANCHI

Costly white truffles, with their distinctive earthy aroma and flavor, are in season for only a few months in the late fall and early winter. Their availability and price will vary, depending on how abundant they are in any particular year. When cooking with white truffles, it's best to do very little to them. This simple pasta, dressed only with butter, is the perfect foil for the white truffle's taste. Truffles are always served very thinly sliced.

½ recipe Fresh Pasta Dough (see pages 167–69), cut into fettuccine, or one
*   10-ounce package prepared fresh fettucine*
6 tablespoons (¾ stick) unsalted butter
Salt and freshly ground black pepper to taste
1 or 2 fresh white truffles, thinly sliced or shaved (see note below)
Freshly grated Parmesan cheese

1. Bring a large pot of water to a boil over high heat. Add a tablespoon of salt and the fettucine and cook, stirring occasionally, for about 5 minutes, until the pasta is tender but firm, *al dente*. Drain well.

2. Melt the butter in a large skillet over medium-high heat. Add the cooked pasta, season with salt and pepper, and toss well to combine. Transfer to individual serving dishes. Divide the shaved truffle among the servings and serve with Parmesan cheese.

MAKES 4 SERVINGS

Note: To shave the truffles, use a single-blade grater such as the single blade on a standard four-sided grater.

Baked Pasta/Pasta al Forno

~ ~ ~

During the Renaissance the Italian meal by law was reduced to three courses—down from the feasts, dating back to Roman times, of five or more courses. Baked pasta was created by the Italian nobility—the only people who could afford ovens—as a way of packing as many different ingredients as possible into the pasta course. Here are some contemporary versions, all of which make perfect dinner party or buffet dishes.

Baked Ziti with Fontina Cheese and Three Squashes

~ ~ ~

PASTICCIO DI ZITI ALLA VALDOSTANA

Three kinds of squash give a confetti-colored effect to this extremely rich and creamy dish.

1 pound uncooked dry ziti

¼ pound (1 stick) unsalted butter

1 small onion, finely chopped

1 clove garlic, minced or pressed

1 medium-size zucchini, coarsely grated or cut into fine julienne strips

1 medium-size yellow squash, coarsely grated or cut into fine julienne strips

1 cup peeled, seeded, and grated fresh pumpkin

Salt and freshly ground black pepper to taste

3 tablespoons all-purpose flour

2 cups hot milk

8 ounces Italian fontina cheese, rind removed and grated

Freshly grated Parmesan cheese

1. Preheat the oven to 350°F.

2. Bring a large pot of water to a boil over high heat. Add a tablespoon of salt and the ziti and cook, stirring occasionally, for 7 to 10 minutes, until the pasta is tender but firm, *al dente*. Drain well and transfer to a large mixing bowl.

3. Melt half of the butter in a large skillet over medium-high heat. Add the onion and garlic and cook, stirring, for about 2 minutes, until the onion begins to soften. Add the zucchini, squash, and pumpkin, season with salt and pepper, lower the heat to medium, and cook, stirring, for about 10 minutes, until the pumpkin is tender. Add the vegetables to the pasta.

4. Melt the remaining butter in a small saucepan over medium-high heat. When the butter foams, add the flour and stir briskly with a wire whisk until it is incorporated. Do not let it brown. Turn off the heat and add the milk ¼ cup at a time, beating with a wire whisk until each addition is absorbed. When all the milk has been added, turn the heat to medium-low and warm the sauce until it thickens and is the consistency of heavy cream, stirring with a wooden spoon. Turn off the heat.

5. Add the white sauce along with the grated fontina to the pasta and toss well to combine. Pour the pasta and vegetables into a deep, 8-cup baking dish and top with grated Parmesan. Bake for about 50 minutes, until the top is brown and bubbly. Let sit a few minutes before serving.

MAKES 6 SERVINGS

Baked Shells with Four Cheeses and Radicchio

~ ~ ~

CONCHIGLIE AI QUATTRO FORMAGGI E RADICCHIO

This recipe was inspired by a dish created by Johanne Killeen and George German at the restaurant Al Forno in Providence, Rhode Island. The combination of the soft shape of the shells and the ripples of red radicchio make for a sensational presentation worthy of your most important guests.

1 pound uncooked dry conchiglie (small dry pasta shells)

2 small heads radicchio (about ½ pound total), shredded

2 cups light cream or half-and-half

4 ounces Gorgonzola cheese, crumbled

4 ounces Asiago fresco (or substitute Bel Paese), cut into small pieces

4 ounces Italian fontina cheese, rind removed and grated

¼ cup freshly grated Parmesan cheese, plus extra for serving

Salt and freshly ground black pepper to taste

1. Preheat the oven to 350°F.
2. Bring a large pot of water to a boil over high heat. Add a tablespoon of salt and the shells and cook, stirring occasionally, for 7 to 10 minutes, until the pasta is tender but firm, *al dente*. Drain well and transfer to a large mixing bowl.
3. Add the radicchio, cream, and cheeses to the pasta, season with salt and pepper, and toss well to combine. Transfer to a large buttered oval baking dish. Cover with aluminum foil and bake for 45 minutes.
4. Turn the oven to 450°F. Uncover the pasta and bake for an additional 15 minutes, until the top is brown. Let sit a few minutes before serving. Serve with Parmesan cheese.

MAKES 6 SERVINGS

Green Lasagna with Fresh Tomato Sauce, Ricotta, and Mozzarella Cheese

~ ~ ~

LASAGNA ALLA NAPOLETANA

The layers of fresh pasta transform this traditional lasagna into an exquisite dish.

½ recipe Spinach Pasta or 1 pound Fresh Pasta Dough (see pages 170 or
167–69), cut into 9-inch lengths, 4 inches wide
One 16-ounce container ricotta cheese
¼ cup heavy cream
Salt and freshly ground black pepper to taste
½ cup freshly grated Parmesan cheese
3 cups Fresh Tomato Sauce (see pages 152–53)
3 cups grated whole-milk mozzarella cheese

1. Lightly butter a 9- × 12- × 3-inch baking dish. Bring a large pot of water to a boil over high heat. Add 1 tablespoon of salt and drop four pieces of pasta at a time into the boiling water. Allow to cook for exactly 3 minutes, drain, and refresh under cold water. Repeat until all the pasta is cooked.

2. In a medium-size mixing bowl, combine the ricotta, cream, salt, pepper, and Parmesan and beat briskly with a wooden spoon until smooth. Set aside. Preheat the oven to 350°F.

3. Arrange two pieces of the pasta in the baking dish to completely cover the bottom. The pasta can overlap, but they should not come up the sides of the dish. Trim the ends with a sharp knife or kitchen shears, if necessary. Spoon about ¾ cup of the tomato sauce over the pasta and cover with another layer of pasta. Spread a third of the ricotta mixture over the pasta with a rubber spatula or wooden spoon and cover with another layer of pasta. Distribute about a third of the mozzarella over the pasta and cover with another layer of pasta. Repeat the layers—tomato sauce, pasta, ricotta, pasta, mozzarella, pasta—two more times. Cover the top with a layer of tomato sauce. There should be about an inch of room

the edge of the dish and the top of the lasagna. Cover with a
aluminum foil.

lace the lasagna in the oven and bake for 45 minutes. Uncover
_____nue baking for about 15 minutes longer, until the pasta is just
beginning to brown. Remove from the oven and allow to stand for 10
minutes before serving.

MAKES 6 SERVINGS

Many Mushroom Lasagna
~ ~ ~
LASAGNA DI FUNGHI

A rich and creamy lasagna brimming with wild mushrooms. This dish
can be prepared a day in advance and refrigerated until ready to cook.

*½ recipe Fresh Pasta Dough (see pages 167–69), or 1 pound fresh pasta
dough, cut into 9-inch lengths, 4 inches wide*

12 tablespoons (1½ sticks) unsalted butter

1 tablespoon olive oil

*3 small, fresh, ripe Italian plum tomatoes, peeled, cored, seeded, and chopped,
or ¼ cup drained, chopped canned tomatoes*

1 large clove garlic, finely minced or pressed

*1 ounce dried porcini mushrooms, soaked in boiling water to cover for 15
minutes, drained, and coarsely chopped*

*1½ pounds wild mushrooms (portobello, shiitake, or crimini), stems removed
and caps coarsely chopped*

Salt and freshly ground black pepper to taste

1 tablespoon chopped fresh oregano or parsley

3 cups milk

¼ cup all-purpose flour

½ cup freshly grated Parmesan cheese

1. Lightly butter a 9- × 12- × 3-inch baking pan and set aside.
2. Bring a large pot of water to a boil over high heat. Add 1 tablespoon

of salt and drop four pieces of pasta at a time into the boiling water. Allow to cook for exactly 3 minutes, drain, and refresh under cold water. Repeat until all the pasta is cooked.

3. Place 4 tablespoons of the butter with the oil in a large skillet over medium-high heat. Add the fresh tomatoes and garlic and cook for about 1 minute. Add the mushrooms and season with salt and pepper. Lower the heat to medium. Cook, stirring frequently, for 7 to 10 minutes, until the mushrooms are tender. Add the oregano (and canned tomatoes, if you're using them) and stir to combine. Turn off the heat and set aside.

4. Place the milk in a medium-size saucepan over medium-high heat. Just before it begins to boil, turn off the heat. (Or heat the milk in the microwave oven in a microwave-safe 4-cup glass measuring cup for 2 minutes on high power.) Place 6 tablespoons of the butter in a large saucepan over medium-high heat. When the butter begins to foam, add the flour and stir with a wire whisk until it is completely incorporated into the butter. Allow the mixture to cook for 1 to 2 minutes, but do not let it brown. Turn off the heat and begin to add the hot milk ¼ cup at a time, stirring well with the whisk after each addition to incorporate the milk into the butter and flour. It will be thick like a paste at first. When the mixture becomes smooth and thin, add all the remaining milk at once. Turn the heat back on to medium-low and cook slowly, stirring frequently, until the sauce has thickened and is the consistency of heavy cream. Turn off the heat, season with salt, and set aside. Preheat the oven to 350°F.

5. To assemble the lasagna, arrange two pieces of the pasta in the baking dish to completely cover the bottom. The pieces of pasta can overlap, but they should not come up the sides of the pan. Trim with a sharp knife or kitchen shears if necessary. Spoon a third of the mushroom mixture over the pasta and pour about ¾ cup of the white sauce over the mushrooms. Using a serving spoon, spread the sauce and mushrooms evenly over the pasta. Sprinkle some Parmesan cheese over the top and cover with another layer of pasta. Spoon another third of the mushroom mixture to cover the pasta and repeat, adding white sauce and Parmesan cheese. Cover with another layer of pasta and another layer of mushrooms, white sauce, and Parmesan. Finish the lasagna with a layer of pasta, the remaining béchamel, and Parmesan cheese and dot with the remaining butter. There should be about an inch of room between the edge of the pan and

the top of the lasagna. Cover the baking dish with a sheet of aluminum foil.

6. Place the lasagna in the oven and bake for 45 minutes. Uncover and bake for about 15 minutes longer, until the pasta is just beginning to brown. Remove from the oven and allow to stand for 10 minutes before serving.

MAKES 6 SERVINGS

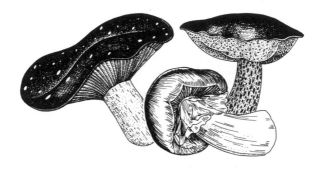

Chapter Nine

~   ~   ~

Risotto, Polenta, Gnocchi, and Beans

Risotto, polenta, gnocchi, and fagioli, along with pasta, are the mainstay of the *primi piatti* (first course dishes) in Italian cuisine. With their individual flavors and comforting textures, they are at once nourishing, satisfying, and, whether they are prepared in a hearty or delicately subtle manner, very versatile. Today you can also find these dishes served as a main course preceded by a simple vegetable *antipasto misto* and accompanied by a crisp green salad.

Risotto

~   ~   ~

As important as pasta is to most of Italy, and bread is to Tuscany, rice is the starch of choice in northern Italy. Of course it isn't just rice that the northern Italians favor, it is risotto—that extraordinary combination of Italian short-grain rice cooked slowly with broth and flavored and enriched with wine, onions, butter, olive oil, and the best Parmesan cheese, as well as with other cheeses, vegetables, seafood, and meats and even fruit.

Risotto is a dish with origins dating back at least to the eleventh century when the Saracens, Moslems who at one time occupied southern Italy, introduced rice to the Italian peninsula. By the fifteenth century, rice growing had been established in the northern region of Lombardy, in the Po River valley near Milan, where conditions are ideal for rice cultivation, helping to make Italy the largest producer of rice in all of Europe.

The story most widely told of the first risotto alleges that the dish was invented in the late sixteenth century in Milan when the magnificent marble-spired *duomo*, the cathedral, was under construction. Supposedly, the master glassworker on the job, who was known for using saffron to enhance his pigments, added saffron to a pot of rice at a big wedding party. The response of the guests was, *"Risus optimus!"*—Latin for "excellent rice"—which was later shortened to *risotto*. To this day, the classic risotto of Milan, made with saffron, is called *risotto alla milanese*.

Risotto is both good and good for you, offering a healthful balance of carbohydrates, protein, and fat. This chapter will give you only a few of the dozens of recipes for risotto with vegetables. (If you find you like the recipes for risotto here, you may wish to go on to the many more vegetable and other recipes to be found in *Risotto: The Classic Rice Dish of Northern Italy* [Collier Books], which I co-authored.)

RISOTTO BASICS

~ ~ ~

RICE/*RISO*. Risotto should be prepared only with Italian short-grain rice. Arborio is the most widely available in the United States as well as in Italy, but recently other Italian rice varieties such as Vialone and Carnaroli, the two types of rice Italian chefs prefer, are also being imported. These varieties are best suited for risotto because they are highly glutinous, a quality that enables the rice to absorb the flavors of the ingredients with which it is cooked to an unusual degree. It also allows the rice to combine with the cooking liquid to create a thick, creamy-smooth consistency that the Italians call *all'onda*—meaning "with waves"—while the individual grains of rice remain firm, *al dente*. It is the combination of the richly flavored and still-firm grains of rice, bound with a creamy-smooth sauce, that gives risotto its special quality.

American-grown long-grain rice can be used in the risotto recipes in this chapter, but it will not give you the texture and consistency of a true risotto. (See page 294 for sources of Italian rice.)

BROTH/*BRODO*. You can use any flavorful broth, vegetable- or meat-based (see pages 10–13). You can also use instant bouillon cubes or canned broth. Whatever you use, be sure you like the flavor of the broth before you use it, since it will be one of the dominant flavors of your finished risotto. Since instant broth tends to be very salty or highly seasoned, I recommend diluting the broth by slightly increasing the amount of the water you use per cube. The broth is always added to risotto very hot.

FLAVORINGS/*SOFFRITTI*. *Soffritti* is the name Italian cooks give to the flavoring base of a dish. In risotto it is usually just onions, but it can be a mixture of onions and other vegetables, including carrots, celery, and garlic, that are chopped up finely and sautéed in olive oil and/or butter. Every risotto begins with a *soffritto*.

FLAVORINGS/*CONDIMENTI*. The *condimenti* are the flavorings—cheeses, vegetables, and herbs—that are added to the risotto to give the dish its special character. Depending on what they are and how long they need to cook, the *condimenti* can be added at the beginning of the cooking, in the middle, or at the end.

COOKING AND SERVING. Please note that the size and type of pot you use for preparing risotto is important. See page 26 for information on risotto pots.

All of the recipes that follow are meant to serve six as a first course and four as a main course. If you want to decrease or increase the quantity, adjust the amount of rice and scale the other ingredients accordingly.

Basic Risotto

~ ~ ~

This is a rich and delicious but simple risotto.

6 tablespoons (¾ stick) unsalted butter

2 tablespoons pure olive oil

½ cup finely chopped onion

2 cups uncooked Italian short-grain rice (Arborio, Vialone, or Carnaroli)

½ cup dry white wine

6½ cups (about) hot broth (see pages 10–13)

½ cup freshly grated Parmesan cheese

1. Place half of the butter and the olive oil in a heavy 4-quart saucepan or casserole over medium-high heat. Add the onion and cook, stirring, for about 3 minutes, until the onion begins to soften. Add the rice and stir, using a wooden spoon, to combine.

2. Add the wine all at once and cook, stirring, until it is absorbed by the rice, about a minute or two. Begin to add the broth, about ¾ cup at a time, stirring well after each addition, until the broth has been absorbed by the rice. Continue to add broth, while stirring, until the rice is tender but firm, *al dente*, about 20 minutes.

3. Turn off the heat, stir in ¼ of broth, the remaining butter, and the Parmesan, and stir well until the butter and cheese melt and are incorporated into the rice. Serve immediately.

PRESSURE COOKER RISOTTO The pressure cooker is the only shortcut method for cooking risotto that I can recommend. I was introduced to this method by Franco and Margaret Romagnoli in their book, *The New Italian Cooking*. It reduces the cooking/stirring time substantially with near-perfect final results. With the exception of the broth, all the quantities of the ingredients listed in the recipe can remain the same when using a pressure cooker. The quantity of broth is always reduced to double the quantity of rice. To prepare risotto in a pressure cooker, follow step 1, then add the wine and cook, stirring, until it is mostly absorbed by the rice. Add the broth (4 cups, in this case) all at once, and stir well. Close the pressure cooker according to the manufacturer's directions and bring the pressure up to full. Cook for exactly 6 minutes. Bring the pressure down immediately (place the cooker in the sink and run cold water over the top). Open the cooker according to the manufacturer's directions. Stir in the remaining butter, broth, and Parmesan (and any prepared vegetable *condimenti* such as those given below). Serve immediately.

Risotto with Many Mushrooms

~ ~ ~

RISOTTO AI FUNGHI

A bounty of mushrooms gives this risotto a wonderful woodsy flavor.

1 ounce dried porcini mushrooms
½ cup boiling water

7 tablespoons unsalted butter

1 large clove garlic, finely minced or pressed

2 pounds wild mushrooms (mixture of portobello, crimini, shiitake, and oyster), stems removed and caps coarsely chopped

Salt and freshly ground black pepper to taste

2 tablespoons pure olive oil

½ cup chopped onion

2 cups uncooked Italian short-grain rice (Arborio, Vialone, or Carnaroli)

½ cup dry white wine

6½ cups (about) hot broth (see pages 10–13)

½ cup freshly grated Parmesan cheese

2 tablespoons chopped fresh parsley

1. Place the porcini in a glass measuring cup with the boiling water and allow to stand for 30 minutes. Drain and rinse well to be sure any dirt or grit has been removed. Strain the soaking liquid through a double thickness of cheesecloth and add to the broth.

2. Melt 4 tablespoons of the butter in a medium-size skillet over medium-high heat. Add the garlic and porcini and wild mushrooms, season with salt and pepper, and cook, stirring, for about 7 minutes, until the mushrooms are tender. Set aside.

3. Melt the remaining butter with the olive oil in a heavy 4-quart saucepan or casserole over medium-high heat. Add the onion and cook, stirring, for about 3 minutes, until it begins to soften. Add the rice and stir well, using a wooden spoon, to combine. Add the wine all at once and cook, stirring, until it is mostly absorbed by the rice, about a minute or two.

4. Begin to add the broth, about ¾ cup at a time, stirring well after each addition until the broth has been absorbed by the rice. Continue to add broth, stirring, until the rice is tender but firm, *al dente*, about 20 minutes.

5. Turn off the heat, stir in one last addition of broth, the mushrooms, Parmesan, and parsley and stir until the cheese melts and is incorporated into the rice. Serve immediately.

Risotto with Spring Vegetables

~ ~ ~

RISOTTO ALLA PRIMAVERA

Lots of fresh vegetables, cut up very finely, give this risotto its special character. This recipe is adapted from La Chiusa, a restaurant and inn in Montefollonico in Tuscany.

7 tablespoons unsalted butter

2 tablespoons chopped scallion, white part only

1 large clove garlic, minced or pressed

1 medium-size artichoke, prepared according to the directions on page 32 and finely chopped

1 medium-size carrot, peeled and finely chopped

¼ cup water

2 small, ripe Italian plum tomatoes, peeled, cored, seeded, and finely chopped

1 medium-size zucchini, finely chopped

2 cups packed fresh spinach leaves, thoroughly cleaned, well drained, stems removed, and coarsely chopped

Salt and freshly ground black pepper to taste

2 tablespoons pure olive oil

½ cup finely chopped onion

2 cups uncooked Italian short-grain rice (Arborio, Vialone, or Carnaroli)

½ cup dry white wine

6½ cups (about) hot broth (see pages 10–13)

½ cup freshly grated Parmesan cheese

2 tablespoons chopped fresh parsley

1. Melt 4 tablespoons of the butter in a medium-size skillet over medium heat. Add the scallion and garlic and cook, stirring, for about 1 minute. Add the artichoke and carrot and stir to combine. Add the water and cook for about 5 minutes, until the water has evaporated and the artichoke is tender. Add the tomatoes, zucchini, and spinach and cook for about 5 minutes longer, until the zucchini is tender. Season with salt and pepper and set aside.

2. Place the remaining butter with the olive oil in a heavy 4-quart saucepan or casserole over medium-high heat. Add the onion and cook, stirring, for about 3 minutes, until it begins to soften. Add the rice and stir well, using a wooden spoon, to combine. Add the wine all at once and cook, stirring, until it is mostly absorbed by the rice, about a minute or two.

3. Begin to add the broth, about ¾ cup at a time, stirring well after each addition until the broth has been absorbed by the rice. Continue to add the broth, stirring, until the rice is tender but firm, *al dente*, about 20 minutes.

4. Turn off the heat, stir in one last addition of broth, the sautéed vegetables, the Parmesan, and parsley, and stir until the cheese melts and the vegetables are incorporated into the rice. Serve immediately.

Risotto with Spinach and Herbs

~ ~ ~

RISOTTO VERDE

Risotto verde is traditionally made with only spinach. I found the herbs add a nice dimension of flavor. Use fresh spinach for the best flavor.

One 10-ounce package fresh spinach, thoroughly washed and stems removed,
or one 10-ounce package frozen spinach, cooked according to the directions
on the package and drained

½ cup chopped fresh parsley

2 tablespoons chopped fresh basil

1 tablespoon chopped fresh marjoram or oregano

2 tablespoons chopped fresh chives

7 tablespoons unsalted butter

Salt and freshly ground black pepper to taste

2 tablespoons pure olive oil

½ cup finely chopped onion

2 cups uncooked Italian short-grain rice (Arborio, Vialone, or Carnaroli)

½ cup dry white wine

6½ cups (about) hot broth (see pages 10–13)

¼ cup mascarpone

½ cup freshly grated Parmesan cheese

1. If using fresh spinach, cook the rinsed spinach in a large saucepan until wilted, 3 to 5 minutes, over medium-high heat. Place the cooked spinach in a food processor fitted with the steel blade, add the herbs and 4 tablespoons of the butter, and pulse the machine on and off several times to chop the spinach and combine it with the herbs and butter. Season with salt and pepper and set aside.

2. Place the remaining butter with the olive oil in a heavy 4-quart saucepan or casserole over medium-high heat. Add the onion and cook, stirring, about 3 minutes, until it begins to soften. Add the rice and stir well, using a wooden spoon, to combine. Add the wine all at once and cook, stirring, until it is mostly absorbed by the rice, about a minute or two.

3. Begin to add the broth, about ¾ cup at a time, stirring well until each addition of the broth has been absorbed. Continue to add the broth, stirring, until the rice is tender but firm, *al dente*, about 20 minutes.

4. Turn off the heat, stir in one last addition of broth, the spinach-and-herb mixture, the mascarpone, and Parmesan, and stir until the cheeses melt and are incorporated into the rice. Serve immediately.

Risotto with Asparagus and Roasted Yellow Pepper

~ ~ ~

RISOTTO AGLI ASPARAGI E PEPERONI

Peppers and asparagus are available most of the year so you can prepare this recipe anytime.

5 tablespoons pure olive oil

1 medium-size yellow bell pepper, cored, seeded, and sliced into
    1-inch-thick strips

Kosher salt

½ pound skinny asparagus spears, trimmed and cut diagonally into
    2-inch lengths

7 tablespoons unsalted butter

½ cup chopped onion

2 cups uncooked Italian short-grain rice (Arborio, Vialone, or Carnaroli)

½ cup dry white wine

6½ cups (about) hot broth (see pages 10–13)

½ cup freshly grated Parmesan cheese

1. Preheat the oven to 450°F. Pour 3 tablespoons of the olive oil into a small baking pan and place the strips of pepper in the pan. Turn them around a few times to be sure they are coated with the oil. Lightly sprinkle with salt and place in the oven. Roast for about 15 minutes, until they begin to brown. Transfer to a small bowl and set aside.

2. Put the asparagus in a small saucepan with just enough water to cover over medium-high heat. Bring to a boil and cook for 5 minutes, until the asparagus is just tender. Drain, refresh under cold water, and set aside.

3. Combine 3 tablespoons of the butter with the remaining oil in a heavy 4-quart saucepan or casserole over medium-high heat. Add the onion and cook, stirring, about 3 minutes, until it begins to soften. Add the rice and stir well, using a wooden spoon, to combine. Add the wine all at once and cook, stirring, until it is mostly absorbed, about a minute or two.

4. Begin to add the broth, about ¾ cup at a time, stirring well until each addition of broth has been absorbed. Continue to add the broth, stirring, until the rice is tender but firm, *al dente*, about 20 minutes.

5. Turn off the heat, add the asparagus, one last addition of broth, the remaining butter, and the Parmesan, and stir until the cheese melts and is incorporated into the rice. Garnish with the roasted pepper and serve immediately.

Risotto with Artichokes and Lemon

~ ~ ~

RISOTTO AI CARCIOFI E LIMONE

The zesty lemon flavor of the artichokes is the perfect complement to the rich-tasting rice.

4 tablespoons olive oil

4 medium-size artichokes (about 1½ pounds), prepared according to the
    directions on page 32, chokes removed, and finely chopped

1 large clove garlic, minced or pressed

Salt and freshly ground black pepper to taste

Juice of ½ lemon

½ cup water

3 tablespoons unsalted butter

½ cup finely chopped onion

2 cups uncooked Italian short-grain rice (Arborio, Vialone, or Carnaroli)

½ cup *dry white wine*

6½ cups *(about) hot broth (see pages 10–13)*

3 ounces *Italian fontina or Taleggio cheese*

½ cup *freshly grated Parmesan cheese*

½ cup *chopped fresh parsley*

1. Heat 3 tablespoons of the olive oil in a medium-size skillet over medium-high heat. Add the artichokes and garlic, season with salt and pepper, and cook, stirring, for a minute or two. Add the lemon juice and water, cover, and simmer over medium-low heat until the artichokes are tender and most of the liquid has cooked away, about 15 minutes.

2. Place the butter and remaining oil in a heavy 4-quart saucepan or casserole over medium-high heat. Add the onion and cook, stirring, about 3 minutes, until it begins to soften. Add the rice and stir well, using a wooden spoon, to combine. Add the wine all at once and cook, stirring, until it is mostly absorbed by the rice, about a minute or two.

3. Begin to add the broth, about ¾ cup at a time, stirring well until each addition of broth has been absorbed by the rice. Continue to add the broth, stirring, until the rice is tender but firm, *al dente*, about 20 minutes.

4. Turn off the heat, stir in ¼ cup of broth, the artichokes and their cooking liquid, fontina, and the Parmesan and stir until the cheeses melt and are incorporated into the rice. Garnish with the parsley and serve immediately.

Risotto with Radicchio
~ ~ ~
RISOTTO AL RADICCHIO

A relatively new classic in the risotto repertoire. The delicately bitter flavor of the radicchio mellows in cooking and its deep red color gives a rosy hue to the rice.

tablespoons unsalted butter

tablespoons pure olive oil

½ cup finely chopped onion

2 cups uncooked Italian short-grain rice (Arborio, Vialone, or Carnaroli)

½ cup dry white wine

1 head radicchio, shredded

6½ cups (about) hot broth (see pages 10–13)

⅓ cup mascarpone

½ cup freshly grated Parmesan cheese

1. Combine the butter with the olive oil in a heavy 4-quart saucepan or casserole over medium-high heat. Add the onion and cook, stirring, for about 3 minutes, until it begins to soften. Add the rice and stir well, using a wooden spoon, to combine. Add the wine all at once and cook, stirring, until it is mostly absorbed by the rice, about a minute or two.

2. Stir in the radicchio and begin to add the broth, about ¾ cup at a time, stirring well until each addition of broth has been absorbed by the rice. Continue to add the broth, stirring, until the rice is tender but firm, *al dente*, about 20 minutes.

3. Turn off the heat. Stir in one last addition of broth, the mascarpone, and Parmesan and stir until the cheeses melt and are incorporated into the rice. Serve immediately.

Risotto with Leeks and Onions

~ ~ ~

RISOTTO AI PORRI E CIPOLLE

This risotto captures all the wonderfully mild sweet flavors of the onion family.

6 tablespoons (¾ stick) unsalted butter

1 medium-size leek, white part only, cleaned (see page 47) and thinly sliced

½ cup thinly sliced red onion

½ cup thinly sliced yellow onion

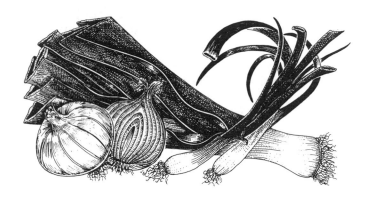

2 scallions, both white and green parts, cut into julienne strips

Salt and freshly ground black pepper to taste

2 tablespoons pure olive oil

½ cup finely chopped onion

2 cups uncooked Italian short-grain rice (Arborio, Vialone, or Carnaroli)

½ cup dry white wine

6½ cups (about) hot broth (see pages 10–13)

½ cup freshly grated Parmesan cheese

¼ cup chopped fresh parsley

1. Melt half of the butter in a medium-size sauté pan over medium-high heat. Add the leek, onions, and scallions and cook, stirring, for about 7 minutes, until the onions are tender. Season with salt and pepper and set aside.

2. Place the remaining butter with the oil in a heavy 4-quart saucepan or casserole over medium-high heat. Add the chopped onion and cook, stirring, for about 3 minutes, until it begins to soften. Add the rice and stir well, using a wooden spoon, to combine. Add the wine all at once and cook, stirring, until it is mostly absorbed by the rice, about a minute or two.

3. Begin to add the broth, about ¾ cup at a time, stirring well until each addition of the broth has been absorbed by the rice. Continue to add the broth, stirring, until the rice is tender but firm, *al dente*, about 20 minutes.

Turn off the heat and stir in one last addition of broth, the leek-and-onion mixture, the Parmesan, and parsley, and stir until the cheese melts and is incorporated into the rice. Serve immediately.

Risotto with Squash

~ ~ ~

RISOTTO ALLA ZUCCA

Three different squashes make this colorful fare for the fall when squash is at its best.

6 tablespoons (¾ stick) unsalted butter

2 cups grated Hubbard squash (about ½ pound)

1 small yellow squash, finely chopped

1 small zucchini, finely chopped

Salt and freshly ground black pepper to taste

2 tablespoons pure olive oil

½ cup finely chopped onion

2 cups uncooked Italian short-grain rice (Arborio, Vialone, or Carnaroli)

½ cup dry white wine

6½ cups (about) hot broth (see pages 10–13)

4 ounces Italian fontina cheese, rind removed and diced

½ cup freshly grated Parmesan cheese

¼ cup chopped parsley

1. Melt half of the butter in a medium-size skillet over medium-high heat. Add the squashes and cook, stirring, for about 5 minutes, until the squashes are tender. Season with salt and pepper and set aside.

2. Place the remaining butter with the oil in a heavy 4-quart saucepan or casserole over medium-high heat. Add the onion and cook, stirring, for about 3 minutes, until it begins to soften. Add the rice and stir well, using a wooden spoon, to combine. Add the wine all at once and cook, stirring, until it is mostly absorbed by the rice, about a minute or two.

3. Begin to add the broth, about ¾ cup at a time, stirring well until each addition of the broth has been absorbed by the rice. Continue to add the broth, stirring, until the rice is tender but firm, *al dente*, about 20 minutes.

4. Turn off the heat and stir in one last addition of broth, the sq
mixture, the fontina, Parmesan, and parsley until the cheeses melt an
incorporated into the rice. Serve immediately.

Risotto with Sun-Dried Tomatoes, Peas, and Goat Cheese

~ ~ ~

RISOTTO AI POMODORI SECCHI, PISELLI, E CAPRINO

The intense taste of the sun-dried tomatoes gives this risotto its
formidable character.

5 tablespoons unsalted butter
2 tablespoons pure olive oil
½ cup finely chopped onion
2 cups uncooked Italian short-grain rice (Arborio, Vialone, or Carnaroli)
½ cup dry white wine
6½ cups (about) hot broth (see pages 10–13)
½ cup coarsely chopped sun-dried tomatoes packed in oil
1 cup fresh shelled peas or defrosted frozen peas
4 ounces creamy goat cheese, crumbled
½ cup freshly grated Parmesan cheese

1. Place 3 tablespoons of the butter with the oil in a heavy 4-quart
saucepan or casserole over medium-high heat. Add the onion and cook,
stirring, for about 3 minutes, until it begins to soften. Add the rice and
stir well, using a wooden spoon, to combine. Add the wine all at once
and cook, stirring, until it is mostly absorbed by the rice, about a minute
or two.

2. Begin to add the broth, about ¾ cup at a time, stirring well until
each addition of broth has been absorbed by the rice. Continue to add the
broth, stirring, until the rice is tender but firm, *al dente,* about 20 minutes.

3. Turn off the heat and stir in one last addition of broth, the remaining butter, the sun-dried tomatos, peas, goat cheese, and Parmesan
until the cheeses melt and are incorporated into the rice. Serve immediately.

Risotto with Strawberries

~ ~ ~

RISOTTO ALLE FRAGOLE

This risotto is bound to surprise—the strawberries lend a fruity but not at all sweet taste.

6 tablespoons (¾ stick) unsalted butter

2 tablespoons pure olive oil

½ cup finely chopped onion

1 cup fresh strawberries hulled, stems removed, and diced

2 cups Italian short-grain rice (Arborio, Vialone, or Carnaroli)

½ cup dry Marsala

6½ cups (about) hot broth (see pages 10–13)

½ cup freshly grated Parmesan cheese

1. Place 3 tablespoons of the butter with the olive oil in a heavy 4-quart saucepan or casserole over medium-high heat. Add the onion and sauté for about 3 minutes, until the onion begins to soften. Add the strawberries and cook for about 1 minute, until they begin to lose their red color. Stir in the rice to combine it with the onion-and-strawberry mixture.

2. Add the Marsala and cook, stirring, until it is absorbed by the rice, about a minute. Begin to add the broth, about ¾ cup at a time, stirring well after each addition until the broth has been absorbed by the rice. Continue to add the broth, stirring, until the rice is tender but firm, *al dente*, about 20 minutes.

3. Turn off the heat, add one last addition of broth, the remaining butter, and the Parmesan, and stir well until the butter melts and the cheese is incorporated into the rice. Serve immediately.

Polenta

~ ~ ~

Polenta is the name ancient Romans gave to the cooked grain cereal they prepared with spelt, a type of wheat. Over time, Italians have used various other grains to make polenta, including barley, oats, buckwheat, and even acorns. When corn was finally introduced into Italy from the New World in the seventeenth century, corn growing became central to the northeastern regions of Italy—Veneto, Trentino-Alto Adige, and Venezia Giulia—and polenta began to be made more and more with cornmeal because its flavor combined so well with those of the cheeses and vegetables of the region. Today polenta is made exclusively with cornmeal and is still an important part of the culinary tradition of northeastern Italy, though it is also enjoyed in other parts of Italy.

Italian cooks are particular about the cornmeal they use in polenta—there are specially ground cornmeals with varying grades of coarseness for different dishes; and some recipes even call for a mixture of coarse and finely ground cornmeal. You can use any cornmeal to prepare the polenta recipes that follow, including stone-ground cornmeal, which you can buy in health food stores. However, the coarseness of the cornmeal will affect the cooking time: the more coarsely ground the cornmeal, the longer the cooking time.

Traditionally, polenta was prepared in a special copper pot called a *paiolo* which heated evenly and helped produce an evenly textured polenta. You don't need a special pot, but a heavy-bottomed pan, preferably one with a nonstick surface, will help the polenta cook evenly without sticking, lumping, or burning.

Polenta is made by boiling cornmeal in a liquid, generally water (milk, broth, or wine can also be used). The boiled polenta can be served directly from the pot dressed with butter and Parmesan cheese, baked with a variety of cheeses and sauces, or allowed to cool until it is firm, then sliced and fried or grilled. Adventurous Italian chefs are producing quite enticing forms of this once modest staple, as in the Fried Polenta with Mushrooms (see pages 206–207) which is the creation of Cesare Casella from the restaurant Vipore outside Lucca.

Although polenta is most typically served as a side dish or first course, it is hearty enough to be a main course entree with a green salad or vegetable antipasto on the side.

Basic Polenta

~ ~ ~

You get perfect—smooth and lump-free—results if you combine the cornmeal with the cold water and heat the two together. This version is simpler and more reliable than most classic recipes, which call for adding the cornmeal very slowly to boiling water. You can easily halve the recipe for a smaller quantity.

2 cups cornmeal

1 tablespoon salt

6 cups cold water

1. Pour the cornmeal into a heavy-bottomed 4-quart saucepan, preferably one with a nonstick surface, add the salt, and gradually add the water, stirring well with a wooden spoon to be sure all the cornmeal is dissolved and there are no lumps.

2. Place the pan over medium-high heat and stir constantly until the cornmeal begins to thicken, about 5 minutes. Lower the heat to medium-low, cover the pan, and simmer, stirring occasionally, for about 20 minutes, until the polenta pulls away from the sides of the pan. Proceed with any of the recipes that follow.

MAKES 6 SERVINGS

Polenta with Butter and Parmesan Cheese

~ ~ ~

POLENTA AL BURRO E FORMAGGIO

Deliciously rich and delicately tasting of corn, this way of preparing polenta is traditional.

1 recipe Basic Polenta (see recipe above)

Salt and freshly ground black pepper to taste

6 tablespoons (¾ stick) unsalted butter, melted

⅓ cup freshly grated Parmesan cheese

1. Prepare the polenta. Taste the cooked polenta and add necessary and season liberally with black pepper. Pour the polent single serving dish or into six individual serving bowls.

2. Make a well in the center of the polenta and add the butter. Sprinkle the Parmesan cheese over the butter. Mix well and serve at once.

MAKES 6 SERVINGS

Layers of Polenta with Mushrooms

~ ~ ~

PASTICCIO DI POLENTA

Slices of cooked polenta are beautifully layered with wild mushrooms and a light creamy sauce. This hearty dish is certain to be a crowd pleaser.

½ recipe Basic Polenta (see page 204)

4 tablespoons (½ stick) unsalted butter

3 tablespoons all-purpose flour

2 cups hot milk

¼ cup pure olive oil

1 clove garlic, finely minced or pressed

4 cups sliced wild mushrooms (portobello, shiitake, crimini, or oyster), stems removed, caps thinly sliced

1 tablespoon chopped fresh parsley

Salt and freshly ground black pepper to taste

Freshly grated Parmesan cheese

1. Pour the cooked polenta into a small bowl, preferably a 4-cup soufflé dish with a flat bottom and straight sides, cover with plastic wrap, and allow to cool completely or refrigerate overnight.

2. Melt the butter in a medium-size sauccpan over medium heat. When the butter begins to foam, add the flour and stir briskly with a wire whisk until the flour is completely absorbed into the butter. Do not let the mixture brown. Turn off the heat and begin to add the milk ¼ cup at a time, beating with the whisk until each addition is incorporated. When the mixture is thin, add all of the remaining milk. Turn the heat to medium

and heat the sauce, stirring with a wooden spoon, until it thickens and is the consistency of heavy cream. Turn off the heat and set aside.

3. Place the oil in a medium-size skillet over medium heat. Add the garlic, mushrooms, and parsley, season with salt and pepper, and cook, stirring, until the mushrooms are tender, 7 to 10 minutes. Turn off the heat and set aside.

4. Preheat the oven to 350°F.

5. When the polenta is completely cool, remove the plastic wrap and run a knife around the edge of the polenta. Invert the dish onto a cutting board, tapping the edges one or two times to release the polenta. It should drop down easily in a solid mass. Using a long, sharp knife, cut the polenta into ¼-inch-thick slices. You should be able to get 10 to 12 slices in all.

6. Butter a 9-inch-square baking dish. Arrange half the slices of polenta in the bottom, cutting them as necessary to fit. Spoon half the mushrooms over the polenta in the baking dish and spoon half the white sauce over the mushrooms. Repeat with another layer of polenta slices and the remaining mushrooms and white sauce. Sprinkle some Parmesan over the top, cover securely with aluminum foil, and bake for 45 minutes. Remove the aluminum foil and bake for 15 minutes longer. Serve with some Parmesan cheese on the side.

MAKES 4 SERVINGS

Fried Polenta with Mushrooms

~ ~ ~

CROSTINI DI POLENTA COI FUNGHI

This is one of my favorite ways to eat polenta. The squares of fried polenta are crispy on the outside and creamy-smooth on the inside. The extraordinarily flavorful topping of mushrooms makes for an outstanding dish. I learned this recipe from Cesare Casella, the owner and chef at the restaurant Vipore outside Lucca in Tuscany. He fries his polenta in peanut oil, but says almost any vegetable oil other than olive is good for frying. Cesare serves these polenta *crostini* as an antipasto while his guests wait for their dinners to arrive. I like to serve them as dinner with a green salad.

1 recipe Basic Polenta (see page 204)

½ cup pure olive oil

2 cloves garlic, very finely minced or pressed

2 small, fresh, ripe Italian plum tomatoes, peeled, cored, seeded, and finely chopped

1 pound fresh wild mushrooms (shiitake, portobello, or crimini), stems removed,
    caps finely chopped

Salt and freshly ground black pepper to taste

2 tablespoons chopped fresh marjoram or 1 teaspoon dried

Vegetable oil for frying

1. Pour the cooked polenta into a small round or rectangular glass or ceramic dish with a flat bottom and straight sides (a soufflé dish works well). Cover with plastic wrap and allow it to cool to room temperature or refrigerate overnight. When it is completely cool, remove the plastic wrap and run a knife around the edge of the polenta. Invert the dish onto a cutting surface, tapping the edges one or two times to release the polenta. It should fall from the dish in a solid mass. With a sharp knife, cut the polenta into ½-inch-thick slices. Cut the slices crosswise into 2-inch-long pieces. Set aside.

2. Place the oil in a large skillet over medium-high heat. Add the garlic and tomatoes and cook, stirring, for about a minute. Add the mushrooms and stir well to combine with the garlic and tomatoes. Season with salt and pepper. Turn the heat to medium-low and cook, stirring, for 7 to 10 minutes, until the mushrooms begin to soften and give up their liquid. Add the marjoram and cook, stirring, for about 5 minutes longer.

3. Pour about ¼ inch of vegetable oil into a large heavy skillet over medium-high heat. When the oil is hot (test it by dropping a small piece of polenta into the oil; if it sizzles, the oil is hot enough), add four pieces of polenta to the oil at once, making sure they do not touch each other, otherwise they will stick. When the underside is golden brown, in about 5 minutes, turn the polenta over and cook for another 5 minutes, until evenly browned on both sides. Using a metal strainer or slotted spoon, remove the fried polenta and place on paper towels to drain. Add four more pieces of polenta and continue frying until all the polenta is cooked.

4. Place the pieces of fried polenta on a serving plate. Top each piece with a heaping teaspoonful of the mushroom mixture and serve.

MAKES 6 SERVINGS

Polenta with Sautéed Onions

~ ~ ~

POLENTA ALLA VENEZIANA

In Venice, polenta is traditionally served with sliced calves liver that has been sautéed with onions. This meatless version is every bit as good. Use mild Vidalia onions when they're available—they lend a wonderful unassertive sweetness to the dish.

6 tablespoons (¾ stick) unsalted butter
1 tablespoon olive oil
4 large Vidalia or other yellow onions (about 2 pounds), thinly sliced
Salt and freshly ground black pepper to taste
1 recipe Basic Polenta (see page 204)
¼ cup chopped fresh parsley

1. Place 2 tablespoons of the butter with the olive oil in a large skillet over medium-high heat. Add the onions and cook, stirring, until the onions begin to soften and are greatly reduced in bulk, about 3 minutes. Lower the heat to medium, season the onions with salt and pepper, and cook for about 30 minutes longer, until the onions are golden brown.

2. While the onions are cooking, prepare the polenta. Stir the remaining butter into the polenta and serve with the onions on top. Garnish with parsley.

MAKES 6 SERVINGS

Polenta with Gorgonzola

~ ~ ~

POLENTA CON LA GORGONZOLA

This recipe was inspired by a dish that's served at Olive's restaurant in Boston. Gutsy Gorgonzola cheese makes this a very flavorful dish.

1 recipe Basic Polenta (see page 204)

1 tablespoon pure olive oil

1 cup Fresh Tomato Sauce (see pages 152–53)

2 to 3 ounces Gorgonzola cheese (or other flavorful strong ch...
    Taleggio or fontina), crumbled or cut into small pieces

Freshly grated Parmesan cheese

1. Preheat the oven to 425°F

2. Pour the cooked polenta into a shallow baking dish that has been coated with olive oil.

3. Spoon the tomato sauce over the top of the polenta and distribute the Gorgonzola over the tomato sauce. Bake for 35 to 40 minutes, or until the Gorgonzola is melted and bubbling. Remove and serve with Parmesan cheese.

MAKES 6 SERVINGS

Gnocchi

~ ~ ~

Gnocchi, the Italian word for dumplings, are prepared in different regions of Italy with different ingredients. In Rome, as well as in other southern Italian cities, you're likely to find gnocchi made with semolina flour, whereas in Tuscany gnocchi might be prepared with cornmeal. But it is the *gnocchi di patate*, or potato dumplings, which are typically found in the northern regions of Italy, that are the most popular version.

Potato gnocchi are not at all difficult to prepare, but you must make them by hand. Don't look for a shortcut with the food processor, which will quickly turn the potatoes into a dense paste.

In their most straightforward form, these gnocchi are made simply with a puree of potatoes combined with flour and egg. You can use almost any type of potato. Russets, Idahos, and Maines seem to work the best. Avoid "new" or red-skinned potatoes, which don't have the right dry texture. Since potatoes vary in moisture content, exactly how much flour to add will also vary.

Following are three variations for potato gnocchi. Once the gnocchi are prepared, they should be boiled in a large kettle of water or baked ıth butter and Parmesan cheese. Gnocchi can be served with fresh tomato sauce, pesto, Gorgonzola and cream sauce, or simply dressed with butter. Whichever you choose, always top the gnocchi with a hefty portion of freshly grated Parmesan cheese.

Basic Potato Gnocchi

~ ~ ~

GNOCCHI DI PATATE

Delicious and straightforward—these are my favorite gnocchi.

1 pound potatoes, preferably Idaho or Russets, peeled and quartered
Salt and freshly ground black pepper to taste
1 large egg
1 cup (about) all-purpose or unbleached white flour

1. Place the potatoes in a deep saucepan and cover with cold water. Bring to a boil over high heat. Reduce the heat to medium and simmer for 10 to 15 minutes, or until the potatoes are tender. Drain.

2. Force the potatoes through a food mill or potato ricer into a medium-size mixing bowl. (Do not use a food processor. It quickly turns the potatoes into a dense paste.) Add the salt, pepper, and egg and, using a wooden spoon, beat briskly until the egg is completely incorporated into the potato puree. Add the flour in ¼-cup increments, stirring well with a wooden spoon after each addition, until the dough forms a ball on the spoon. Some of the flour may be left over. Turn the dough onto a well-floured work surface and knead for about 3 minutes, adding more flour if necessary, until the dough is smooth and soft and not sticky to the touch.

3. Divide the dough into six equal pieces. Flour your hands and gently roll each piece between your hands into a log shape measuring 6 to 8 inches long and 1 inch around. Cut each log into approximately 1-inch pieces. Gently roll the cut pieces on the work surface to flour the cut sides. Form into gnocchi by gently pressing each piece onto the floured work surface with the tines of a dinner fork. You want to press just hard enough to leave ridges in the dough. Transfer the gnocchi to a well-floured sheet of waxed paper until ready to cook. These may be prepared ahead

of time, covered, and refrigerated for a day or frozen for several months.

4. Bring a large pot of water to a boil. Drop 12 gnocchi at a time into the water. They will sink to the bottom but within a couple of minutes they will rise to the surface. Once they come to the surface, cook for 5 minutes. Using a skimmer or slotted spoon, remove and drain the cooked gnocchi and place on a warm serving platter. Add more uncooked gnocchi to the boiling water and repeat until all the gnocchi are cooked.

MAKES 6 SERVINGS

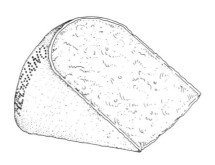

Potato Gnocchi with Butter and Parmesan

~ ~ ~

GNOCCHI AL BURRO E FORMAGGIO

4 tablespoons (½ stick) unsalted butter
1 recipe Basic Potato Gnocchi (see preceding recipe)
Salt and freshly ground black pepper to taste
Freshly grated Parmesan cheese

Melt the butter in a medium-size skillet over medium heat. When the butter begins to foam, turn off the heat and add the cooked, drained gnocchi. Shake the pan in a back-and-forth motion until all the gnocchi are coated with the butter. Season with more salt and pepper. Transfer to a serving dish and serve with Parmesan cheese.

MAKES 6 SERVINGS

VARIATION: Preheat the oven to 350°F. Toss the gnocchi with the butter, above, and transfer to a baking dish just large enough to hold them in a single layer. Generously sprinkle with Parmesan cheese. Bake about 15 minutes until the cheese is lightly brown.

Potato Gnocchi with Pesto

~ ~ ~

GNOCCHI AL PESTO

1 recipe Basic Potato Gnocchi (see pages 210–11)
1 recipe Pesto (see pages 154–55)
¼ cup freshly grated Parmesan cheese
Salt and freshly ground black pepper to taste

Prepare the gnocchi and cook them according to the directions on pages 210–11. Drain well and transfer to a preheated serving bowl. Toss with pesto and cheese. Season with salt and pepper and serve immediately.

MAKES 6 SERVINGS

Potato Gnocchi with Gorgonzola and Cream

~ ~ ~

GNOCCHI ALLA GORGONZOLA

4 ounces Gogonzola cheese
¼ cup heavy cream
2 tablespoons unsalted butter
1 recipe Basic Potato Gnocchi (see pages 210–11)
Freshly grated Parmesan cheese

1. Place the Gorgonzola, cream, and butter in a large heav
over medium heat. Using a fork, mash the Gorgonzola to combin
the cream and butter. Whisk the mixture into a thick, creamy con
and heat through.

2. Add the drained cooked gnocchi to the skillet with the Gorgonzola
sauce and toss well to combine. Serve with freshly grated Parmesan cheese.

MAKES 6 SERVINGS

Green Spinach Gnocchi

~ ~ ~

GNOCCHI DI PATATE E SPINACI

Gorgeous green gnocchi have a delicate fresh spinach flavor. Serve
them with tomato sauce for a colorful effect.

1 pound potatoes, preferably Idaho or Russets, peeled and quartered
2 cups fresh spinach leaves, well rinsed, cooked, chopped, and drained of any
*   excess liquid*
Salt and freshly ground black pepper to taste
1 large egg
1½ cups Fresh Tomato Sauce (see pages 152–53)
Freshly grated Parmesan cheese

1. Place the potatoes in a deep saucepan and cover with cold water.
Bring the water to a boil over high heat, then turn the heat down to
medium and simmer for 10 to 15 minutes, or until the potatoes are tender.
Drain.

2. Force the potatoes through a food mill or potato ricer into a
medium-size mixing bowl. (Do not use a food processor; it will turn the
potatoes into a dense paste.) Add the spinach, salt, pepper, and egg. Using
a wooden spoon, beat briskly until the egg and spinach are completely
incorporated into the potato puree. Add the flour in ¼-cup increments,
stirring with a wooden spoon after each addition until the dough forms a
ball on the spoon. Some of the flour may be left over. Turn the dough
onto a well-floured work surface and knead for about 3 minutes, adding

more flour if necessary, until the dough is smooth and soft and not sticky to the touch.

3. Divide the dough into six equal pieces. Flour your hands and gently roll each piece between your hands into a log shape measuring about 6 to 8 inches long and 1 inch around. Cut each log into approximately 1-inch pieces. Gently roll the cut pieces on the work surface to flour the cut sides. Form into gnocchi by pressing each piece onto the work surface with the tines of a dinner fork. You want to press hard enough to leave ridges in the dough. Transfer the gnocchi to a well-floured sheet of waxed paper until ready to cook. These may be prepared ahead of time, covered, and refrigerated for a day or frozen for several months.

4. Bring a large pot of water to a boil. Drop 12 gnocchi at a time into the water. They will sink to the bottom, but within a couple of minutes they will rise to the surface. Once they come to the surface, cook for 5 minutes. Using a skimmer or slotted spoon, remove and drain the cooked gnocchi and place on a warm serving platter. Add more uncooked gnocchi to the boiling water and repeat until all the gnocchi are cooked.

5. While the gnocchi are cooking, place the tomato sauce in a small saucepan over medium-high heat and heat through. Pour over the cooked gnocchi and serve immediately with freshly grated Parmesan cheese.

MAKES 6 SERVINGS

GNOCCHI WITH THE ESSENCE OF PORCINI MUSHROOMS/*GNOCCHI DI FUNGHI*
Place ½ ounce dried porcini mushrooms in a heatproof measuring cup with ½ cup boiling water, and let stand for 30 minutes. Drain, straining the liquid through a double thickness of cheesecloth, and reserving the mushrooms for the sauce. Follow the directions above, omitting the spinach and adding the mushroom liquid when you add the egg to the potatoes. Instead of saucing with the tomato sauce, melt 4 tablespoons (½ stick) unsalted butter in a medium-size sauté pan over medium heat until it begins to bubble. Add the soaked mushrooms and cook, stirring, for 2 to 3 minutes. Turn off the heat and add the drained gnocchi. Shake the pan in a back-and-forth motion until all the gnocchi are coated with butter. Season with salt and pepper, transfer to a warm serving dish, and serve with freshly grated Parmesan cheese.

Beans/Fagioli

~ ~ ~

Beans and dried legumes have been a staple of Italian cooking for thousands of years. Apicius, who documented the eating customs of ancient Rome, described several dishes prepared with dried beans. *Tisanum*, for which he gave the recipe, was a stew of lentils, chickpeas, favas, and barley. During the Renaissance, when Catherine de' Medici attempted to refine Italian cuisine along the lines of French cooking, beans of all varieties came to be regarded as strictly peasant fare, and fell out of favor with the nobility and aristocracy. Today the popularity of beans has been firmly reestablished, and they are widely recognized to be a delicious, healthful, and economical source of protein.

The most popular beans in Italy include *borlotti* beans, which are pale pink with red speckles (similar to our pinto beans); *cannellini*, white kidney beans, which are usually associated with Tuscan cooking; *ceci*, chickpeas, which are eaten with pasta as well as with soups and are a staple of southern Italian cooking; *lenticchie*, brown lentils, which are grown mostly in Umbria near Spoleto; and favas, broad, flat beans that are among the most flavorful of beans. Unlike the other beans, favas are eaten when they are fresh as well as dried. In Rome and other regions, a rite of spring is to eat uncooked young fresh favas with olive oil and pecorino cheese.

The preparation of the bean recipes below starts with cooked beans. With a little advance preparation, you can easily make your own. You can also use canned cooked beans, although to my taste these tend to be overly salty and overly cooked, and you cannot always get the specific variety of beans used in Italy. If you use canned beans, always drain and rinse them in a colander or strainer before cooking.

Most of the bean dishes make a hearty and satisfying main course entree at lunch or dinner when served with a green salad.

QUANTITY. Whether you cook your beans in a conventional pot or in a pressure cooker, in general, you can figure 1 cup dried beans will yield 2 to 3 cups cooked beans.

SOAKING BEANS FOR COOKING. With the exception of lentils and split peas, beans should be soaked before cooking. This reduces the cooking time by several hours. To soak beans, place the dried beans in a large bowl, amply cover with water, and allow to stand for 8 hours or overnight. You can cut the soaking time in half if you add boiling water to cover the beans.

The soaking water should always be drained and discarded before cooking the beans.

COOKING BEANS. Beans are cooked in plenty of water to give them ample room to expand. Exact quantities are not critical since you can add more liquid if necessary. You can cook the beans with a variety of different flavorings including onions, carrots, celery, herbs, and garlic. You should never add salt or acidic ingredients, such as tomatoes, until the beans are almost fully cooked; these ingredients will retard the cooking process and the beans will not become tender, no matter how long you cook them.

To cook beans, place the soaked, drained beans in a large saucepan or small stockpot with 4 cups of water for every cup of beans. Bring to a boil over medium-high heat. Reduce the heat to medium-low and simmer, partially covered, until tender. The cooking time varies with the size of the beans, so it follows that the small white beans take less time to cook than the broad fava bean. Cooking times are as follows:

Cannellini (white kidney)	1 to 1½ hours
Chickpeas	1½ to 2 hours
Fava	1½ to 2 hours
Great Northern	1 to 1½ hours
Lentils (unsoaked)	30 to 40 minutes
Peas (split)	30 to 40 minutes
Peas (whole)	1½ to 2 hours
Pinto beans	1 to 1½ hours
Small white	¾ to 1 hour

PRESSURE COOKING BEANS. The fastest way to soak and cook beans is to use a pressure cooker (see page 19). It cuts the soaking and cooking times dramatically and enhances the natural flavor of the beans since almost nothing cooks away. Always follow the manufacturer's directions for using your pressure cooker, and never fill the cooker more than two-thirds full.

To presoak the beans, add the beans to the pot with just enough water to cover; close the pressure cooker according to the manufacturer's directions and bring the pressure up to full; cook for 1 minute, then bring the pressure down immediately by placing the cooker in the sink and running cold water over the top until the safety latches indicate that the pressure has dropped and you can open the top.

To pressure-cook beans, drain the beans and discard the water; return the beans to the pot and add 4 cups of fresh cold water for every cup of beans; follow the manufacturer's instructions for using the pressure cooker. Close the cooker, bring the pressure up to full, and start timing the cooking once the pressure has reached its maximum point, according to the manufacturer's directions; when cooking time is complete, immediately bring the pressure down by placing the cooker in the sink and running cold water over the top of the pressure cooker. Times for cooking beans in the pressure cooker are as follows:

Cannellini (white kidney)	12 to 15 minutes
Chickpeas	20 to 25 minutes
Fava	16 to 22 minutes
Great Northern	14 to 18 minutes
Lentils (unsoaked)	10 minutes
Peas (split)	10 minutes
Peas (whole)	16 to 18 minutes
Pinto beans	7 to 10 minutes
Small white	14 to 18 minutes

White Beans with Tomatoes and Sage
~ ~ ~
FAGIOLI ALL'UCCELLETTO

This is a typical Tuscan way to prepare beans. The name *uccelletto*, which means "little birds," comes from the sage and tomato flavorings that are traditionally used in cooking game birds.

½ cup pure olive oil

2 cloves garlic, finely minced or pressed

6 fresh sage leaves

4 cups cooked white kidney beans (see pages 216–17), or two 16-ounce cans
    cannellini beans

1 cup chopped canned tomatoes with their juice

Salt and freshly ground black pepper to taste

1. Place the oil in a large saucepan with a cover over medium-high heat. Add the garlic and sage and cook for 1 minute.

2. Add the beans and tomatoes, season with salt and pepper, and stir well to combine. Reduce the heat to medium-low, cover, and simmer, stirring occasionally, for about 10 minutes, or until the beans are heated through and you can smell the aroma of the sage.

MAKES 4 SERVINGS

Small White Beans with Leeks

~ ~ ~

FAGIOLI CON PORRI

This is a hearty bean dish perfect for a winter dinner. Prepare it a day in advance—it's even better the next day.

2 tablespoons pure olive oil

2 medium-size leeks, white part only, trimmed, cleaned (see page 47), cut in
    half lengthwise, and thinly sliced

1 medium-size carrot, finely chopped

2 cloves garlic, finely minced or pressed

4 cups cooked small white beans (see pages 216–17), or two 16-ounce cans
    cannellini beans

2 cups broth (see pages 10–13)

1 pound tomatoes (about 3 medium-size), peeled, cored, seeded, and chopped

2 tablespoons tomato paste

2 sprigs fresh thyme or ½ teaspoon dried

1 teaspoon salt

Freshly ground black pepper to taste

1. Place the oil in a large pot or casserole over medium-high heat. Add the leeks, carrot, and garlic and cook, stirring, for about 5 minutes, until the leeks are wilted.

2. Add the beans, broth, tomatoes, tomato paste, and thyme and bring to a boil over high heat. Turn the heat to medium-low and simmer, uncovered, for 30 minutes. Season with salt and pepper.

MAKES 6 SERVINGS

Lentils Cooked with Soffritto

~ ~ ~

LENTICCHIE ALL'UMBRIA

This is the way our family most enjoys eating lentils. Lentils come in a variety of sizes. I like to use the smallest lentils for this dish because they keep their firmness.

2 tablespoons pure olive oil

1 medium-size onion, finely chopped

1 rib celery, finely chopped

2 cups smallest dried brown lentils

4 cups chicken broth (see pages 11–12)

1. Place the oil in a large heavy saucepan over medium-high heat. Add the onion and celery and cook, stirring, for 2 to 3 minutes, until the onion begins to soften.

2. Place the lentils in a strainer and rinse under cold running water, then add to the saucepan. Stir in the broth and bring to a boil. Lower the heat to medium-low, cover the pan, and simmer for 30 to 40 minutes, until the lentils are tender. Leave them to stand, covered, for about 10 minutes before serving.

MAKES 6 SERVINGS

Lentils with Tubular Pasta

~ ~ ~

LENTICCHIE E TUBETTI

I first tasted this robust dish in Rome at the Ristorante Otello. You can serve it either hot or at room temperature in the summer with a drizzle of your best olive oil.

¾ cup pure olive oil

1 medium-size onion, finely chopped

2 cloves garlic, minced or pressed

1 small, ripe Italian plum tomato, peeled, cored, seeded, and finely chopped

1 cup dried brown lentils

2 cups water

Salt and freshly ground black pepper to taste

1 pound uncooked dry tubetti (short macaroni)

Freshly grated Parmesan cheese

1. Place the oil in a large saucepan over medium-high heat. Add the onion and garlic and cook, stirring, for about 3 minutes, until the onion begins to soften. Add the tomato, lentils, and water. When the liquid comes to a boil, stir, reduce the heat to medium-low, cover, and simmer for 25 to 30 minutes, until the lentils are tender. Add salt and pepper.

2. Meanwhile, bring a large pot of water to a boil over high heat. Add a tablespoon of salt and the tubetti and cook, stirring occasionally, for 7 to 10 minutes, or until the pasta is tender but firm, *al dente*. Drain and transfer to a large serving bowl and cover to keep warm.

3. When the lentils are done, taste and add more salt and pepper if necessary. Pour the lentils over the tubetti, toss well, and serve with Parmesan cheese.

MAKES 6 SERVINGS

White Beans with Escarole and Garlic

~ ~ ~

FAGIOLI E SCAROLA

This recipe was given to me by Jane Lavine, a food consultant in Boston who passed it on from her Italian grandmother. The escarole and white beans combine to make a very robust dish. Serve with a drizzle of your best olive oil.

½ cup pure olive oil

2 large cloves garlic, minced or pressed

1 head escarole, coarsely chopped

4 cups cooked (see pages 216–17) white kidney beans, or two 16-ounce cans
　　cannellini beans

Salt and freshly ground black pepper to taste

1. Place the olive oil in a medium-size casserole with a heavy bottom over medium heat. Add the garlic and cook, stirring, for 1 minute. Add the escarole and cook for about 5 minutes longer, until the escarole is wilted and tender.

2. Add the beans and stir well. Cover and cook for 5 minutes longer, or until the beans are heated through. Season with salt and pepper, then serve.

MAKES 6 SERVINGS

Sicilian-Style Pureed Fava Beans

MACCÙ

There are many variations of this traditional Sicilian dish. You can thin it with broth and serve it as a soup, or combine it with macaroni for an even heartier dish. As it is, *maccù* makes a perfect lunch when served with crusty bread.

4 cups cooked fava beans (see pages 216–17), or two 16-ounce cans
　　fava beans

⅓ cup pure olive oil

1 medium-size onion, finely chopped

1 cup chopped canned tomatoes with their juice

Salt and freshly ground black pepper to taste

2 tablespoons chopped fresh parsley

2 tablespoons extra virgin olive oil

1. Put the beans through a food mill or mash through a sieve to puree and remove the tough outer skins. (Do not use a food processor.)

2. Place the oil in a medium-size saucepan over medium-high heat. Add the onion and cook, stirring, for about 3 minutes, until the onion begins to soften. Add the pureed favas and the tomatoes, season with salt and pepper, and cook, stirring, until the mixture is combined and heated through. Stir in the parsley and transfer to a serving dish. Drizzle the oil over the beans before serving.

MAKES 6 SERVINGS

Fresh Uncooked Baby Favas, Pecorino, and Olive Oil

~ ~ ~

FAVE AL PECORINO

A rite of spring in Italy, fresh favas with pecorino need only really good olive oil and salt and pepper. I have been able to find fresh favas in local ethnic produce markets in the spring and early summer. The long, soft pods are easy to peel, but you need a lot of them. Pungent pecorino cheese is also essential.

3 pounds fresh fava beans in their pods
½ pound fresh imported pecorino cheese, thinly sliced
⅓ cup extra virgin olive oil
Salt and freshly ground black pepper to taste

1. Remove the favas from their pods and divide them equally on six individual serving plates. Arrange the cheese slices around the beans.

2. Combine the olive oil, salt, and pepper and pour over the beans.

MAKES 6 SERVINGS

Chickpeas with Pasta

~ ~ ~

CECI E PASTA

The sumptuous smooth puree of chickpeas makes a rich, flavorful sauce for the corkscrew pasta.

4 cups cooked chickpeas (see pages 216–17), or two 16-ounce cans chickpeas
½ cup pure olive oil
2 cloves garlic, minced or pressed
1 cup chopped canned tomatoes with their juice
Salt and freshly ground black pepper to taste
2 tablespoons chopped fresh parsley
1 pound uncooked dry imported rotini

1. Bring a large pot of water to a boil over high heat.
2. Put the chickpeas through a food mill or mash through a sieve (do not use a food processor) to puree the beans and remove the tough outer skins.
3. Place the oil in a large saucepan over medium-high heat. Add the garlic and cook, stirring, for 1 minute. Add the pureed chickpeas and the tomatoes, season with salt and pepper, and cook, stirring, for about 10 minutes. Stir in the parsley and set aside.
4. When the water comes to a boil, add a tablespoon of salt and the rotini. When the water returns to the boil, cook for 7 to 10 minutes, or until the pasta is tender but firm, *al dente*. Drain well and transfer to a large serving bowl. Add the chickpeas, toss well, and serve immediately.

MAKES 6 SERVINGS

Chickpeas with Chicory

~ ~ ~

CECI E CICORIA

This southern Italian dish can also be prepared with favas.

⅓ cup pure olive oil

2 cloves garlic, minced or crushed

4 cups cooked chickpeas (see pages 216–17), or two 16-ounce cans chickpeas

4 cups chopped fresh chicory

½ cup chopped canned tomatoes with their juice

1. Place the oil in a large saucepan over medium-high heat. Add the garlic and cook, stirring, for about 1 minute.

2. Add the chickpeas and chicory, reduce the heat to medium, and cook, stirring, for 5 to 10 minutes, until the chicory is wilted. Add the tomatoes, stir well to combine, and cook for 5 minutes longer. Serve immediately.

MAKES 6 SERVINGS

Chapter Ten

~ ~ ~

Savory Pies and Omelettes

Torte e Frittate

EVERY CUISINE has its savory—not sweet—pastries. The French have their quiches, the Chinese dim sum. For Italians, it is the versatile pies, known as *torte*, and the egg cakes, or *frittate*, that are studded with all manner of fresh herbs and well-seasoned vegetables. These richly flavored preparations can be served as a first course, as part of a brunch, as a luncheon entree, or as a light supper, which is when egg dishes are traditionally served in Italy.

Savory Pies/Torte

~ ~ ~

Torta is the generic Italian name for any cake or pie, and it refers to sweet as well as savory pastries. The savory *torta* is a creation of early Renaissance cooking. Originally they were prepared in the grandest manner imaginable: extravagantly large fabrications with two crusts, embellishments that made them look like decorated layer cakes, and fillings composed of all types of ingredients, including meats and pastas. Traditionally presented at important banquets, they were whole meals in themselves.

Over the centuries, *torte* have been simplified. Today, with the exception of the traditional Easter multilayered, festively decorated *torta pasqualina*, *torte* are typically prepared with a single crust and a simple, flavorful vegetable or pasta filling bound together with eggs and cheese. All can be prepared with the same basic pastry shell of *pasta frolla*.

Basic Tart Pastry

~ ~ ~

PASTA FROLLA

1¼ cups all-purpose flour

1 teaspoon salt

¼ pound (1 stick) well-chilled unsalted butter, cut into 8 pieces

¼ cup ice water (preferably carbonated)

1. Combine the flour and salt in a mixing bowl. Add the butter, working it into the flour with a pastry blender or fork until the mixture is the texture of cornmeal. Add the water while mixing until the dough holds together. (If you are using a food processor, combine the flour and salt in the workbowl fitted with the steel blade. Add the butter, then turn the machine on for approximately 15 seconds, until the butter-and-flour mixture resembles the texture of cornmeal. With the machine running, add the water and allow the machine to run until the dough forms a ball on the blade. Turn off the machine. Remove the dough from the machine.) Wrap the dough in plastic wrap or waxed paper, press it into a flat, circular shape with your hands, and refrigerate for at least 30 minutes before rolling out..

2. Preheat the oven to 425°F.

3. Unwrap the dough, lightly flour it on both sides, and place it on a well-floured work surface. Using a rolling pin, roll out the dough to form a circle, turning it frequently and lightly flouring on both sides. When the dough is approximately 12 inches in diameter and ¹⁄₁₆ inch thick, fold it in half, then in half again so you have a quarter-circle, and place the folded corner of the dough in the center of a 10-inch tart pan. (You can use any straight-sided pan, a metal tart pan with a removable bottom, or a glass or ceramic pan.)

4. Open the dough so that it fits inside the tart pan. Press the dough lightly into the pan, trim the edges, fold down, and crimp to form a decorative edge around the pan. Prick the pastry all over with the tines of a fork. Cover with plastic wrap and refrigerate or freeze until ready to bake. The crust does not need to be defrosted before baking.

MAKES ONE 10-INCH CRUST

Angel Hair Tart with Sun-Dried Tomatoes and Goat Cheese

~ ~ ~

TORTA DI CAPELLI DI ANGELO AI POMODORI SECCHI E CAPRINO

Pasta tarts were originally created as a way of using up leftover pasta. This tart, made with freshly prepared capellini (angel hair), has a deliciously tangy flavor from the sun-dried tomatoes and goat cheese. The top gets wonderfully crunchy while the inside stays moist and creamy.

1 recipe Basic Tart Pastry (see preceding recipe)

4 ounces uncooked capellini (angel hair pasta), dried or fresh

1 cup ricotta cheese

4 ounces mild goat cheese

4 ounces oil-packed sun-dried tomatoes, drained and chopped

2 large eggs, lightly beaten

1. Preheat the oven to 425°F.

2. Cover the pastry with waxed or parchment paper, fill with dried beans, uncooked rice, or other baking weights, and bake for 15 minutes. Remove the weights and waxed paper and allow the pan to stand on a cooling rack until ready to fill.

3. Bring a large pot of water to a boil over high heat. Add a tablespoon of salt and the capellini and cook, stirring occasionally, for about 5 minutes, until the pasta is tender but firm, *al dente*. Drain and transfer to a large mixing bowl.

4. Add the remaining ingredients and mix vigorously with a wooden spoon until they are all combined. Pour into the prepared crust and bake for 30 to 35 minutes, until the top is evenly browned. Allow to cool slightly before serving.

MAKES ONE 9-INCH TART, OR 6 SERVINGS

Artichoke Pie

~ ~ ~

TORTA DI CARCIOFI

A wonderfully rich pie, inspired by Marcella Hazan's recipe, this is one of the best ways to enjoy artichokes.

1 recipe Basic Tart Pastry (see page 227)

3 tablespoons pure olive oil

4 medium-size artichokes (1½ to 2 pounds total), prepared according to the directions on page 32, halved lengthwise, chokes removed, and sliced lengthwise as thinly as possible

1 clove garlic, finely minced or pressed

Salt and freshly ground black pepper to taste

Juice of ½ lemon

¼ cup water

1 cup ricotta

2 large eggs, lightly beaten

¼ cup freshly grated Parmesan cheese

¼ cup chopped fresh parsley

1. Preheat the oven to 425°F.

2. Cover the pastry with waxed or parchment paper, fill with dried beans or other baking weights, and bake for 15 minutes. Remove the

weights and waxed paper and allow the pan to stand on a cooling rack until ready to fill.

3. Place the olive oil in a medium-size saucepan over medium-high heat. Add the artichokes and garlic, season with salt and pepper, and cook for about 5 minutes, stirring occasionally to keep the artichokes from browning. Add the lemon juice and water, cover the pan, and reduce the heat to medium-low. Simmer for 20 minutes, or until the artichokes are tender. Transfer to a large mixing bowl and allow to cool slightly.

4. Add the remaining ingredients to the artichokes and stir well to combine. Pour the artichoke mixture into the prebaked pie crust and bake for 30 to 35 minutes, or until the top is lightly browned. Allow to cool slightly before serving.

MAKES ONE 9-INCH PIE, OR 6 SERVINGS

Mushroom Tart

~ ~ ~

TORTA DI FUNGHI

The robust, woodsy flavor of the porcini and wild mushrooms gives this tart a hearty, earthy taste.

2 tablespoons unsalted butter

1 tablespoon pure olive oil

1 ounce dried porcini mushrooms, soaked in 1 cup boiling water for 30 minutes, drained, and coarsely chopped

1 pound fresh wild mushrooms (portobello, shiitake, or crimini), stems removed and caps thinly sliced

Salt and freshly ground black pepper to taste

¼ cup chopped fresh parsley

1 tablespoon chopped fresh oregano

3 large eggs, lightly beaten

⅔ cup heavy cream

⅓ cup freshly grated Parmesan cheese

1 recipe Basic Tart Pastry (see page 227)

1. Preheat the oven to 350°F.

2. Place the butter and olive oil together in a medium-size saucepan over medium-high heat. Add all the mushrooms, season with salt and pepper, and cook, stirring, for 7 to 10 minutes, until the fresh mushrooms are tender. Transfer to a medium-size mixing bowl, stir in the parsley and oregano, and allow to cool for about 15 minutes.

3. Add the eggs, cream, and Parmesan to the mushroom mixture and mix well with a wooden spoon. Pour the mixture into the prepared unbaked pie crust. Place in the oven and bake for approximately 45 minutes, until the filling is set and the crust is lightly browned. Allow to cool slightly before serving.

MAKES ONE 9-INCH TART, OR 6 SERVINGS

Spinach Tart

~ ~ ~

TORTA D'ERBAZZONE

Fresh and light, this *torta* is the perfect centerpiece for a springtime lunch.

1 recipe Basic Tart Pastry (see page 227)

One 10-ounce package fresh spinach, thoroughly washed and stems removed, or one 10-ounce package frozen chopped spinach

3 tablespoons pure olive oil

1 medium-size onion, chopped

1 cup ricotta

2 large eggs, lightly beaten

¼ cup freshly grated Parmesan cheese

Salt and freshly ground black pepper to taste

1. Preheat the oven to 425°F.

2. Cover the pastry with waxed or parchment paper, fill with dried beans or other baking weights, and bake for 15 minutes. Remove the weights and waxed paper and allow the pan to stand on a cooling rack until ready to fill.

3. Cook the spinach in a large saucepan over medium-high heat for about 5 minutes, until wilted. Drain as much liquid as possible from the spinach and chop. (If you are using frozen spinach, cook according to the directions on the package and drain.) Transfer the spinach to a large mixing bowl.

4. Place the oil in a small saucepan over medium-high heat. Add the onion and cook, stirring, for 7 to 10 minutes, until translucent. Add the onion to the spinach, along with the remaining ingredients, and stir vigorously with a wooden spoon to combine. Pour into the pie crust and bake for about 30 to 35 minutes, until the filling is set and the crust and top are browned. Allow to cool slightly before serving.

MAKES ONE 9-INCH TART, OR 6 SERVINGS

Omelettes/Frittate
~ ~ ~

The *frittata*, which is often referred to as an Italian version of the French omelette, actually more closely resembles the Spanish *tortilla* because it is always served whole and round, rather than folded.

You make *frittate* with whole eggs—only lightly beaten so as not to incorporate too much air into them—that are combined with herbs and vegetables and freshly grated Parmesan cheese. A *frittata* is traditionally flipped to cook both sides, but that awkward technique can be sidestepped by finishing the cooking of the *frittata* under the oven broiler. Be careful not to overcook the frittata as it becomes dry and less flavorful. A *frittata* is one of my favorite brunch dishes, served with sliced fresh tomatoes.

Asparagus Frittata
~ ~ ~

FRITTATA AGLI ASPARAGI

2 tablespoons pure olive oil

1 pound skinny asparagus spears, tough bottom parts removed and cut into
  2-inch pieces

6 large eggs

1 tablespoon water

¼ cup freshly grated Parmesan cheese

Salt and freshly ground black pepper to taste

2 tablespoons unsalted butter

2 tablespoons chopped fresh parsley

1. Place the olive oil in a 10-inch skillet or omelette pan, preferably one with a nonstick surface, over medium-high heat. Add the asparagus and cook, stirring occasionally, for 5 minutes, or until the asparagus is tender.

2. Preheat the oven broiler.

3. Break the eggs into a medium-size mixing bowl. Add the water, Parmesan, salt, and pepper and lightly beat. Using a fork or slotted spoon, transfer the asparagus to the egg mixture and stir with a wooden spoon to combine. Pour off any excess oil remaining in the pan.

4. Melt the butter in the skillet over medium heat. When the butter begins to foam, add the egg-and-asparagus mixture. Reduce the heat to low and cook slowly, without stirring, for about 7 minutes, or until the eggs are set and only the egg at the top is uncooked. Place the pan in the oven and broil for 1 to 3 minutes, watching closely, until the top is lightly browned and the eggs are set.

5. Loosen the underside of the *frittata* with a large spatula and gently slide it onto a preheated round serving dish. Sprinkle the parsley over the top and serve at once.

MAKES 6 SERVINGS

Savory Pies and Omelettes

Parsley, Marjoram, Chives, and Basil Frittata

~ ~ ~

FRITTATA ALLE ERBE

A variety of herbs give this *frittata* a fresh flavor. Vary the herbs, depending on what is available.

6 large eggs

1 tablespoon water

¼ cup freshly grated Parmesan cheese

1 cup packed chopped fresh herbs (a mixture of parsley, basil, chives, marjoram, thyme, oregano, sage)

Salt and freshly ground black pepper to taste

2 tablespoons pure olive oil

1 tablespoon unsalted butter

1. Break the eggs into a medium-size mixing bowl and lightly beat with a fork. Stir in the water, Parmesan, herbs, salt, and pepper.

2. Preheat the oven broiler.

3. Place the oil and butter in a 10-inch skillet or omelette pan, preferably one with a nonstick surface, over medium-low heat. When the butter begins to foam, add the egg mixture, reduce the heat to low, and cook slowly, without stirring, for 7 to 10 minutes, until the eggs are mostly set and only the egg on the top is uncooked. Place the pan under the broiler for 1 to 3 minutes, watching closely, until the top is lightly browned and the eggs are set.

4. Loosen the underside of the *frittata* with a large spatula and gently slide it onto a preheated round serving dish. Serve immediately.

MAKES 6 SERVINGS

Fennel Frittata

~ ~ ~

FRITTATA DI FINOCCHIO

The lightly sautéed fennel gives this *frittata* a wonderfully mild anise flavor and tender texture.

¼ cup olive oil

1 small fennel bulb, stalks and leaves cut away and discarded, and sliced crosswise as thinly as possible

Salt and freshly ground black pepper to taste

6 large eggs

1 tablespoon water

¼ cup freshly grated Parmesan cheese, plus extra for serving

2 tablespoons unsalted butter

1. Place the olive oil in a 10-inch sauté or omelette pan, preferably one with a nonstick surface, over medium-high heat. Add the sliced fennel, season with salt and pepper, and cook for about 10 minutes, stirring occasionally, until the fennel is tender and just beginning to brown.

2. Break the eggs into a medium-size mixing bowl and beat lightly with a fork. Stir in the water and Parmesan cheese, season with salt and pepper, and beat lightly. Using a slotted spoon, transfer the fennel to the egg mixture and stir well to combine. Pour off any excess oil remaining in the pan.

3. Preheat the oven broiler.

4. Melt the butter in the sauté pan over medium heat. When the butter foams, add the egg-and-fennel mixture. Reduce the heat to low and cook slowly, without stirring, for 7 to 10 minutes, until the eggs are set and only the egg at the top is uncooked. Place the pan under the oven broiler and broil for 1 to 3 minutes, watching closely, until the top is lightly browned and the eggs are set.

5. Loosen the underside of the *frittata* with a large spatula and gently slide it onto a preheated round serving dish. Serve at once with Parmesan cheese.

MAKES 6 SERVINGS

Leek Frittata

~ ~ ~

FRITTATA DI PORRI

The mild oniony flavor of the leeks infuses the eggs with a delicious flavor.

3 tablespoons pure olive oil

2 large leeks, white part only, cleaned (see page 47) and sliced as thinly as possible

6 large eggs

1 tablespoon water

¼ cup freshly grated Parmesan cheese, plus extra for serving

2 tablespoons chopped fresh chives

Salt and freshly ground black pepper to taste

2 tablespoons unsalted butter

1. Place the oil in a 10-inch sauté or omelette pan, preferably one with a nonstick surface, over medium-high heat. Add the leeks and cook, stirring, for 5 to 7 minutes, until the leeks are completely tender.

2. Break the eggs into a medium-size mixing bowl and beat lightly with a fork. Stir in the water, Parmesan cheese, and chives, season with salt and pepper, and beat lightly. Using a slotted spoon, transfer the leeks to the egg mixture and stir well to combine. Pour off any excess oil remaining in the pan.

3. Preheat the oven broiler.

4. Melt the butter in the sauté pan over medium heat. When the butter foams, add the egg-and-leek mixture. Reduce the heat to low and cook slowly, without stirring, for 7 to 10 minutes, until the eggs are set and only the egg at the top is uncooked. Place the pan under the oven broiler and broil for 1 to 3 minutes, watching closely, until the top is lightly browned and the eggs are set.

5. Loosen the underside of the *frittata* with a large spatula and gently slide it onto a preheated round serving dish. Serve at once with Parmesan cheese.

MAKES 6 SERVINGS

Mushroom Frittata

~ ~ ~

FRITTATA DI FUNGHI

A very mushroomy dish—even the eggs take on the pale taupe color of the *funghi*.

3 tablespoons pure olive oil

½ pound fresh wild mushrooms (portobello, shiitake, or crimini), stems removed and caps thinly sliced

Salt and freshly ground black pepper to taste

6 large eggs

1 tablespoon water

¼ cup freshly grated Parmesan cheese

¼ cup chopped fresh parsley

2 tablespoons unsalted butter

1. Place the oil in a 10-inch sauté or omelette pan, preferably one with a nonstick surface, over medium-high heat. Add the mushrooms, salt, and pepper and cook, stirring, for about 7 minutes, until the mushrooms are tender.

2. Break the eggs into a medium-size mixing bowl and beat them lightly with a fork. Stir in the water, Parmesan, and parsley. Transfer the mushrooms to the egg mixture with a slotted spoon and pour off any excess oil remaining in the pan.

3. Preheat the oven broiler.

4. Melt the butter in the sauté pan over medium heat. When the butter foams, add the egg-and-mushroom mixture. Reduce the heat to low and cook slowly, without stirring, for 7 to 10 minutes, until the eggs are set and only the egg at the top is uncooked. Place the pan under the oven broiler and broil for 1 to 3 minutes, watching closely, until the top is lightly browned and the eggs are set.

5. Loosen the underside of the *frittata* with a large spatula and gently slide it onto a preheated round serving dish. Serve at once.

MAKES 6 SERVINGS

Pasta Frittata

~ ~ ~

FRITTATA DI PASTA

This satisfying *frittata* makes a perfect light supper dish. It's also a great way to use leftover pasta, if you have some on hand.

¼ cup pure olive oil

1 tablespoon unsalted butter

2 cups cooked penne (or other leftover pasta)

6 large eggs

Salt and freshly ground black pepper to taste

1 tablespoon water

¼ cup freshly grated Parmesan cheese

2 tablespoons chopped fresh parsley

1. Place the oil and butter in a 10-inch sauté or omelette pan, preferably one with a nonstick surface, over medium-high heat. Add the pasta and cook, stirring, for 5 to 7 minutes, until the pasta is just beginning to brown.

2. Preheat the oven broiler.

3. Break the eggs into a medium-size mixing bowl. Season with salt and pepper, add the water and Parmesan, and beat lightly. Pour the eggs over the pasta, reduce the heat to low, and cook slowly, without stirring, for 7 to 10 minutes, until the eggs are set and only the egg at the top is uncooked. Place the pan under the oven broiler and broil for 1 to 3 minutes, watching closely, until the top is lightly browned and the eggs are set.

4. Loosen the underside of the *frittata* with a large spatula and gently slide it onto a preheated round serving dish. Sprinkle the parsley over the top and serve at once.

MAKES 6 SERVINGS

Potato and Onion Frittata

~ ~ ~

FRITTATA DI PATATE E CIPOLLE

A hearty and deliciously satisfying dish that will appeal to any palate.

3 *tablespoons pure olive oil*

1 *large baking potato, peeled and thinly sliced*

1 *medium-size onion, thinly sliced*

Salt and freshly ground black pepper to taste

6 *large eggs*

1 *tablespoon water*

¼ *cup freshly grated Parmesan cheese*

2 *fresh sage leaves, shredded*

2 *tablespoons unsalted butter*

2 *tablespoons chopped fresh parsley*

1. Place the oil in a 10-inch sauté or omelette pan, preferably one with a nonstick surface, over medium-high heat. Add the potato and onion, season with salt and pepper, and cook for 10 to 12 minutes, stirring frequently, until the potatoes are tender.

2. Break the eggs into a medium-size mixing bowl. Add the water, Parmesan, and sage and beat lightly. Using a slotted spoon, transfer the potato-and-onion mixture to the bowl with the eggs. Stir well to combine. Pour off any excess oil remaining in the pan.

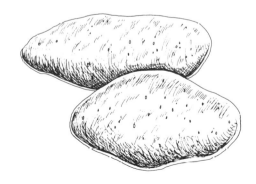

3. Preheat the oven broiler.

4. Melt the butter in the sauté pan over medium heat. When the butter foams, add the egg-and-potato mixture. Reduce the heat to low and cook slowly, without stirring, for 7 to 10 minutes, until the eggs are mostly set and only the egg at the top is uncooked. Place the pan under the oven broiler and broil for 1 to 3 minutes, watching closely, until the top is lightly browned and the eggs are set.

5. Loosen the underside of the *frittata* with a large spatula and gently slide it onto a preheated round serving dish. Sprinkle the parsley over the top and serve at once.

MAKES 6 SERVINGS

Zucchini Frittata

~ ~ ~

FRITTATA DI ZUCCHINE

Green and fresh tasting—this is one of my favorite *frittate*. Add a lot of fresh basil for a delicious accent of flavor.

½ pound zucchini (about 2 small), sliced as thinly as possible, preferably in a food processor with a slicing disk or on a mandoline

Salt

3 tablespoons pure olive oil

6 large eggs

1 tablespoon water

¼ cup freshly grated Parmesan cheese

2 tablespoons chopped fresh basil

¼ cup chopped fresh parsley

Salt and freshly ground black pepper to taste

2 tablespoons unsalted butter

1. Place the zucchini in a strainer, sprinkle liberally with salt, and allow to stand for 30 minutes or longer, until it releases its water. Pat the zucchini dry with paper towels.

2. Heat the oil in a 10-inch sauté or omelette pan, preferably one

with a nonstick surface, over medium heat. Add the zucchini and cook, stirring, for 7 to 10 minutes, until the zucchini is tender.

3. Preheat the oven broiler.

4. Break the eggs into a medium-size mixing bowl and beat them lightly with a fork. Stir in the water, Parmesan, basil, parsley, salt, and pepper. Using a slotted spoon, transfer the zucchini into the mixing bowl with eggs. Pour off any excess oil remaining in the pan.

5. Melt the butter in the sauté pan over medium heat. When the butter foams, add the egg-and-zucchini mixture. Reduce the heat to low and cook slowly, without stirring, for 7 to 10 minutes, until the eggs are set and only the egg at the top is uncooked. Place the pan under the oven broiler and broil for 1 to 3 minutes, watching closely, until the top is lightly browned and the eggs are set.

6. Loosen the underside of the *frittata* with a large spatula and gently slide it onto a preheated round serving dish. Serve at once.

MAKES 6 SERVINGS

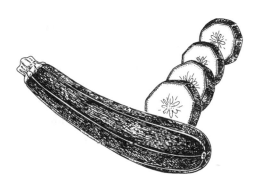

Chapter Eleven

~ ~ ~

Salads

Insalate

THE ROMANS HAVE a saying that it takes four people to make a proper salad: a miser for the vinegar, a spendthrift for the olive oil, a wiseman to season it, and a madman to toss it.

At its most basic, an Italian *insalata* is either an *insalata verde*, leafy greens, or an *insalata mista*, which consists of greens with the addition of chicory (red and green), diced raw cucumber, sliced celery, grated carrots, radishes, and sliced tomatoes. These salads are typically seasoned only with salt, high-quality olive oil, and vinegar. In Italy, they are almost always served as a *contorni*, or accompaniment to the main course.

Insalata can also be more varied, and can consist of almost any chilled combination of ingredients, including rice, beans, pasta, or bread combined with cooked or raw vegetables and cheeses. These *insalate*, however, are more substantial dishes than the mixed greens, and are usually served either as the first course to a multicourse meal or as the main course lunch.

Mixed Green Salad

~ ~ ~

INSALATA MISTA

This is probably the most common salad found in Italy. The greens should always be crisp and fresh, and well rinsed in several changes of cold water to be sure no dirt or grit is left on the leaves, then patted or spun dry. Just as important is the dressing, which is a delicate combination of mostly olive oil with just a hint of vinegar or lemon juice and salt as a seasoning. The dressing should wet—never drown—the greens.

8 cups greens (combination of redleaf, Boston, or romaine lettuce, curly-leaf chicory, radicchio, and arugula), stems removed and torn into bite-size pieces

1 scallion, white and green parts, finely chopped

Salt to taste

3 tablespoons extra virgin olive oil

1 teaspoon red wine vinegar

1. Combine the greens and scallion in a serving bowl. Refrigerate, uncovered, until ready to serve.

2. Just before serving, season the salad with salt. Pour the olive oil and then the vinegar over the lettuce. Toss well and serve.

MAKES 4 SERVINGS

Wild Greens with Grilled Goat Cheese

~ ~ ~

INSALATA MISTICANZA CON CAPRINO ALLA GRIGLIA

Traditionally, a *misticanza* is a Roman salad made with a variety—sometimes as many as twenty—of wild greens. Specialty greengrocers in many areas of this country now sell what they are calling mesclun and restaurants call field greens. It is the closest we can get to approximating the Italian *misticanza*. If you can't find mesclun, use a mixture of lettuce greens, arugula, radicchio, dandelion, and fresh herbs. The grilled goat cheese is my own addition. I like the way its sharp flavor complements the sweetness of the balsamic vinaigrette and the mildly bitter taste of the greens.

6 cups mesclun (see note below)

4 ounces goat cheese, preferably log shape, cut into 4 even-size pieces

½ cup plain bread crumbs

Salt to taste

3 tablespoons extra virgin olive oil

1 teaspoon balsamic vinegar

1. Preheat the oven broiler.

2. Place the greens in a serving bowl and refrigerate until ready to serve.

3. Place the goat cheese pieces on a flat plate and pour the bread crumbs over them, turning the pieces once to coat both sides. Using your fingers, gently press the bread crumbs into the cheese. Transfer the cheese to a piece of aluminum foil and place under the broiler. Broil for 3 to 5 minutes, until the bread crumbs are brown.

4. Season the salad greens with salt, add the oil and vinegar, and toss well. Arrange the greens on four individual serving plates, top each serving with a piece of goat cheese, and serve.

MAKES 4 SERVINGS

Note: Mesclun comes washed and ready to serve. However, if you are using lettuce and other greens, they should be rinsed in several changes of cold water and dried.

Salad of Tomatoes, Garlic, Basil, Olives, and Salty Ricotta

~ ~ ~

INSALATA SICILIANA

Salty ricotta is a strong, distinctively flavored cheese. You can substitute Greek feta or a fresh mozzarella for a milder taste.

1 pint cherry tomatoes, stems removed and halved

½ cup Gaeta olives, pitted

4 ounces salty hard ricotta (see note below)
1 tablespoon chopped fresh basil
1 clove garlic, minced or pressed
Freshly ground black pepper to taste
3 tablespoons pure olive oil

Place the tomatoes in a serving bowl with the olives, cheese, basil, and garlic. Season with black pepper and add the olive oil. Toss well and serve.

MAKES 4 SERVINGS

Note: Hard ricotta is available in Italian food stores and some good cheese shops.

Tomato, Basil, and Mozzarella Salad
~ ~ ~
INSALATA CAPRESE

A popular salad everywhere, this is the traditional version. When delicious, ripe tomatoes are not available, substitute sun-dried tomatoes or roasted yellow peppers.

und (about) buffalo mozzarella (see page 8), cut into ¼-inch-thick slices

!ium-size ripe tomatoes, cored and sliced ¼ inch thick

nd freshly ground black pepper to taste

. . ...p extra virgin olive oil

4 large fresh basil leaves, shredded

1. Arrange the mozzarella slices in a single layer on a serving platter, alternating a piece of cheese with a slice of tomato. This can be prepared ahead of time and refrigerated until ready to serve.

2. When you are ready to serve, sprinkle the cheese and tomato slices with salt and pepper and drizzle the oil over the top. Garnish with the basil and serve.

MAKES 4 SERVINGS

Salad of Raw Artichokes, Radicchio, and Parmesan Cheese

~ ~ ~

INSALATA DI CARCIOFI, GRANA, E RADICCHIO

Use only very fresh, small artichokes and the best Parmesan. This salad has a delicious lemony taste. The recipe was inspired by a dish I tasted at the restaurant Le Madri in New York City.

12 carciofini, very small artichokes (about 2 inches high)

½ cup extra virgin olive oil

¼ cup fresh lemon juice

1 cup shredded radicchio leaves

One 4-ounce (about) piece Parmigiano-Reggiano cheese, shaved into
    paper-thin slices

Salt and freshly ground black pepper to taste

1. Prepare the artichokes according to the directions on page 32. When you are finished trimming them, they should be about the size of a large egg.

2. Pat the artichokes dry with a paper towel. Cut them in half length-

wise and slice them as thinly as possible so that they are almost shredded. Transfer the sliced artichokes to a bowl and immediately add the olive oil and lemon juice. Mix well.

3. Combine the radicchio and most of the cheese with the artichokes and stir to combine. Season lightly with salt. Be careful not to oversalt since the cheese will also add saltiness to the salad.

4. Divide the mixture evenly among six plates. Place some of the remaining Parmesan cheese on each serving. Serve immediately with freshly ground black pepper.

MAKES 6 SERVINGS

Salad of Fresh Mushrooms and Parmesan Cheese

~ ~ ~

INSALATA DI FUNGHI E PARMIGIANO REGGIANO

I first tasted this salad in a hotel restaurant in Sirmione, a medieval walled city on Lake Garda in northern Italy. I have no idea what variety of mushrooms they served, but I have made this salad many times and have used most of the "wild" varieties available in my grocery store, as well as plain white mushrooms, all with wonderful results. Use the freshest, best-quality mushrooms, since the taste of the mushrooms really comes through.

1 pound fresh mushrooms (crimini, portobello, shiitake, or white cultivated, or
*   a mixture of two or more varieties), stems removed, caps thinly sliced*
¼ pound Parmigiano-Reggiano cheese, shaved paper thin
⅓ cup extra virgin olive oil
3 tablespoons fresh lemon juice
Freshly ground black pepper to taste
Salt

1. Place the mushrooms and cheese in a medium-size serving bowl.
2. Combine the oil, lemon juice, and a few grinds of the black pepper

in a small mixing bowl. Pour over the mushroom-and-cheese mixture and toss gently but thoroughly to distribute the dressing. Add more oil, a tablespoon at a time, if the mixture seems too dry. Season lightly with salt. Be careful not to oversalt since the cheese will also add saltiness. Serve immediately.

MAKES 6 SERVINGS

Pasta Salad with Broccoli and Sweet Red Pepper

~ ~ ~

FUSILLI AI BROCCOLI E PEPERONI

Lively green and red colors make this a festive dish. The garlicky dressing clings to the ridges of the pasta.

1 bunch fresh broccoli, thick stems removed and cut into small florets
1 pound uncooked dry imported fusilli (corkscrew pasta)
1 cup fresh parsley leaves
1 clove garlic, peeled
½ cup extra virgin olive oil
1 teaspoon red wine vinegar
Salt and freshly ground black pepper to taste
1 large red bell pepper, cored, seeded, and thinly sliced

1. Place the broccoli florets in a large mixing bowl, cover with cold water, and allow to stand for 30 minutes. Drain. Place the broccoli in a

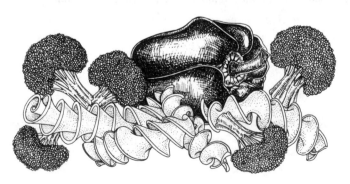

medium-size saucepan fitted with a steamer basket or tray over boiling water. Cover and cook for 5 minutes. Drain and refresh under cold water. Set aside.

2. Bring a large pot of water to a boil over high heat. Add a tablespoon of salt and the fusilli and cook, stirring occasionally, for 7 to 10 minutes, until tender but firm, *al dente*. Drain well and transfer to a large mixing bowl.

3. Combine the parsley and garlic in a food processor fitted with the steel blade. Turn the machine on and process for about 15 seconds, until the parsley and garlic are finely chopped. With the machine running, add the olive oil in a steady stream and the vinegar. Pour over the pasta, mix well, and allow to cool to room temperature. Add the broccoli to the pasta, season with salt and pepper, and toss to combine. Transfer to a serving dish and garnish with the red pepper slices.

MAKES 6 SERVINGS

Salad of Cold Pennoni with Fresh Tomatoes and Basil

~ ~ ~

INSALATA DI PENNONI FREDDE AL POMODORO E BASILICO

The perfect summertime salad. I ate it first on a steamy July day in a trattoria in Florence. Use the ripest, reddest tomatoes and lots of the freshest basil.

1 pound uncooked imported pennoni (large penne)
1/4 cup extra virgin olive oil, plus a little extra
2 pounds fresh, ripe tomatoes, peeled, cored, seeded, and coarsely chopped
1/2 cup packed fresh basil leaves, julienned or coarsely chopped
1 clove garlic, finely minced or pressed
Salt and freshly ground black pepper to taste

1. Bring a large pot of water to a boil over high heat. Add a tablespoon of salt and the pennoni and cook, stirring occasionally, for 7 to 10 minutes, until tender but firm, *al dente*. Drain and transfer to a large serving bowl. Drizzle some olive oil over the pasta, toss well, cover, and allow to cool to room temperature.

2. Combine the olive oil with the tomatoes, basil, garlic, salt, and pepper in a small mixing bowl. When the pasta is cool, add the tomato mixture, toss well, and serve.

MAKES 6 SERVINGS

Rice Salad

~ ~ ~

INSALATA DI RISO

Tender grains of rice studded with a confetti of fresh, crisp vegetables and ripe black olives make this a colorful, fresh-tasting salad.

1 cup uncooked Italian short-grain rice (Arborio, Vialone, or Carnaroli)

3 cups water

Salt to taste

3 small, fresh Italian plum tomatoes, cored, seeded, and finely chopped

½ cup finely chopped zucchini

⅓ cup finely chopped yellow bell pepper

½ cup grated carrot

½ cup pitted Gaeta olives, chopped

Freshly ground black pepper to taste

¼ cup extra virgin olive oil

1 tablespoon red wine vinegar

1. Combine the rice and water with salt in a medium-size saucepan and bring the water to a boil over medium-high heat. Then stir the rice once, cover, reduce the heat to medium-low, and simmer for about 18 minutes, until the rice is tender but firm, *al dente*. Drain the rice in a colander and refresh under cold water. Transfer to a large serving bowl, cover, and allow to cool slightly.

2. When the rice is at room temperature, add the tomatoes, zucchini, pepper, carrot, and olives, then season with salt and pepper. Add the olive oil and vinegar, toss well, and serve.

MAKES 6 SERVINGS

Bread Salad

~ ~ ~

PANZANELLA

This Tuscan salad makes a very satisfying lunch on a hot day. Traditional versions call for the bread to be soaked first in water. I like to use dry, crusty bread: it adds delicious texture to the salad.

3 cups cubed crusty bread (sourdough, French, or peasant bread; see pages 4–5)

6 small Italian plum tomatoes, cored, seeded, and diced

1 large cucumber, seeded and diced

1 medium-size red onion, finely chopped

¼ cup chopped fresh parsley

Salt and freshly ground black pepper to taste

¼ cup extra virgin olive oil

1 tablespoon red wine vinegar

1. Preheat the oven to 350°F. Spread the bread cubes on an ungreased jelly roll pan in a single layer and place in the oven for 10 minutes. Transfer to a large serving bowl and allow to cool slightly.

2. Add the tomatoes, cucumber, onion, and parsley, season with salt and pepper, pour in the oil and vinegar, and toss well. Allow to stand for at least 15 minutes before serving. Toss again and serve.

MAKES 6 SERVINGS

Lentil Salad

~ ~ ~

INSALATA DI LENTICCHIE

Simple but very satisfying. Serve this salad on a bed of crisp greens with some fresh crusty bread.

1 cup brown lentils

4 cups water

Salt and freshly ground black pepper to taste

¼ cup chopped red onion

½ cup finely chopped carrot

1 tablespoon chopped fresh parsley

¼ cup extra virgin olive oil

1 tablespoon red wine vinegar

1. Combine the lentils and water in a large saucepan and bring the water to a boil over high heat. Then cover the pan, reduce the heat to medium-low, and simmer for 30 to 35 minutes, until the lentils are tender. Drain well, cover, and allow to cool to room temperature.

2. Transfer the lentils to a medium-size serving bowl and season with salt and pepper. Add the onion, carrot, parsley, olive oil, and vinegar and toss well to combine before serving.

MAKES 4 SERVINGS

Salad of White Beans and Green Onions

~ ~ ~

INSALATA DI CANNELLINI

This is my husband's favorite Saturday lunch, served with fresh crusty bread. Tuna is traditional, but not essential. In Venice we ate it with smoked tune roe, *bottarga*.

2 cups cooked white kidney beans (see pages 216–17), or one 16-ounce can

cannellini beans, drained and rinsed

2 large scallions, white and green parts, finely chopped

One 3-ounce can tuna, drained and flaked (optional)

Salt and freshly ground black pepper to taste

3 tablespoons olive oil

1 teaspoon vinegar

Combine the beans, scallions, and tuna in a medium-size serving bowl, season with salt and pepper, and add the olive oil and vinegar. Toss well and serve.

MAKES 4 SERVINGS

Fennel and Cucumber Salad

~ ~ ~

INSALATA DI FINOCCHIO E CETRIOLI

The aromatic anise flavor of the *finocchio* gives this refreshing salad its distinctive taste. Serve this as a first course in combination with one or more other salads or antipasti.

1 medium-size fennel bulb, stalks and leaves removed

1 large cucumber, peeled

3 tablespoons extra virgin olive oil

Juice of 1 lemon

1 clove garlic, minced or pressed

1/4 cup chopped fresh parsley

Salt and freshly ground black pepper to taste

1. Cut the fennel bulb in half lengthwise and slice across the bulb as thinly as possible, preferably in a food processor fitted with a slicing disk or with a mandoline. Cut the cucumber in half lengthwise, cut out and discard the seeds, and slice crosswise as thinly as possible.

2. Combine the sliced fennel and cucumber in a medium-size serving bowl. Add the oil, lemon juice, garlic, and parsley and season with salt and pepper. Toss well to combine, cover, and allow to stand for at least an hour at room temperature, stirring occasionally, before serving.

MAKES 4 SERVINGS

Salad of Sliced Red Onion and Oranges

~ ~ ~

INSALATA DI CIPOLLINE E ARANCE ALLA SICILIANA

One of the simplest and best salads there is. This recipe comes from Sicily, where most of Italy's oranges grow.

6 Valencia oranges, peeled and thinly sliced
1 medium-size red onion, thinly sliced
¼ cup extra virgin olive oil
¼ cup pitted oil-cured olives

Arrange the orange and onion slices on a large serving plate in a single layer, alternating them in an overlapping fashion. Drizzle the olive oil over the top, sprinkle with the olives, and serve.

MAKES 6 SERVINGS

Asparagus Vinaigrette

~ ~ ~

INSALATA DI ASPARAGI

A traditional and popular way to eat asparagus in Italy. Use the freshest, fattest asparagus spears you can find.

2 pounds fresh asparagus, tough bottom parts trimmed away and, if the spears
　　are thick, peeled
Salt and freshly ground black pepper to taste
⅓ cup extra virgin olive oil
2 teaspoons red wine vinegar

1. Cook the asparagus according to the directions on page 34.
2. Transfer the cooked asparagus to a serving platter and sprinkle
with salt and pepper.
3. Combine the oil and vinegar in a small bowl and pour over the
asparagus. Turn the spears around a few times to be sure they are evenly
coated. Cover and allow the asparagus to cool to lukewarm or room temperature before serving.

MAKES 6 SERVINGS

Salad of Grated Raw Zucchini
~ ~ ~
INSALATA DI ZUCCHINE FRESCHE

This salad captures all the best flavor of zucchini. Use only the
smallest, just-picked zucchini, if you can find them, for the freshest taste.
This recipe comes from the restaurant Vipore outside Lucca, Italy.

4 small zucchini (1 inch in diameter by about 6 inches long), grated
Salt
1 small clove garlic, minced or pressed
2 tablespoons extra virgin olive oil
1 small, ripe tomato, peeled, cored, seeded, and chopped
2 tablespoons chopped fresh parsley
Freshly ground black pepper to taste

lace the grated zucchini in a colander. Sprinkle liberally with salt
/ to stand for 30 minutes, until it releases its water. Lightly pat
th paper towels.

?ut the zucchini in a small serving bowl and add the garlic, olive
oil, tomato, and parsley. Toss well to combine the ingredients. Season
with pepper and more salt, if necessary, and serve.

MAKES 4 SERVINGS

Potato and String Bean Salad

~ ~ ~

INSALATE DI PATATE E FAGIOLINI

This is a favorite summer salad to serve with grilled fish or meat. The
potatoes and string beans are cooked just until they are tender and are
dressed while they're still warm so they absorb the delicious flavors of the
sharp wine vinegar and fruity extra virgin olive oil.

3 pounds small red potatoes (all about the same size, 2 inches in diameter)

1 pound fresh string beans, trimmed

Salt and freshly ground black pepper to taste

⅓ cup extra virgin olive oil

1 teaspoon red wine vinegar

2 scallions, white and green parts, chopped

2 tablespoons chopped fresh parsley

1. Place the potatoes in a large saucepan with water to cover and
bring the water to a boil over high heat. Turn the heat down to medium-
low and simmer for about 20 minutes, just until the potatoes are tender
when pierced with a sharp knife. Watch carefully so that the potatoes do
not crack and fall apart. Drain and allow to stand until cool enough to
handle with your bare hands. Cut the potatoes into quarters and place
them in a large mixing bowl.

2. Meanwhile, place the string beans in a steamer basket over boiling
water. Cover and cook for 8 minutes. Put the beans in a colander and rinse
under cold running water. Add the beans to the bowl with the potatoes.
Season with salt and pepper.

3. Combine the oil and vinegar in a small mixing bowl, and pour over the potatoes and beans. Toss well and allow to stand, loosely covered with plastic wrap or waxed paper, until completely cool. Just before serving, add the scallions and parsley and toss well.

MAKES 6 SERVINGS

Chapter Twelve

~ ~ ~

Fruit Desserts
Dolci di Frutta

FROM THE MOUNTAINOUS northern regions of Piedmont, Lombardy, and the Veneto to the lush fields and orchards of Campania, Reggio-Calabria, and Sicily, fruits of all kinds grow in abundance in Italy. Particularly renowned are the pears and apples from the Valle d'Aosta, cherries from Lazio, peaches and plums from the Marches, figs from Liguria and Tuscany, raspberries from Lombardy, oranges and lemons from Sicily, walnuts from Sorrento, chestnuts from Tuscany, and grapes from everywhere.

Much of the fruit found in Italian cuisine today is indigenous to Italy and has been eaten there since the days of the Roman Empire. For centuries Italians have been enjoying cherries, peaches, pears, and figs. Lemons, native to southern Italy, were cherished by the Romans for their medicinal properties.

In ancient Rome, fresh fruits were treated like vegetables, served at the beginning of a meal and prepared with savory seasonings. It wasn't until the eighteenth century that fruit became the mainstay of Italian desserts.

A bowl of fresh, unadulterated fruit in season—wonderful brown Bosc pears or grapes in the fall and winter, juicy, pink-blushed peaches and apricots and sweet, luscious berries in the spring and summer—and a fresh fruit salad, *macedonia*, are the most common desserts found in Italy. The more elaborate cakes, pastries, and sweet breads that are rarely part of an Italian meal but are essential for midmorning or afternoon snacks, special occasions, and religious holidays are typically prepared at least in part with dried, candied, or fresh fruit. And fruit dominates the many flavors of *gelati*, *sorbetti*, and *granite*.

Nuts, particularly almonds, walnuts, and hazelnuts, grow in abundance throughout the Italian peninsula, and pistachios grow in Sicily. And, like fresh fruit, they are also an important ingredient in the variety of baked sweets. In season, nuts are also often enjoyed on their own after a meal with a glass of good dessert wine.

Apples

~ ~ ~

MELE

Apples are a staple of the cuisine of northern Italy, with the greatest variety of apple desserts coming from the regions of Lombardy, Piedmont, and the Valle d'Aosta. When apples are in season there, they're prepared in rich apple tarts and sweet, baked apples. Elsewhere in Italy, apples are a mainstay of the fall fruit salad. In Liguria, you might also find apples dipped in batter and deep-fried as part of a savory *fritto misto* (a mixture of fried fruit and vegetables).

Apricots

~ ~ ~

ALBICOCCHE

Apricots, unlike most of the fruits that grow in Italy today, were brought there from other parts of the world. The apricot is said to have come to Italy with the Saracens from the Middle East around A.D. 700 or 800, and for centuries was primarily coveted for medicinal purposes.

Today apricots grow in abundance in the southern and central regions of Italy, and are almost always eaten raw. When Italian cooks prepare apricots, they typically make fruit tarts, crystallized fruit, or preserves, which in turn are used to sweeten other desserts such as the Neapolitan custard cream, *zuppa inglese*.

Berries: Strawberries, Raspberries, Blueberries

~ ~ ~

FRAGOLE, LAMPONI, MIRTILLI

A variety of berries grow throughout Italy and are enjoyed there as much as they are here. They are usually eaten naturally and uncooked. Sometimes they are dressed with a little bit of lemon juice and sugar and embellished with a hearty serving of sweet cream or mascarpone whipped with fresh cream.

Basically, there are two varieties of strawberries grown in Italy. The preferred is the diminutive wild *fragolina di bosco*, which has a pronounced, perfumy aroma and almost not-quite-sweet flavor. Much more available are the cultivated, large *fragoline*. Strawberries are also used in cooking some savory dishes such as *risotto alle fragole*.

Raspberries, *lamponi*, are grown mostly in Piedmont and Lombardy and are available for only a short time in the spring, when they are very expensive.

Finally, blueberries, or *mirtilli*, are generally not cultivated in Italy. They grow wild on low bushes in the mountains in the north, much the way they grow in the northeastern part of the United States.

Cherries

~ ~ ~

CILIEGIE

Most cherries found in Italy today are sweet and similar to our own Bing cherries. Although cherries are usually eaten uncooked out of hand, one of the most popular recipes for cherries is to cook them in a wine syrup with cinnamon—a recipe that originated with the Italian cook Vincenzo Corrado in the late eighteenth century. Cherries are also preserved in a vinegar base and served as an accompaniment to *bollito misto*, a mixture of boiled meats.

Figs

~ ~ ~
FICHI

What is supposed to be the oldest fig tree in the world stands in a garden in Palermo, Sicily.

The best and sweetest figs are the ones that come off the tree fully ripe. However, because figs are so perishable at that point, few fully ripe figs ever reach the markets. Instead, figs that are not-quite-ripe, called *fioroni*, are picked and shipped. The fully ripe ones are usually dried. Figs are in season and available in the late summer and fall.

Typically, fresh figs are served uncooked, with prosciutto or *salame* as an antipasto, but they are also enjoyed as a dessert. They can be cooked—poached or baked into a custard—but my own preference is to eat them fresh, just peeled and uncooked. A perfectly ripe fig should yield slightly when pressed, but should not feel soft.

Grapes

~ ~ ~
UVA

Grapevines, like olive trees, are a fixture of the Italian landscape. The ancient Romans called Italy Enotria, "land of the vine," because so much of the landscape was covered with vines. Grapevines still stretch for miles on end across the hillsides from the far northern regions to the south and Sicily. Many varieties of grapes grow in Italy. Most are pressed into wine; many are eaten fresh. Grapes are also dried to become raisins.

Lemon

~ ~ ~
LIMONE

An ancient medicinal ingredient, the lemon has been grown in southern Italy, particularly Sicily, which has been growing most of the Italian citrus crop since the seventh century. It has become an essential culinary ingredient both for savory as well as sweet dishes from meat and fish, pasta and risotti, to fruits and desserts. My own favorite way to enjoy lemons is in a *granita di limone* (see pages 288–89), which is the perfect antidote to a hot summer day.

Melons

~ ~ ~

MELONE

With their sweet, satisfying flavor, tender, juicy texture, and aromatic odor, melons are one of the most universally enjoyed fruits.

The Romans are credited with being the first on the European continent to grow melons, which were originally a fruit from the Middle East. A lot has been written about how melons were a favorite food of the Emperor Tiberius, who grew them under glass so that he could eat them all year long.

Although many varieties of melons are found in markets in Italy, the two most popular types are the *napoletano*, which is like an orange-fleshed honeydew, and the *cantalupo*, or cantaloupe melon, named for the gardens of Cantalupo near Tivoli, outside Rome.

Italians typically eat melon before the meal—with prosciutto—as an antipasto. Melon is also eaten as a dessert, usually in a *macedonia*, or fruit salad.

Choosing a perfect melon depends a lot on experience and even more on instinct. I go by smell. A ready-to-eat melon should have a mild aroma. I occasionally buy unripe melons with no aroma for a day or two down the line. Leave an unripe melon to stand at room temperature until it develops an aroma and then eat or refrigerate it. I usually avoid buying melons with a strong or perfumy aroma. That signals to me that it is probably already overripe. Always avoid buying melons with shriveled or bruised skins. Store cut melons in the refrigerator.
or bruised skins. Store cut melons in the refrigerator.

Nuts

~ ~ ~

NOCI

From the chestnuts in the northern regions of Italy to the almonds in the south, numerous types of nuts are grown in Italy. Nuts are one of the most essential ingredients in Italian cuisine. They are the basis of countless desserts, cookies, and confections; they are also inseparable from some of the best-known savory sauces including pesto. Nuts can be enjoyed straight from the shell or served as a dessert with an after-dinner drink.

Nuts in the shell can keep for weeks and even months in a cool (not refrigerated) dry place. Once nuts are shelled, they should be kept in an airtight container in the freezer section of your refrigerator.

ALMOND/*MANDORLA*. There are two varieties of almonds grown throughout the Central and Southern regions of Italy. The *mandorle dolci*, sweet almonds, are used in cooking and baking, ground to make *pasta di mandorle* or *marzapane* (marzipan), and eaten from the shell or as candy when they are coated. The *mandorle amare* are the bitter almonds and they are used to flavor liqueur or to give a more intense almond flavor to some sweets.

CHESTNUT/*CASTAGNA*. Chestnuts grow in northern Italy, which is why most of the recipes for chestnuts come from Piedmont and Lombardy. There are both savory and sweet recipes for chestnuts: they are served as an accompaniment to meats and game, as well as in confections. In season, roasted chestnuts are served in their shells after dinner as a dessert. And like the French who grow chestnuts just across the border in Alsace, the Italians of Piedmont make a version of *marrons glacées*, or candied chestnuts, and Monte Bianco, like the French Mont Blanc, is the pureed chestnut Italian dessert. Italians also dry chestnuts so that they can be available all year long.

HAZELNUT/*NOCCIOLA*. Hazelnuts are mostly used in Italian cooking in the preparation of candies, of which *torrone* and *gianduiotti* are the best known. They are also used in cakes—a traditional chocolate cake from the northern city of Turin is made with hazelnut flour. Today hazelnuts are principally incorporated into sweets, but in the past hazelnuts were also widely used in the preparation of savory dishes including sauces, stuffings, and coatings for meats.

PINE NUTS/*PINOLI* or PIGNOLI. Pine nuts—which are not nuts in the true sense of the word because they do not have shells—are the seeds from stone pine trees which grow along the Italian Mediterranean and Adriatic coasts. They have a characteristic rich, creamy flavor and soft texture. Pine nuts are important in many Italian dishes, but are best known as an essential ingredient in pesto (see pages 154–55). They are also a part of many sweets and desserts. Pine nuts are also added to some dishes as a garnish. When using pine nuts as a garnish, always toast them lightly in a dry, heavy pan before serving. It gives them better flavor.

PISTACHIOS/*PISTACCHIO*. Pistachio nuts, with their brilliant, bright green color, are the fruit of a small tree that grows almost exclusively in Sicily. Originally from the Middle East, pistachios are mostly used in flavoring and coloring ice cream. They are also used in the preparation of Sicilian *cassata* and *cannoli*.

WALNUT/*NOCE*. Walnuts grow profusely throughout the regions of southern Italy. They are harvested in the fall and are eaten from September through to the spring. Walnuts are typically eaten from the shell, with fruit, for dessert. They are also used in savory sauces such as *salsa di noce* (see pages 178–79), which is a Ligurian pasta sauce. They go into many desserts and candies, the best known being *torta di noci*, walnut cake (see page 283), a version of which is made in every region of Italy.

Oranges

~ ~ ~

ARANCE

Oranges have been grown in Italy since bitter oranges (*arance amare*, what we sometimes call Seville oranges) were brought to Sicily around the year 1000 by the Saracens. Oranges then became a symbol of wealth and opulence in Italy; during the Renaissance the Medicis incorporated five bright oranges into their coat of arms. The common sweet juice orange was ultimately introduced into Italy in the seventeenth century.

Today many varieties of oranges are grown in southern Italy, principally in Sicily and Calabria. The distinctive Italian "blood" oranges, with their vivid red flesh, are grown in Sicily. One of the now-classic Sicilian dishes is a salad made with sliced oranges and red onions that are dressed with olive oil, salt, and pepper (see page 254 for the recipe). More typically, however, oranges are used for juice, or in a *macedonia*, or fruit salad (see page 267).

For most Italian recipes you can use the California-grown Valencia oranges, which are available during most of the year.

Peaches and Nectarines
~ ~ ~
PESCHE E PESCHE NOCI

There are two basic types of peaches grown in Italy: the *pesca gialla*, yellow peach, is most like American-grown peaches and is widely grown and available, in season, throughout Italy; the *pesca bianca*, white peach, is less common, but a cherished delicacy where available. Peaches are predominantly grown in the southern and south-central regions of Italy.

The sweet flavor and firm texture of peaches make them easy to use in cooking. The most common way of serving peaches in Italy is either to poach them in wine and sugar or simply to peel, slice, and dress them with a flavoring of sugar, liqueur, or wine.

Peaches (and nectarines, which are similar to peaches, although not related botanically, and can be used in place of them) are a summer fruit and are best, and most reasonably priced, during July, August, and September. When buying peaches, look for freestones, what the Italians call *spaccatelle*. They are easier to cut and serve. I always choose peaches that are firm but not hard, with a blush all over the skin. Underripe peaches will ripen when stored at room temperature in a brown paper bag for a day or two. Ripe peaches should be refrigerated.

HOW TO PEEL PEACHES. Bring 2 quarts of water to a boil in a large saucepan on top of the stove. Place 3 to 4 peaches at a time in the boiling water. Wait 1 minute. Using a slotted spoon or strainer, remove the peaches from the water, place in a colander, and refresh under cold water. Add more peaches to the boiling water and repeat the process. When the peaches are cool enough to handle, using a sharp knife, gently pull the skin off each peach. The skin should come away easily.

Pears

~ ~ ~

PERE

Many varieties of pears are grown throughout Italy. Some are sweet and juicy with a buttery texture, others are more granular and hard. Pears are usually eaten in their natural state—uncooked and unadulterated. They are brought to the table whole, usually in a bowl of fresh ice water, and served with a sharp knife. The custom is to peel the pear, cut it into quarters, and carefully trim away the core, making sure that as little as possible of the pear is discarded. Each quarter is cut into slices, and every bit is consumed. Pears are also served with different cheeses. In addition, pears can be poached in red wine or baked into a tart or cake.

Most pears in our markets tend to be hard and unripe and should be left to ripen at room temperature for up to several days. Pears develop an aroma when they are ripe which quickly becomes an unappealing smell when they are overripe. The trick is to eat pears before they reach that point.

For eating raw, our firmer-textured Bosc and Comice pears are probably the best. For baking or cooking, the softer D'Anjou and Bartlett pears are preferred. You can poach any type of pear (see pages 272–73), even the smallest Seckle pears, which are available for a short time during the late fall.

Plums

~ ~ ~

PRUGNE

It is the small purple prune plum that is mostly grown and eaten in Italy. Harvested in the late summer, it is usually poached in a wine syrup or simply dried. Dried prunes can be stewed in wine or with sliced lemons.

Fruit Salad/ Macedonia di Frutta

~ ~ ~

Fall/Winter Fruit Salad

~ ~ ~

MACEDONIA DI FRUTTA D'AUTUNNO

Of all the prepared fresh fruit desserts, the fruit salad is probably the most popular and common in Italy. While *macedonie* are invariably flavored with sugar and fresh orange and lemon juices, the nature of the fruit salad changes from season to season, depending on what fruit is fresh and available. This *macedonia* is a delicious and refreshing way to treat fall fruit. The lemon juice keeps the fruit from discoloring. After preparing the fruit salad, allow it to stand, refrigerated, for at least three hours before serving.

> *3 medium-size Granny Smith apples, peeled, cored, quartered, and cut into small pieces*
>
> *3 medium-size Bosc pears, peeled, cored, quartered, and cut into small pieces*
>
> *1 small bunch red seedless grapes (about 1 cup), stemmed and quartered*
>
> *1 cup fresh orange and lemon juice (made with juice of 1 lemon plus enough orange juice to make 1 cup)*
>
> *½ cup sugar*

1. Place all the fruit in a large mixing bowl.
2. In a 2-cup glass measuring cup, combine the juices with the sugar

and stir to dissolve as much of the sugar as possible. Pour the juice over the fruit and stir well to combine. Cover with plastic wrap and refrigerate for several hours. Stir well again before serving.

MAKES 6 SERVINGS

Cooked Summer Fruit Compote

~ ~ ~

MACEDONIA DI FRUTTA D'INVERNO "COTTA"

A delicious way to enjoy the variety of summer fruits—peaches, nectarines, plums, apricots, and blueberries. Serve chilled or warm over rich vanilla ice cream or tangy mascarpone cheese. Fruit compote can be kept for up to a week in the refrigerator and reheated, or not, just before serving.

3 pounds fresh summer fruit
Juice of ½ lemon
½ cup sugar
¼ cup water

1. Prepare the fruit: Peel the peaches and nectarines (see directions on page 265–66), if you are using them, remove the pits, and cut the fruit into halves or quarters. Rinse the blueberries and remove any stems or leaves.

2. Combine the lemon juice, sugar, and water in a medium-size nonaluminum saucepan over medium-high heat. Cook for about 3 minutes, until the sugar dissolves. Add the fruit and stir well to combine with the liquid. Reduce the heat to medium-low and cook slowly, stirring frequently so it does not stick, for about 20 minutes, until the fruit is tender but not mushy. Transfer to a serving bowl. Serve immediately or cool and refrigerate before serving.

MAKES 6 SERVINGS

MICROWAVE TECHNIQUE: The microwave oven can quickly and evenly cook the fruit. Combine the fruit in an 8-cup microwave-safe container with high sides (such as a soufflé dish). The high sides of the dish prevent the fruit, when it is cooking and bubbling up, from overflowing. Stir in the lemon juice, sugar, and water. Stir well to coat all the fruit with the mixture. Cover the dish securely with microwave-safe plastic wrap or a tight-fitting cover. Place the dish in the microwave and cook on high power for 6 minutes. Uncover and stir well. Serve immediately or cool and chill before serving.

Baked Apples Stuffed with Raisins and Pine Nuts

~ ~ ~

MELE AL FORNO CON UVETTA E PIGNOLI

The raisins and pine nuts give these baked apples an Italian flavor. Serve them warm at the end of a hearty midwinter meal.

6 large Cortland or Rome apples

3 tablespoons pine nuts

3 tablespoons walnut pieces

⅓ cup golden raisins

¼ cup sugar

2 cups apple cider

1. Preheat the oven to 350°F.

2. Using an apple or zucchini corer, cut out the cores and seeds from the apples. Peel the skin from around the tops and bottoms. Arrange the apples in a glass or ceramic baking dish. Combine the pine nuts, walnuts, raisins, and sugar in a food processor fitted with the steel blade. Pulse the machine on and off a few times so that the mixture is coarsely chopped. Using a teaspoon, fill the cavities of the apples with the nut mixture from both the top and bottom ends and gently press the mixture to pack it firmly. Leave a little of the filling spilling out of the apple tops.

3. Pour the apple cider into the baking pan. Bake the apples for 1 hour. Serve warm or at room temperature. These can be refrigerated and reheated before serving.

MAKES 6 SERVINGS

Fruit Desserts 269

Marinated Oranges

~ ~ ~

ARANCE MARINATE

A refreshing dessert that makes these oranges very flavorful.

10 Valencia oranges, peeled and thinly sliced into rounds
1 cup sugar
Rind of 1 lemon, grated
Juice of 1 lemon
¾ cup (about) fresh orange juice

1. Arrange one-third of the orange slices in a single overlapping layer in a large oval serving dish. Sprinkle ⅓ cup of the sugar over the oranges and a third of the lemon rind. Repeat two more times to have three layers of oranges.
2. Combine the lemon juice with enough orange juice to make 1 cup. Pour over the oranges, cover, and refrigerate for at least 6 hours or overnight. Serve chilled.

MAKES 8 SERVINGS

Peaches Poached in White Wine and Filled with Mascarpone

~ ~ ~

PESCHE RIPIENE

This is a simple dessert to prepare, but very elegant. Serve it in large goblets for an impressive effect.

1 cup dry Italian white wine, such as Pinot Grigio or Chardonnay
½ cup sugar
6 large peaches (about 2 pounds), peeled (see pages 265–66), halved, and
*   pitted*
1 cup mascarpone
¼ cup finely chopped walnuts

1. Combine the wine and sugar in a large, shallow, nonaluminum saucepan with a cover. Place over medium heat and stir until the sugar dissolves. Place the peaches in the pan, cut side down. Cover the pan, raise the heat to medium-high, and bring the liquid to a boil. Reduce the heat to medium-low, keep covered, and simmer the peaches for 10 minutes. Turn the peaches over and cook for an additional 10 minutes. Turn off the heat and let cool. Refrigerate for at least 3 hours before serving.

2. Just before serving, place the peaches, cut side up, with some of the cooking liquid in individual serving dishes. Place a heaping tablespoon of the mascarpone-and-nut mixture in the center of each peach half. Garnish with chopped walnuts.

MAKES 6 SERVINGS

VARIATION: Omit the mascarpone-and-nut mixture and serve the poached peaches with fresh raspberries or blackberries and some of the poaching liquid.

Oven-Poached Pears in Red Wine

~ ~ ~

PERE IN VINO ROSSO

Oven poaching is not traditional, but it cooks the pears gently and evenly, and infuses them with a fantastic amount of flavor.

1 cup sugar

3 cups dry Italian red wine, such as Chianti or Spanna

Rind of 1 lemon, coarsely chopped

6 pears (Bosc, Bartlett, or Comice), preferably with stems and all about the same size, or 12 Seckle pears

1. Preheat the oven to 300°F.

2. Combine the sugar, wine, and rind in a heavy casserole large enough to hold the pears in a single layer. Place over medium-low heat and stir until the sugar is dissolved.

3. Peel the pears, leaving them whole with the stems on. Place the pears in the pot with the sugar-and-wine mixture and add enough water

(1 to 2 cups) to bring the liquid up to the tops of the pears. Cover the casserole and place in the oven. Bake for 3 hours, or until the pears are tender when pierced with a sharp knife. Allow the pears to cool to room temperature, then chill for several hours before serving.

MAKES 6 SERVINGS

Note: For a thick, syrupy sauce for the pears, remove the pears from the pot once they cool and set them in a serving bowl or in individual serving dishes. Place the casserole on the stove over medium-high heat, bring the wine mixture to a boil, and cook briskly for 5 to 7 minutes, until the mixture is thick and syrupy. Pour the syrup over the pears, allow to cool, and refrigerate before serving.

Poached Fresh Figs in Red Wine

~ ~ ~

FICHI FRESCHI IN VINO ROSSO

I can eat fresh figs every day when they are in season from July through the early fall months, but even then I can't seem to get enough. This is the best way to cook fresh figs—they're only lightly cooked so you don't lose the fresh taste. They need only a few minutes to become infused with the flavor of the wine.

1 cup sugar

3 cups dry Italian red wine (such as Chianti or Spanna)

18 fresh ripe figs

1. Combine the sugar and wine in a large heavy-bottomed non-aluminum casserole or saucepan that is large enough to hold the figs in one layer. Place over medium-high heat and cook, stirring, until the sugar is dissolved. Holding the figs by their stems, place the figs into the wine-and-sugar mixture. Reduce the heat to medium, cover the casserole, and cook for 7 to 10 minutes, until the figs are tender and a deep brown color.

2. Using a slotted spoon, carefully transfer the figs to a large serving platter. Raise the heat under the casserole to medium-high and cook for 5 to 7 minutes longer, until the liquid becomes thick and syrupy. Pour the wine syrup over the figs and allow to cool to room temperature before serving.

MAKES 6 SERVINGS

Strawberries, Raspberries, and Blackberries with Raspberry Sauce and Mascarpone

~ ~ ~

FRUTTA DI BOSCO E MASCARPONE

A berry lover's delight—just fresh, sweet summer berries and some mascarpone for a touch of richness.

1 quart fresh strawberries, stemmed and cut in half lengthwise

1 pint fresh blueberries

2 pints fresh raspberries (or 1 pint each raspberries and blackberries)

½ cup confectioner's sugar

2 cups mascarpone

¼ cup plain yogurt

1. Combine the berries in a large mixing bowl, reserving 1 pint of the raspberries to make a sauce.

2. Combine the remaining pint of raspberries with the sugar in a blender or food processor fitted with the steel blade. Process for about 30 seconds, until the raspberries are smooth and the sugar is dissolved.

3. Combine the mascarpone and yogurt in a small mixing bowl. Using a wire whisk, beat until the mixture is smooth.

4. To serve, spoon some of the raspberry sauce onto each individual serving plate. Place some of the berry mixture over the sauce and top with a heaping tablespoon of the mascarpone.

MAKES 6 SERVINGS

Strawberries with Balsamic Vinegar

~ ~ ~

FRAGOLE AL BALSAMICO

This recipe dates from the Renaissance. Although it is traditionally prepared with the precious, specially aged balsamic vinegar, your standard supermarket variety balsamic vinegar can do justice to the berries. This is the best way to treat berries that look beautiful but lack taste. The vinegar somehow finds the flavor hiding within the fruit and brings it out.

2 quarts fresh strawberries, stems removed and cut in half lengthwise
¼ cup confectioner's sugar
3 tablespoons balsamic vinegar

Place the strawberies in a large serving bowl. Sprinkle the sugar over the berries and pour the vinegar over the top. Toss well and chill for at least an hour. Toss well again before serving.

MAKES 6 SERVINGS

Cherries Stewed in Red Wine with Cinnamon

~ ~ ~

CILIGIE IN VINO ROSSO E CANNELLA

This is a classic Italian preparation for cherries that dates back to the eighteenth century when fruit was moved from its traditional place at the beginning of the meal to its now customary place at the end. Cinnamon brings out the best cherry flavor. Pit the cherries first with a cherry-pitting tool (see page 25).

1 cup sugar

3 cups dry Italian red wine (such as Chianti or Spanna)

1 cinnamon stick, about 3 inches long

2 pounds bing (dark red) cherries, stems removed and pitted

1. Combine the sugar, wine, and cinnamon stick in a large, heavy, nonaluminum casserole or saucepan. Place over medium-high heat and cook, stirring, until the sugar is dissolved. Add the cherries, lower the heat, and cook, covered, about 10 minutes, until the cherries are tender and lose their bright red color.

2. Use a slotted spoon and transfer the cherries to a large serving bowl, leaving the cinnamon stick in the casserole. Cook the wine-and-sugar mixture with the cinnamon over medium-high heat 7 to 10 minutes, until the liquid is thick and syrupy. Remove the cinnamon stick and discard. Pour the syrup over the cherries and allow to cool to room temperature or chill before serving.

MAKES 6 SERVINGS

Baked Cherry Custard

~ ~ ~

SFORMATO DI CILIGIE

A version of the French clafoutis, this rich-tasting dish is easy to prepare. A cherry-pitting tool makes it that much easier (see page 25).

1 pound bing (dark red) cherries, stems removed and pitted

5 tablespoons granulated sugar

1 teaspoon ground cinnamon

¼ cup all-purpose flour

Pinch of salt

2 cups whole milk, light cream, or half-and-half

3 large eggs, lightly beaten

Confectioners' sugar for garnish

1. Preheat the oven to 375°F. Generously butter a shallow 10-inch glass or ceramic baking dish (such as a pie plate or tart pan).

2. Arrange the cherries in a single layer in the bottom of the baking dish. Sprinkle 2 tablespoons of the sugar and the cinnamon over the cherries.

3. Put the flour and salt into a large mixing bowl. Using a wire whisk or hand mixer, slowly add the milk and beat to combine with the flour. Add the eggs and beat vigorously for 2 to 3 minutes, until the mixture is light and foamy. Beat in the remaining sugar. Pour the egg-and-milk mixture over the cherries. Place on the middle shelf in the oven and bake 35 to 45 minutes, or until lightly brown and puffy. Allow to cool slightly. Sprinkle heavily with confectioners' sugar and serve warm.

MAKES 6 SERVINGS

Roasted Chestnuts

~ ~ ~

MARRONI ARROSTITI

This is one of the simplest desserts. Roasted chestnuts make a delicious fall dessert, especially when served with a dessert wine and dried figs.

2 pounds fresh chestnuts in their shells

1. Preheat the oven to 400°F.
2. Using a sharp knife, cut an X in the top side of the chestnut shell. Arrange the chestnuts in a single layer in a baking pan and place them in the oven. Roast for 20 minutes. Allow to cool slightly and serve warm in their shells. Shells will peel off easily.

MAKES 6 SERVINGS

Fruit Pies/Torte di Frutta

~ ~ ~

Italian fruit pies offer a wonderful combination of a cookie-like crust and a fresh-tasting fruit filling that's not overly sweet so that the taste of the fresh fruit comes through.

Basic Pie Pastry

~ ~ ~

PASTA FROLLA

This is a very rich pastry with a crumbly-cookie texture.

2 cups all-purpose flour
⅓ cup sugar
¼ pound (1 stick) unsalted butter, at room temperature and cut into 8 pieces
2 large eggs, lightly beaten

1. Combine the flour and sugar in a food processor fitted with the double-edge steel blade. Process for about 10 seconds to combine. Add the butter and process for 15 seconds, until the texture of the flour resembles that of cornmeal. Add the eggs and process for about 30 seconds, until the dough forms a ball on the blade.

2. Remove the dough, wrap securely in plastic wrap, and flatten into a circle with your hands. Refrigerate for at least 30 minutes before rolling out. If you refrigerate longer than 30 minutes, the dough will become quite stiff and you will need to leave it at room temperature for about 30 minutes before rolling.

3. Unwrap the dough and place it on a well-floured work surface. Roll about ¼ inch thick, then place the dough in a 9-inch pie pan. With your fingers, press the dough as evenly as possible into the pan. Press it up the sides to form a decorative edge.

MAKES ONE 9-INCH CRUST

Apple Tart

~ ~ ~

TORTA DI MELE

This is my favorite tart. The layer of applesauce makes a delicate filling and the sliced apples give a decorative finished appearance.

1 recipe Basic Pie Pastry (see preceding recipe)
1 cup prepared unsweetened applesauce (preferably the kind you make yourself)
2 or 3 large, crisp, tart apples (McIntosh, Macoun, Empire, or Granny Smith)
Juice of ½ lemon
¼ cup sugar
½ cup apricot preserves

1. Preheat the oven to 375°F. Prepare the pie pastry, roll it out, and line a 9-inch tart pan. Crimp the edges.

2. Spread the applesauce over the bottom of the pastry. Cut the apples in quarters, peel, and cut away the cores. Cut each piece of apple into evenly thin slices and arrange in an overlapping fashion over the

applesauce in concentric circles. Squeeze the juice over the apple slices, sprinkle the sugar evenly over the top, and place on the middle rack of the oven. Bake for about 1 hour, until the pastry is golden brown and the edges of the apple slices begin to brown. Remove from the oven and cool on a rack.

3. Just before serving, heat the preserves (you can do it easily in the microwave: put the preserves in a microwave-safe, heatproof glass measuring cup, heat on high power for about 1 minute, until the preserves are melted and bubbling), and use a teaspoon to spread evenly over the top of the apples. Serve from the pan.

MAKES ONE 9-INCH TART, OR 6 TO 8 SERVINGS

Peach, Apricot, and Plum Tart
~ ~ ~
TORTA DI PESCHE E ALBICOCCHE E PRUGNE

All the best flavors of summer fruit are combined in this wonderful pie. This tart was prepared for my husband and myself at a wonderful lunch prepared by Lorenza de' Medici in Tuscany.

1 recipe Basic Pie Pastry (see pages 277–78)
3 pounds total peaches, nectarines, apricots, and/or plums
½ cup sugar
Juice of ½ lemon

1. Prepare the pie pastry, roll it out, and press it into a 9-inch springform pan with removable sides. Leave enough dough aside to make strips for a lattice-top crust.

2. Prepare the fruit: Peel the peaches and nectarines according to the directions on pages 265–66. Remove all the pits and cut the fruit into thick slices. Put the fruit into a large nonaluminum saucepan. Add the sugar and lemon juice, stir well to combine, and place over medium-high heat. Cook, while stirring, until the fruit begins to give up its liquid and the sugar is dissolved, about 5 minutes. Reduce the heat to medium-low and continue cooking for about 20 minutes longer, stirring occasionally, until the fruit is tender but not mushy and the liquid in the pan has become quite thick.

3. Preheat the oven to 375°F.

4. Pour the fruit filling into the crust. Cover the filling with strips of the dough to make a lattice-top crust and crimp the edges of the pastry. Place the pan on the middle rack in the oven and bake for about 1 hour, or until the crust is evenly golden brown and the filling is bubbling. Allow to cool completely before removing the sides of the pan. When cool, run a sharp knife between the crust and the pan. Open the pan latch and remove.

MAKES ONE 9-INCH TART, OR 6 TO 8 SERVINGS

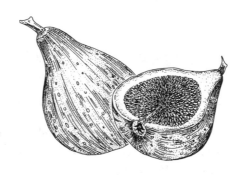

Fig Tart with Hazelnuts

~ ~ ~

TORTA DI FICHI SECCHI E NOCI

This is a wonderfully rich and hearty dessert—dense with figs and infused with orange flavor—to make in the winter when only dried figs are available. It comes from a great chef, Jody Adams, who runs the kitchen at Michela's restaurant in Cambridge, Massachusetts, where her cooking is earthy and delicious.

CRUST

¼ cup hazelnuts
1½ cups all-purpose flour
1 teaspoon salt

2 tablespoons sugar

6 tablespoons (¾ stick) unsalted butter, cut into tablespoon-size pieces

2 tablespoons water

FILLING

½ pound dried figs, stems removed and cut into quarters

Zest of 1 orange, finely chopped

Juice of 1 orange

3 large eggs

½ cup mascarpone

Juice of 1 lemon

1 tablespoon all-purpose flour

Pinch of salt

½ cup sugar

½ cup toasted coarsely chopped hazelnuts

1. Preheat the oven to 400°F. Place all the hazelnuts on a baking sheet. Place in the oven and toast for 10 minutes. Cool slightly. Grind or chop in a food processor.

2. To prepare the crust, combine the ground nuts, flour, salt, and sugar in a medium-size bowl. Add the butter and work it through your fingers into the dough until the mixture resembles coarse meal. Add the water and toss through your fingers into the dough. Squeeze some dough in your hand. If it holds together fairly well, you've added enough water. If not, add more water, a tablespoon at a time, until it does hold together. Place the dough on a counter top. Using the heel of your hand, smear the dough across the counter. Repeat. Form the dough into a flat cake and refrigerate at least 1 hour.

3. Preheat the oven to 400°F. Roll out the dough and line a 9-inch springform pan with it. Refrigerate until ready to fill.

4. In a large mixing bowl, combine the figs with the orange zest and juice and toss well. Allow to macerate for 30 minutes.

5. In a large mixing bowl, beat the eggs with the mascarpone, lemon juice, flour, salt, and the orange juice from the figs. Gradually beat in the sugar.

6. Distribute the figs evenly over the bottom of the prepared crust. Sprinkle over the hazelnuts. Pour the mascarpone-and-egg mixture over the figs, then fold the pastry down to form a nice edge. Bake for 10 minutes, then reduce the oven to 350°F and bake for an additional 20 to 30 minutes, until set. Serve with vanilla ice cream.

MAKES ONE 9-INCH TART, OR 8 SERVINGS

Lemon Tart

~ ~ ~

TORTA DI LIMONE

A very lemony, rich tart, this recipe was inspired by the lemon custard that was served for dessert at La Chiusa in Montefollonico.

1 recipe Basic Pie Pastry (see pages 277–78)
4 large eggs, lightly beaten
½ cup sugar
3 lemons, squeezed and zest finely chopped
¼ pound (1 stick) unsalted butter, melted
1 cup almonds, ground as finely as possible

1. Preheat the oven to 350°F.
2. Prepare the pastry, roll it out, and press into a 9-inch tart pan.
3. Combine the eggs with the sugar, lemon zest, juice, butter, and almonds. Mix well and pour into the prepared pie crust. Bake for 25 to 30 minutes, until the crust and the top of the tart are golden brown. Serve from the pan.

MAKES ONE 9-INCH TART, OR 6 TO 8 SERVINGS

Walnut Tart

~ ~ ~

TORTA DI NOCI

Dense with walnuts, this traditional tart is more of a cake than a pie. It is deliciously moist and rich and not too sweet. Dust the top with powdered sugar before serving.

3 cups walnut pieces

4 large eggs, separated

1 cup plus 1 tablespoon granulated sugar

Rind of 1 lemon, grated

Powdered sugar for garnish

1. Preheat the oven to 350°F. Lightly butter and flour a 9-inch spring-form pan.

2. Place the walnut pieces in a blender or food processor fitted with the steel blade and chop them finely, being careful not to overprocess them into a paste. Set aside.

3. Beat the egg yolks and sugar with an electric mixer until light and fluffy. Add the lemon rind and walnuts and mix only enough to combine.

4. In a separate bowl, beat the egg whites with an electric mixer until stiff. Fold them into the egg yolk–and–walnut mixture. Pour into the prepared pan. Bake for 1 hour, or until golden brown. Cool on a rack. Remove the sides of the pan, dust with powdered sugar, and serve.

MAKES ONE 9-INCH TART, OR 6 TO 8 SERVINGS

Apple Fritters

~ ~ ~

FRITTELLE DI MELE

Wonderfully light and delicately crisp, these fritters are not too sweet and make a delicious ending to any meal.

3 tablespoons sugar

Juice of ½ lemon

3 medium Granny Smith apples, peeled, cored, and sliced into rounds about ¼ inch thick

⅔ cup all-purpose flour

1 cup cold water

Vegetable oil for deep frying

Confectioners' sugar

1. Combine the sugar and lemon juice in a medium-size nonaluminum mixing bowl. Stir to dissolve the sugar. Add the apple slices, mix well, and allow to stand for 30 minutes.

2. Put the flour in a small mixing bowl and gradually add the water, beating with a wire whisk until the batter has the consistency of heavy cream.

3. Pour enough vegetable oil to fill a deep, heavy saucepan 1 inch deep and place over medium-high heat. Test the oil by dropping some batter into the oil. If it bubbles it's ready. When the oil is hot, slip the apple slices one at a time into the batter. Using a pair of kitchen tongs, remove the slices from the batter, letting any excess drip off, then put only as many apple slices into the hot oil as can fit in a single layer without touching. Cook until the underside is golden brown, 7 to 10 minutes, then turn and continue cooking until brown all over, another 3 to 5 minutes. Take the apple slices from the oil, drain on paper towels, and let cool slightly. Repeat until all the apple slices are cooked. Dust with confectioners' sugar and serve warm.

MAKES 6 SERVINGS

Dried Prunes Poached in Red Wine

PRUGNE SECCHI AL VINO ROSSO

These prunes make a wonderful topping for vanilla ice cream.

1 pound dried pitted prunes
1½ cups light Italian red wine, such as Chianti or Spanna

Combine the prunes and wine in a small nonaluminum saucepan and place over medium heat. When the wine comes to a boil, reduce the heat to low, cover the pan, and simmer for 10 minutes. Turn off the heat and allow to stand until cool. Chill and serve with vanilla ice cream.

MAKES 6 SERVINGS

Dried Prunes with Lemon

PRUGNE SECCHI E LIMONE

The lemon adds a zesty contrast to the flavor of the prunes. My grandmother used to make these for breakfast. You can also serve them as a dessert at lunch or dinner.

1 pound dried pitted prunes
1 lemon, sliced into thin rounds
Boiling water to just cover

1. Place the prunes and lemon slices in a medium-size nonaluminum, heatproof mixing bowl.
2. Add the boiling water. Stir the prunes once, cover the bowl, and allow to stand at room temperature until cool. Stir again, transfer to a storage container, and refrigerate until ready to serve. Can keep in the refrigerator for at least a week.

MAKES 4 TO 6 SERVINGS

Fruit Ices/Sorbetti e Granite di Frutta

~ ~ ~

Italian ices have been a traditional treat in Italy for centuries. The distinction between *sorbetti* and *granite* is not exactly clear. I like to think of a sorbet as having a puree of fruit as the base and a *granita* only fruit juice. *Sorbetti* need to be frozen in an ice cream maker, whereas *granite*, which are more icy and granular, can be frozen in a bowl in your freezer. Whichever you choose, these cold confections are a perfect ending to any meal. Serve with almond *biscotti* (see pages 291–92).

Note: If you prepare a sorbet or *granita* a day or more in advance, it will become too hard to scoop and serve. In that case, allow it to defrost slightly for 2 to 3 hours in your refrigerator before serving.

Sugar Syrup

~ ~ ~

SCIROPPO DI ZUCCHERO

Most of the sorbet and *granita* recipes that follow call for the addition of sugar syrup—a cooked combination of sugar, water, and lemon juice. It combines with the fruit or juice without leaving any undissolved sugar granules in the finished product. You should make your sugar syrup ahead of time because it must be cool or preferably cold when it is added to the fruit or fruit juice. It will keep for several weeks in your refrigerator.

1¾ cups sugar
1 cup cold water
Juice of ½ lemon

Combine the sugar, water, and lemon juice in a small nonaluminum saucepan. Stir well. Bring to a boil over high heat. Allow it to boil briskly for 2 to 3 minutes, until the mixture turns clear. Cool completely, or refrigerate. It can keep in the refrigerator for several months.

MAKES ABOUT 2 CUPS

Strawberry Sherbet

~ ~ ~

SORBETTO DI FRAGOLE

The sweet sensation of fresh strawberries makes this *sorbetto* spectacular. You can even use out-of-season berries with excellent results. The quantity of sugar syrup may vary, depending on how sweet the strawberries are.

1 quart fresh strawberries, stems removed, hulled, and cut in half

¾ cup (about) Sugar Syrup (see preceding recipe)

1 tablespoon sweet liqueur, such as kirsch (optional)

1. Place the strawberries in a food processor fitted with the double-edge steel blade or a blender and puree. With the machine running, add the sugar syrup slowly. Taste and add more if necessary. Add the liqueur and continue processing for about 5 seconds longer. The mixture will be quite thin.

2. Freeze the strawberry mixture in an ice cream maker according to the manufacturer's directions. Transfer to a plastic container with a tight-fitting lid and allow the *sorbetto* to harden in the freezer for several hours before serving.

MAKES ABOUT 1 QUART OR 6 SERVINGS

Peach Sherbet

~ ~ ~

SORBETTO DI PESCHE

A luscious treat with a lot of sweet peach flavor. Make this in the summer when fresh peaches are plentiful. Serve with fresh raspberries.

2 pounds fresh peaches, peeled (see pages 265–66) and pitted

1 tablespoon amaretto or other almond liqueur

1 teaspoon fresh lemon juice

¾ cup (about) Sugar Syrup (see page 286)

1. Place the peaches in a food processor fitted with the steel blade. Cover and process for about 30 seconds, until the peaches are pureed and smooth. Add the amaretto and lemon juice and process for 5 seconds longer. With the machine running, add the sugar syrup slowly. Taste and add more if necessary. Transfer the peach mixture to a mixing bowl and refrigerate until the mixture is cold.

2. Pour the peach mixture into your ice cream maker and freeze according to the manufacturer's directions. When frozen, transfer to a plastic container with a tight-fitting lid and allow to harden for several hours in your freezer before serving.

MAKES ABOUT 1 QUART, OR 6 SERVINGS

Lemon Ice

~ ~ ~

GRANITA DI LIMONE

Deliciously tart and tangy, this is a refreshing palate pleaser.

1½ cups Sugar Syrup (see page 286)
1 cup fresh lemon juice with pulp
2½ cups cold water

1. Combine the sugar syrup, lemon juice, and water in a medium-size plastic or metal mixing bowl and stir well to combine. Place the bowl,

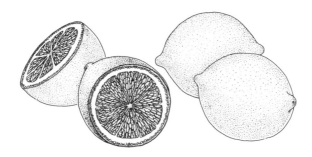

uncovered, in the freezer and freeze for 3 to 4 hours, stirring the mixture occasionally, until slushy. (Because of the amount of sugar syrup in it, the mixture will not freeze solid.)

2. Transfer the slushy lemon ice to a blender or a food processor fitted with the steel blade and process for about 30 seconds, until frothy and smooth. Pour the mixture back into the plastic container, cover, and freeze for 1 to 2 hours, until firm but not hard.

MAKES ABOUT 1 QUART, OR 6 SERVINGS

Grapefruit Ice
~ ~ ~
GRANITA DI POMPELMO

The refreshing taste of this grapefruit *granita* quenches and cools.

4 cups fresh grapefruit juice, with the pulp and seeds removed
1 cup (about) Sugar Syrup (see page 286)

1. Combine the grapefruit juice with the sugar syrup in a large non-aluminum plastic or metal mixing bowl. Taste and add more syrup if the mixture seems too sour. Mix well and place the bowl, uncovered, in your freezer.

2. After an hour the mixture will have begun to freeze around the sides of the bowl. Using a wooden spoon, free the ice from the sides of the bowl. Stir the mixture well and return it to the freezer. Repeat this

step every hour for the next 4 to 6 hours, until the mixture is quite thick and slushy.

3. Transfer the grapefruit juice mixture to a food processor fitted with the double-edge steel blade and process for about 15 seconds, until the mixture is light and frothy. Transfer to a plastic container, cover tightly, and return to the freezer until ready to serve. If you don't intend to serve it the same day, refrigerate 2 hours before serving so that you can scoop it.

MAKES 6 TO 8 SERVINGS

ORANGE AND CAMPARI ICE/*GRANITA DI ARANCIA E CAMPARI.* Bitter Campari cuts the sweetness of the orange juice to make a surprisingly new flavor that will delight and refresh. Substitute 4 cups fresh orange juice and ¼ cup Campari for the grapefruit juice and continue with the recipe as directed above.

Pistachio Ice Cream

~ ~ ~

GELATO DI PISTACCHIO

Pistachios come from Agrigento—a town also worth visiting to see the ancient Roman mosaics—in Sicily, where they grow in abundance. Sicilian pistachios are not widely available in the United States, but Middle Eastern ones are and they are an excellent substitute. Use only unsalted pistachios.

1 cup shelled pistachio nuts (unsalted)

2 cups milk

4 large egg yolks

½ cup sugar

1. Preheat the oven to 350°F. Combine the pistachios with enough water to cover in a small saucepan over medium-high heat. As soon as the water boils, turn off the heat and drain the pistachios. Place them in a cloth dish towel and rub them briskly between your hands to remove the skins. If the skins do not come off, pick them off individually. Place half

the nuts in a food processor fitted with a metal blade or blender and grind as finely as possible. Place the remaining nuts on a baking sheet and bake for 10 minutes. Allow to cool and coarsely chop.

2. Warm the milk over medium heat in a heavy saucepan until the milk begins to bubble around the top, about 5 minutes. (To heat the milk in the microwave, place it in a heatproof glass measuring cup, uncovered, and heat on high for 2 to 3 minutes.) Turn off the heat, add the ground pistachios, and allow to steep for 10 minutes. Pour through a fine wire-mesh strainer, reserve the strained milk, and discard the ground nuts.

3. Combine the egg yolks with the sugar in a medium-size mixing bowl and beat with an electric mixer at high speed until the mixture is thick and pale lemon colored. With the machine running, gradually pour the strained milk into the yolk mixture. Pour the milk-and-egg-yolk mixture back into the saucepan. Place over medium-low heat and cook, stirring constantly, until the mixture is thick and custardlike, 8 to 10 minutes.

4. Immediately set the saucepan in a bowl of cold water to stop the cooking and continue stirring for 1 to 2 minutes, until the custard begins to cool. Pour the custard back into the mixing bowl and chill the custard in the refrigerator for at least 1 hour or overnight until cold.

5. Pour the custard into an ice cream freezer and freeze according to the manufacturer's directions. Just before you take the *gelato* from the freezer, add the toasted pistachios and mix well. Transfer to a plastic freezer container with a tight-fitting lid. Freeze for several hours before serving.

MAKES 4 SERVINGS

Almond Cookies

~ ~ ~

BISCOTTI DI PRATO

Prato, just to the northwest of Florence, is famous for its deliciously dry and crunchy, almond-studded *biscotti*. Although *biscotti* has come to refer to almost any Italian cookie, *biscotti* means "twice cooked" and originally referred only to cookies like these that are literally baked twice. These Tuscan *biscotti*, adapted from Carol Field's version in *The Italian Baker*, are traditionally served for dipping in Vin Santo, the sweet dessert wine of the region, but I find they are also a wonderful complement to any fruit dessert.

1 cup whole almonds

2¼ cups sifted unbleached white flour

1 cup sugar

½ teaspoon baking powder

Pinch of salt

3 large eggs

1 teaspoon vanilla extract

1 large egg yolk beaten with 1 tablespoon water

1. Preheat the oven to 350°F.

2. Spread the almonds out on a baking sheet in a single layer and bake them for 7 minutes. Allow to cool while you prepare the *biscotti* dough.

3. Combine the flour, sugar, baking powder, and salt in a large bowl. If you are using an electric mixer, turn the machine on to the slowest speed and mix the dry ingredients. Add the eggs, one at a time, beating well after each addition. When the dough forms a ball on the beaters, add the vanilla and almonds and continue beating until they are distributed throughout the batter. The batter will be quite sticky. (A hand mixer is probably not strong enough to handle this dough. You can mix the dough by hand.)

4. Scrape the batter out of the bowl onto a heavily floured work surface. Using a pastry scraper or rubber spatula, divide the dough into two equal pieces. Flour your hands and roll each piece of dough into the flour to completely coat it. Form each piece into a log approximately 10 inches long Place the logs side by side on a well-greased baking sheet. They will spread slightly. Brush with the egg yolk-and-water mixture. Bake for 25 to 30 minutes, until golden brown. Remove the pan from the oven and transfer the logs to a cutting board.

5. Using a large chef's knife, slice the logs crosswise on the diagonal into ½-inch-thick pieces. Place the cut pieces, cut side down, back onto the baking sheet with about 1 inch of space between the pieces. Lower the heat to 325°F and bake for 15 minutes longer. Cool on racks. These will keep frozen for several months.

MAKES ABOUT 2 DOZEN

Chocolate Almond Cookies

~ ~ ~

BACI DI CIOCCOLATO

These wonderful bite-size chocolate cookies come from the restaurant Coco Pazzo in New York City and were created by pastry chef Susan Spungen.

6 cups almond flour (see pages 295–96 for sources)

4½ cups sugar

1 cup cocoa powder

6 ounces semisweet chocolate, melted

6 tablespoons honey

Dash of vanilla

9 egg whites

1. Preheat the oven to 350°F.
2. Combine the flour, sugar, and cocoa powder in a large mixing bowl and stir with a wooden spoon to combine.
3. Add melted chocolate and honey and mix well. Add egg whites and mix until a dough is formed.
4. Drop by rounded teaspoonfuls, or use a melon baller, onto baking sheets lined with parchment or aluminum foil. Bake 8 to 10 minutes. They should still be soft when you take them from the oven. Cool slightly before serving. Serve them warm.

MAKES 3 DOZEN

Almond Macaroons

~ ~ ~

AMARETTI

These crisp cookies, dense with almonds, are the perfect accompaniment to the tart taste of citrus *granite*.

1 ⅓ cups (8 ounces) blanched almonds (see note below)

1 tablespoon confectioners' sugar

2 large egg whites

⅓ cup granulated sugar

1 teaspoon almond extract

1. Preheat the oven to 300°F. Arrange the oven shelves in the middle third of the oven. Line two baking sheets with parchment or aluminum foil, shiny side up.

2. Grind the almonds with the confectioners' sugar until they become a fine powder. Set aside.

3. Beat the egg whites until they form soft peaks. Gradually beat in the granulated sugar until the whites are shiny. Fold in the ground almonds and almond extract.

4. Transfer the mixture to a 14-inch pastry bag fitted with a straight ½-inch tube and pipe the mixture out into 2-inch rounds. Bake for 30 minutes, until the cookies are lightly browned and hard. Cool on racks.

MAKES 24 COOKIES

Note: Blanched almonds can be bought in most large supermarkets. To make your own, cover almonds with water in a small saucepan. Bring to a boil over medium-high heat. Immediately drain, let cool a bit, and then rub off the skins.

Mail-Order Sources for Specialty Foods

~ ~ ~

Imported Italian specialty foods are beginning to be available locally in greater numbers of markets and food shops. Following is a list of mail-order sources for some of the foods and ingredients called for in the recipes in this book that may not be sold in stores in your area.

BALDUCCI'S
424 Sixth Avenue
New York, NY 10011
212-673-2600

DEAN AND DELUCA
560 Broadway
New York, NY 10012
800-221-7714 (outside New York)
212-431-1691 (in New York)

Most specialty Italian foods, including olive oil, Gaeta olives, flours (almond, durum, and semolina), cheeses, Arborio rice, and dried imported pastas, can be purchased from Dean and DeLuca. They do not offer a catalog, but if you know specifically what you want they will send it out to you. Cheeses will be sent next-day mail.

MOZZARELLA COMPANY
2944 Elm Street
Dallas, TX 75226
214-741-4072

They carry mozzarella, ricotta, and pecorino cheeses. A catalog is available.

TODARO BROTHERS MAIL ORDER
555 Second Avenue
New York, NY 10016
212-679-7766

Semolina and durum flours can be purchased through Todaro Brothers. A catalog is available.

WILLIAMS-SONOMA
P.O. Box 7456
San Francisco, CA 94120-7456
(and in many cities nationwide)
800-541-2233

All equipment and a limited selection of food products—special pizza yeast, Arborio rice, olive oil, and balsamic vinegar—are available by mail order. A catalog is available.

Index

~ ~ ~

Gnocchi, potato (cont.)
    with Gorgonzola and cream, 212
    with pesto, 212
Goat cheese
    about, 8–9
    angel hair tart with sun-dried tomatoes and, 228
    green ravioli filled with basil and, 174
    grilled, wild greens with, 243
    Olive's pizza with olive pâté, caramelized onions, and, 147
    pizza with fresh tomatoes, sun-dried tomatoes, mozzarella, and, 144
    risotto with sun-dried tomatoes, peas, and, 201
    spread, crostini with herb-flavored, 124
Gorgonzola
    about, 7–8
    polenta with, 208
    potato gnocchi with cream and, 212
Grana, about, 6–7
Grapefruit ice, 289
Grapes, about, 261
Grater, cheese, 23
Green(s)
    salad, mixed, 242
    wild, with grilled goat cheese, 243
Green bean(s)
    about, 43
    linguine with pesto and, 155
    and potato salad, 256
    with tomato sauce, 89
Green onions, salad of white beans and, 252
Grill, 24
Grilling vegetables, 20

Hazelnuts
    about, 263–64
    fig tart with, 280
Herb(s, -ed). See also specific herbs
    about, 29, 44–47
    goat cheese spread, crostini with, 124
    risotto with spinach and, 193
    spaghettini with, 158
    tomatoes baked with bread crumbs, garlic, and, 90
History of vegetables in Italy, 28–30

Ice
    grapefruit, 289
    lemon, 288
    orange and Campari, 290
Ice cream, pistachio, 290
Ingredients
    bread, 3–4
    broth, 10–12
    butter, 9
    cheese, 5–9
    flour, 13
    olive oil, 1–2

    for pizza, 131
    salt and pepper, 14
    vegetable oil, 3
    vinegar, 14–15
    wine, 15

Kidney beans, red, and barley soup, 118
Knives, 24

Lasagna
    green, with fresh tomato sauce, ricotta, and mozzarella cheese, 183
    many mushroom, 184
Leek(s)
    about, 29, 47
    with a green caper sauce, 75
    to clean, 47
    frittata, 236
    with lemon vinaigrette, 74
    -potato croquette, 85
    risotto with onions and, 198
    roasted, 75
    white beans with, 219
Lemon
    about, 261–62
    artichokes cooked in olive oil and juice of, Venetian-style, 59
    dried prunes with, 285
    ice, 288
    risotto with artichokes and, 196
    spinach with oil and lemon, 88
    tart, 282
    vinaigrette, leeks with, 74
Lentil(s)
    cooked with soffritto, 220
    salad, 252
    soup, 115
    with tubular pasta, 220
Lettuce, about, 47–48
Linguine with pesto and green beans, 155

Macaroons, almond, 293
Maccù, 222
Mail-order sources, 295–96
Marjoram
    about, 45
    frittata with parsley, chives, basil, and, 234
Mascarpone
    peaches poached in white wine and filled with, 270
    strawberries, raspberries, and blackberries with raspberry sauce and, 273
Meat broth, 10
Melons, about, 262
Microwave oven, 25
    steaming vegetables in, 17–19
Minestra, 98–99
Minestrone, about, 107
Mint, about, 45

Index